PUBLICATIONS OF THE WERTHEIM COMMITTEE

Strategy and Collective Bargaining Negotiation

CARL M. STEVENS

Professor of Economics
Reed College

GREENWOOD PRESS, PUBLISHERS
WESTPORT, CONNECTICUT

Library of Congress Cataloging in Publication Data

Stevens, Carl M
    Strategy and collective bargaining negotiation.

    Reprint of the ed. published by McGraw Hill, New
York, which was issued in the Publications of the
Wertheim Committee.
    Bibliography: p.
    Includes index.
    1. Collective bargaining. I. Title.
II. Series: Wertheim Committee. Publications.
[HD6483.S68 1978]   331.89   78-5304
ISBN 0-313-20377-6

Reprinted in 1978 by Greenwood Press, Inc.
51 Riverside Avenue, Westport, CT 06880

Printed in the United States of America

10 9 8 7 6 5 4 3 2 1

Foreword

Professor Stevens' volume is a significant contribution because it develops and applies theoretical tools to the collective bargaining process. It provides a body of concepts and insights to interpret the strategy of the parties and their tactics at varying stages of agreement-making.

There have been few careful descriptions of what actually happens at the bargaining table, in smoke filled rooms, in the caucuses of each side, or at side bar conferences. There is widespread perplexity over the fact that negotiations often continue down to a strike deadline late at night, that negotiations take so long, and there is curiosity over what people can possibly accomplish in marathon sessions. Negotiators from labor and management, and mediators as well, have not provided any systematic interpretation of the events to which they have been so close. There is accordingly great need for imaginative theoretical work on the collective bargaining process to provide interpretation of the events and to separate the general and characteristic from the unique and the particular.

In recent years theories have been developed to encompass all negotiations: from those involved in parlor games to transactions between nations. At some level of abstraction such generality is no doubt useful as the "theory of games" has demonstrated. But such models, it is fair to say, have not helped much in illuminating labor and management bargaining. This is not to say that "games" in which the participants have both common interests and conflicting interests are not of some relevance to an analysis of collective bargaining. But there is need for a theoretical framework more specialized to collective bargaining and to industrial relations systems.

Professor Stevens examined a variety of particular negotiations in the course of his research, and his theoretical framework has grown from ideas confronting experience. It is a fruitful notion to regard the negotiation process as a succession of stages or games in which the parties and others, including government, are involved in shaping or reshaping the rules of play. The course or path of negotiations often shifts in locale, in top level representatives of the parties, in the appearance of mediators, fact finders or other government or private representatives, and a work stoppage or other change in the work relationship may develop. Each of these situations is a different game, and the agreement-making process often involves the search for a new stage or game.

Professor Stevens' emphasis upon communication and information in the negotiation process is also a fruitful element of analysis. The information and views which the parties hold with regard to their objective environments and their views of each others' intentions are decisive to the results of negotiations. Professor Stevens' analysis also illuminates the mediation process and links it directly to the tactics and strategy of the parties.

This volume should be of interest to practitioners involved in collective bargaining as well as to those who only write about the subject. A theoretical analysis of collective bargaining negotiations is a contribution to the participants because it reveals the essential characteristics and stages of the agreement-making process; it should assist them to see in a detached way what they have been doing. Such analysis should assist the public generally to understand better the gyrations of the parties, and to mediators and other government officials a theoretical model should facilitate the process and timing of intervention. Professor Stevens' volume serves all these purposes.

John T. Dunlop

Contents

Tables

Figures

Author's Preface

This is an inquiry into the tactics and strategy of conflict (and cooperation) as they relate to collective bargaining negotiation. At the level of
systematic analysis, this is not a well developed field. Therefore, some
prefatory remarks are essential.

Research in collective bargaining (and in industrial relations more
generally) tends toward fragmentation—essentially descriptive accounts
which lack sharp focus. Here I am attempting to develop at least some of
the major components of a more systematic approach to the subject.

The important procedural features of collective bargaining negotiation,
common to many instances of such negotiation, are comprehended under
the rubric "rules for play" of the negotiation game. To so comprehend
these features it makes it necessary to explain what otherwise might be taken
for granted. Operating within the rules-for-play framework, the parties
resort to "tactics" in the process of negotiation. I have developed a
classification-of-tactics scheme and tried to distinguish various tactical entities. I have then gone on to give particular attention to the later stages of
negotiation and the agreement process.

Much of the conceptual development needed is essentially taxonomical.
On the theoretical side, suggestions have been incorporated from disparate
sources. While not usefully considered a "game" in the technical sense,
collective bargaining is a game-like interaction involving strategy. Hence
the potential contributions of game theory to the analysis of collective
bargaining negotiation have been considered. Particular attention has
been given to the negotiation process in terms of intrapersonal conflict—
choice theory as developed in psychology. In addition, theoretical suggestions have been taken from bargaining theory based upon utility theory
and from studies focused on collective bargaining.

Although considerable emphasis has been placed throughout on theoretical analysis, this study is nevertheless empirically oriented. This is because the focus throughout is upon the particular set of institutional ar-

rangements that comprise collective bargaining negotiation (for the most part, as practised in this country); and theoretical constructs are illustrated in terms of these institutions. There are a number of important social interactions in addition to collective bargaining in which negotiatory phenomena are important, such as political processes both intranational and international, relations between firms in the economy, and so on. Much of the analysis pertinent to each of these areas will be pertinent to the others as well. For this reason, although the empirical reference maintained throughout is as indicated, this inquiry should be viewed as a contribution to the development of a general theory of negotiation.

I have attempted to contrive a balance between theoretical and institutional material to bridge the unfortunate hiatus which has developed in the analysis of collective bargaining negotiation. On the one hand, there is considerable literature of an institutional and descriptive sort relating to collective bargaining negotiation. In this literature, little or no attention is paid to developments in the theory of bargaining and negotiation, or to game theory. On the other hand, there is a good deal of theoretical literature relating to games of conflict and strategy, to bargaining and negotiation, to decision problems under risk and uncertainty, and so forth—theory which, though for the most part not so focused, might cast some light upon collective bargaining negotiation. In this literature, empirical reference tends to be diffuse and casual, and reference to collective bargaining, if any, is confined to parenthetical-type suggestions that it is perhaps illustrative of particular problems or formulations under consideration. The task of attempting to relate results in the two areas has fallen largely unattended into a gap between the investigators.

This is understandable. Game theorists, for example, are interested in games in general, and empirical catholicism is appropriate to their interests. This inquiry is vulnerable to criticism from both sides. For the tastes of the institutionally oriented investigator, it may appear too abstract, too lacking in sufficient contact with "reality," whereas the theoretically oriented investigator may deem it lacking in rigor and regret its failure to pursue theoretical topics in greater depth. Nevertheless, I feel it is necessary for progress in the analysis of collective bargaining to pull theoretical and institutional results more closely together. It is my hope that, as a result of this study, a bridge across this gap will have been begun.

My thinking on choice theory generally and on the theory of negotiation more particularly has been influenced by many people in many ways.

To account for intellectual indebtedness by even tolerably complete enumeration of these persons and ways would be impossible.

My interest in psychological choice theory and in application of conflict-choice theory to analysis of interpersonal conflict derives from the years (1951–1954) that I was fortunate to spend as a Post-doctoral Fellow in the Institute of Human Relations, Yale University. More recently, I have found the work of Professor Thomas C. Schelling on bargaining theory and on "reoriented" game theory a source of stimulation. During the preparation of the manuscript, I was privileged to have several discussions with Professor George W. Taylor which contributed greatly to my understanding of aspects of the negotiation problem. My thinking about problems in this area of analysis has been greatly assisted also by R. Duncan Luce and Howard Raiffa's estimable *Games and Decisions*.

I reserve for last acknowledgment the contributions of Professor John T. Dunlop. These go back many years, to my graduate school days, during which he was responsible for my interest in labor economics and collective bargaining. His contributions with respect to this book have been invaluable. During the preparation of the manuscript I had numerous helpful discussions with him concerning the problems and issues involved. He read the entire manuscript and provided detailed comment. Without his encouragement and enthusiasm this book might never have been completed.

This study was undertaken during my tenure (1959–1960) of a Brookings Institution National Research Professorship. I am grateful for the opportunity thus afforded me, and I am also indebted to the Committee of the Jacob Wertheim Fellowship in Industrial Relations for assistance during the period of manuscript revision.

Carl M. Stevens

CHAPTER I

Subject Matter Context
and the Negotiation Model

SUBJECT MATTER OF THIS INQUIRY

Negotiation and Bargaining Distinguished

This is an inquiry into tactics, strategy, and collective bargaining negotiation over terms and conditions of employment. Although in a general way the empirical reference of "collective bargaining negotiation" is apparent, ambiguities do arise in the interpretation of this term. "Negotiation" has a more restricted reference than "bargaining" in that although only certain exchange transactions are featured by negotiation, all may be viewed as instances of bargaining.[1] In any exchange transaction —for example, an ordinary retail purchase—a bargain regarding the terms of exchange is struck, and, hence, a kind of bargaining may be said to have taken place. However, as in this instance, there need be no negotiation involved.

In order to conclude any transaction, the parties must exchange minimal information—namely, their terms and their subsequent acceptance or rejection of the other's terms.[2] However, they may be said to negotiate if they exchange further information relevant to the transaction. An analysis of negotiation is in large part an analysis of the content and function of such additional information and of the tactical "moves," agreement problems, and so forth, reflected in it.

Just as negotiation is only one aspect of the total collective bargaining relationship, that relationship itself is set into a larger context which is well defined by John T. Dunlop's concept of an "industrial relations system."[3] An industrial relations system determines the "web of rules" governing the work place (including among these rules the terms of compensation). In Dunlop's model, the workers and their organizations, managers and their organizations, and governmental agencies concerned with the work place and work community interact within three related environmental contexts: the technology, the market or budgetary constraints and power relations in the larger community, and their own derived status. In an industrial relations system such as that of the United States, the collective bargaining interaction between workers and their organizations and managers and their organizations is an important part of the rule-making procedure. Negotiation in turn plays a vital role in this bargaining interaction.

To define precisely the way in which analysis of negotiation fits into analysis of bargaining generally, and into analysis of industrial relations systems even more generally, would require a volume addressed to "the economics of collective action"—a study far beyond that intended here.[4] Nevertheless, enough can be said in short compass to provide the orientation necessary to understand this inquiry. Some conflict of interest between labor and management is inherent in an industrial relations system. In collective bargaining more income for one side generally means less for the other (although collective bargaining is by no means a zero-sum game in either the technical or the general sense). The power "pie" is as important as the source of conflict.[5] In pursuit of its objectives, each side may use various pressures in operating upon its opposite number. Classification of types of social power is important, but need not detain us here. A few examples will suffice. The environmental context provided by technology and by market organization will importantly condition, in any particular collective bargaining relationship, the economic power which may be brought to bear by refusal to deal, for instance. The ideological content of community mores provides a source of "ethical," "moral" power which may be harnessed by the disputants. In laying hold of power weapons, the parties are constrained by government, by the rules of law (both common and statutory) which define the "allowable area of economic conflict."

Collective bargaining negotiation is a social-control technique for reflecting and transmuting the basic power relationships which underlie the conflict of interest inherent in an industrial relations system. It is a technique for directing, controlling, and exploiting power in the formulation of the web of rules governing the work place. It is also a technique for containing conflict, for resolving it short of overt trials of industrial warfare if this be possible, or to handle such trials if necessary. Negotiation is also a technique for the accommodation of labor and management organizations in pursuit of common organizational objectives.[6] Although negotiation reflects and transforms the basic power relationships inherent in the situation, we should recognize that "negotiation power" is a type of power in its own right. Negotiation power, *per se*, comes from facility and shrewdness in the execution of negotiation tactics such as manipulation of the communications structure of the situation to achieve commitment of a threat, use of rationalization of a position to win allies, and so forth. Negotiation power, along with other kinds of power, determines the final result.

From the above discussion, it should be clear that a theory of collective bargaining negotiation is not a general theory of wage determination under collective bargaining. It is a crucial part of such a theory, along with other aspects suggested—for example, by Dunlop's concept of an industrial relations system. It should also be clear that an analysis of collective bargaining negotiation will take as given (not to be explained) certain elements which a general theory of the collective bargaining relationship would treat as variables. Generally speaking, an analysis of collective bargaining negotiation will take as given the basic power positions upon which the bargaining is based, although these would have to be explained in an over-all analysis of collective bargaining.

Take, for example, the ordinary bargaining strike. A party's stated intention to strike is a negotiation tactic which may be analyzed in terms of its effect upon the opponent's position. Among the tactical problems scrutinized in this context will be those of bluff, notbluff, apparent commitment to course of action, and so forth. To analyze negotiation, the fact that some strikes are within the "allowable area of economic conflict" can be taken as given, although, as we noted above, a general analysis of the collective bargaining relationship would treat this "rule" as something to be explained. Thus, when we come to the "rules for play" of the negotiation game, we must have in mind an empirical reference more restricted than that which would be comprehended by the rules for the whole collective bargaining game. The techniques whereby a party may attempt to establish his opponent's expectations about the impact of a strike are a proper subject for analysis in a theory of collective bargaining negotiation. The same may be said of a party's efforts to modify the course of an expected strike, for instance, by statements designed favorably to dispose the general public. The actual impact of a strike, as it depends upon technology and market structure, may be taken as given in an analysis of negotiation. In a more general analysis of the power structure of an industrial relations system this impact might have to be treated as a variable—to be explained in market structure (or other) terms.

Although we may distinguish the concepts "bargaining" and "negotiation," these analytical boxes are not analogues to watertight containers. In other words, classification of particular moves, strategies, or acts may not always be unequivocal in these terms. The broad outline of the foregoing analytical context is provided with the hope that it sufficiently orient the reader to avoid any major misunderstandings of the scope and focus of this study.

Analysis Restricted to "Mature" Bargaining Relationship

Of primary concern is the "mature" collective bargaining relationship, which, generally speaking, is one of considerable duration with parties who will have had sufficient bargaining experience. It is less important to enumerate the properties characteristic of the mature relationship than it is to indicate those excluded by this definition. Excluded are cases in which the parties do not possess the ordinary negotiating skills and/or are confused by unrealistic interpretations of the environmental and tactical situation. A case in point would be the management negotiator who bases his strategy on the belief that his employees will repudiate their union on a "last-offer" vote required by law as a part of the Labor Management Relations Act emergency strike procedure. Also excluded are cases in which the leaders do not strive to represent the best interests of their respective organizations, and/or cases in which the members of the organizations have no control over the leadership. An example in this category would be the negotiator who wants a strike because he thinks it will serve his personal interests—even though he knows that such a strike would not benefit the membership of the organization.[7]

Also excluded are cases in which one or both parties are unwilling participants in the negotiation process. In these instances a party may be more concerned with the destruction of his opponent than in negotiating with him. There are also cases in which political party aims are the only objective of the union.

Whatever else it may be, the mature relationship is not a state of disorderly conflict, but rather an effort to contain conflict by resort to the negotiation of collective agreements. Mature bargaining relationships may exist under various mixtures of competitiveness, antagonism, and cooperation. A mature relationship may be what Harbison and Coleman have called the "armed truce" type.[8] In this relationship, management views collective bargaining as a necessary evil, and the union leadership feels that one of its main jobs is to challenge and protest management decisions. There is disagreement over the appropriate scope of joint determination as against management prerogative. There is rivalry between the parties for the loyalty of the workers and a frank admission that settlements of major disputes are made on the basis of the relative power positions of the parties. In spite of the competitive nature of the relationship, it is stable, and the parties have a mutual desire to work out an orderly method for living together under the terms of a collective agreement.

Less competitive is the mature relationship termed "working harmony" by Harbison and Coleman. In this relationship, the parties are more impressed with the extent to which the well-being of each organization depends upon the other and more convinced that compromises benefit both sides. There is a tendency to broaden the scope of issues subject to joint determination and a real mutual appreciation of organizational problems. Still less competitive is the union–management cooperation type of relationship in which a real feeling of "partnership" develops in the attempt to solve joint problems. If union and management cooperate to the extent where organizational goals become identical and there is no differentiation of organizational function, then the case is not one for analysis in this context. With this reservation, the various degrees of competitiveness suggested above are admissible. We should expect the "tactic mix" employed during the course of negotiation to vary depending upon the relationship. (The union–management cooperation type is, in any event, relatively rare.)

Periodic Agreement Conference of Central Interest

Collective bargaining is a continuing, day-in-day-out relationship. In discussion and analysis (and in practice by the parties) it is important to distinguish periodic contract negotiation (legislative activity) and contract administration (in part, quasi-judicial activity). In prescriptive principle and to a large extent in practice this distinction is recognized and accepted by the parties. Yearly or at longer regular intervals the parties negotiate the major terms and conditions of employment which will prevail for the duration of the agreement. In the interim, problems of contract administration arise. The contract language must be given meaning when applied to concrete instances, disputes may start over such meaning, problems not covered by the contract may arise, and so forth. In a mature bargaining relationship the grievance machinery is set up to facilitate the function of contract administration.[9] Such machinery may vary in approach from a narrow, "legalistic" approach aimed principally at interpreting contract language to an approach aimed more at the substantive resolution of whatever problems arise.

The kinds of pressure appropriate for periodic contract negotiation are not similarly appropriate for the differences arising in day-to-day contract administration.[10] Also, techniques like final and binding arbitration, appropriate for contract administration under the grievance machinery are not similarly useful in periodic contract negotiations. In this inquiry we are concerned with contract negotiation and with the periodic agreement conferences.

Why Strike Negotiations Are Not Analyzed

The following discussion is organized in terms of successive "stages" of negotiation. Analysis is carried down only to the prestrike stage. The decision thus to limit the scope of inquiry in no way means to imply that strike negotiations are uninteresting or unimportant. It reflects the fact that a different analytical apparatus from that developed in the following pages is probably necessary for adequate consideration of strike negotiations.

A strike is not an autonomous event. If it does occur, it is an integral part of the negotiation process—a consequence of what has gone before. Nevertheless, once a strike has occurred, the psychological milieu changes radically. As Stagner has pointed out, the strike is an unstable situation. That is, often neither side has a clear-cut picture of what is happening, communications are disrupted, propaganda may become relatively more effective, and increasing tensions may lead to various forms of aberrant behavior—violent reactions.[11] It has seemed to the author that, from the point of view of the contribution this inquiry can make, extension of the conceptual format to comprehend such phenomena would only result in a confusing proliferation and heterogeneity in the basic theoretical structure underlying the inquiry.

THE NEGOTIATION MODEL

Collective bargaining negotiation is a game-like interaction involving strategy.[12] To analyze it, we will need a model—or, better, a description of this process which will serve as a model. In this chapter we undertake a brief description of the component parts of this model to give the reader an idea of how the analysis is organized and of the directions in which it is extended.

There exists no general theory of the negotiation process which will serve as a fair and reasonably complete working description. Much of the conceptual development needed involves an essentially taxonomical operation—not model construction in the sense of exhibiting a postulational structure from which propositions may be had as theorems. In the following analysis, suggestions will be drawn from disparate sources like game theory, utility analysis in nongame contexts, intrapersonal conflict-choice theory, and descriptive discussion of collective bargaining negotiation tactics.

In a fully developed general theory of negotiation, precise restrictions implied by characterizing the players would be detailed. In much of the following context, this is not so. The parties are labor and management organizations and the negotiators representing them. The objective of each party is to make the outcome as near to his own preferred position as possible. Although the objective of each party has here been stated in terms of preferences, preference functions enter into much of the subsequent analysis only incidentally. For example, A in his negotiations with B may be depicted as representing or misrepresenting his own preferences, or as attempting to alter B's preferences, and so on. Discussion of such tactical operations on preference functions does not require narrow restrictions on the shapes of these functions, nor does it require general discussion of the other determinants of these functions. However, some of the subsequent analysis is based upon theories which do incoporate critical assumptions characterizing the parties, for instance, rationality and extent of knowledge or information. When the author has found these assumptions necessary, they will be described.

Conflict-Choice Theory

As will be explained in Chapter II, theories of choice behavior can be divided into two classes—conflict choice and nonconflict choice. A part of the task involved in construction of a theory of negotiation is to characterize the kind of choice situation in which the parties are supposed to find themselves. Economic analysis of choice behavior generally, including analysis of interpersonal conflict situations as developed in game theory, is predicated upon modern-utility theory. This theory is essentially a nonconflict-type theory of individual-choice behavior.

However, analysis of negotiation (and of interpersonal conflict situations generally) is perhaps better predicated upon a theory of individual-choice behavior of the conflict type. In Chapter II the application of a particular conflict-choice theory model to the analysis of negotiation is suggested. Since conflict-choice theory is seldom employed in the analysis of economic-choice behavior and is not generally familiar to students of such behavior, an attempt has been made to present a reasonably self-contained description of the model in question. This model characterizes the negotiation-choice situation in a categorical sense, and it exhibits an equilibrium for the negotiation-choice situation. However, it does not by itself constitute a complete theory of negotiation. Following development of the model in Chapter II, it will be referred to in the subsequent analysis.

Rules for Play of the Negotiation Game

A number of procedural features of collective bargaining negotiation like the bargaining strike deadline, setting of the agenda for each forum by initial demand and counterdemand, and so on, are common to many instances of such negotiations. These customary procedural features, although not really "rules" in the sense of formal statement and promulgation by authority, are nevertheless usefully comprehended under the rubric "rules for play" of the negotiation game. These rules will be discussed in Chapter III.

To comprehend these features as rules may seem a rather gratuitous exercise in semiformality. Were the rules to be discussed the only possible ones—were the framework constituted by these rules the only one within which the transactions in question could be resolved—this might be the case. However, the rules to be adduced, although characteristic of much collective bargaining, are clearly not the only possibilities. Since there is a variety of sets of rules within the contexts of which the transactions could be resolved, it is incumbent upon the analysis to explain why the choice of this particular set of rules instead of another. The very device of designating these features as "rules for play" demands an explanation of what might otherwise be taken for granted as given.

The Negotiation Process: Tactics

The rules for play of the negotiation game establish a framework within which the process of negotiation takes place. We will need a scheme to analyze and organize information about this "process." The problem here is one of response definition or what, for want of a better term, we may call the "instrumental" significance of a negotiation response. It was previously suggested that parties to a transaction may be said to negotiate if they exchange information relevant to that transaction in addition to the minimal information necessary to resolve the transaction on a take-it-or-leave-it basis. Understanding that the process of negotiation involves an exchange of information, we need some scheme to categorize the functions or effects of this exchange.

For present purposes, a rather informal approach to this categorization will serve. Most discussions of bargaining and negotiation, and of related concepts such as bargaining power and the manipulation of bargaining power, suggest that each party "operates" upon his opposite number by the use of "tactics" to influence the least favorable terms upon which his opponent will settle.

A Note on Terminology

Although some classification of tactics is necessary for analysis of negotiation, one is tempted to shirk a systematic approach to this essentially taxonomical task in favor of straightforward resort, without elucidation, to such terms as "threat," "bluff," and so forth.

Such terms may convey the desired meaning without the tedious definition of concepts. However, they also carry ambiguous connotations. From the point of view of focus, the threat seems to connote contingency. The bluff may or may not involve contingency, but the central feature seems to be deception. The promise is associated with a specified course of action, but the term does not connote so much a particular class of courses of action as it does a means to commitment to a course of action (in a culture in which the assertion "I promise" carries weight). Since the obvious bluff is not effective, nor the incredible threat, nor the unconvincing promise, all these devices—the bluff, the threat, and the promise—may involve problems of commitment. But, in addition, the term commitment has been given independent status, being used to mean an unconditional course of action (and thus distinguished from the threat). And beyond this, since commit also has a verb sense, the awkward terminological situation of talking about A's means for committing himself to a commitment may arise. Perhaps one may illustrate the nature of the problem by describing a "single" tactic in the negotiations between A and B in this way: A's threat was only a bluff since, although he seemed to commit himself to a course of action by his promise, he had no intention of carrying it out.

In short, a terminological morass is in the making with the continued use of these terms, and the need for some carefully defined and agreed-upon terminology is apparent. Nevertheless, these terms are used with such frequency in the literature that it is awkward and perhaps even confusing to discuss negotiation tactics without reference to them. As a result, the author uses these terms and attempts to define them within the context of the classification-of-tactics scheme, although he hesitates to present this as an attempt to establish conventions with respect to their usage.

The "Mixed" Relationship and the Negotiation Cycle

Negotiation tactics will be discussed in Chapters IV (Classification of Tactics, Early Stages of Negotiation and Persuasion versus Rationalization), V (Tactics of Coercion: Bluff and Notbluff), and VI (The Later Predeadline Stages of Negotiation). Two sets of general considerations underlie the organization of the analysis in these chapters.

First, analysis of negotiation tactics must take into account the fact that collective bargaining is a "mixed" or symbiotic relationship, one involving both tactics of competition and conflict and tactics of cooperation and coordination. That is, it is an interdependent relationship in which both parties stand to gain by cooperation to the extent of preserving the fact of the relationship. But there are also elements of competition involved—namely, those over the "terms of trade" upon which the cooperation shall take place. The fact that the parties to collective bargaining are symbionts in their basic relationship implies that the collective bargaining negotiation game will be "mixed." [13]

Second, analysis of negotiation tactics must take into account a phenomenon which may be termed the negotiation "cycle." No two instances of collective bargaining contract negotiation are precisely the same. However, as the titles of Chapters IV and VI suggest, there tends to be a progression of events, a succession of "stages" common to many contract negotiations.[14] Although an attempt to trace the negotiation cycle in detail would not be warranted in the present context, certain general features of this cycle should be noted. The negotiation cycle involves a movement from earlier stages with emphasis upon the competitive aspects of negotiation to the later stages where the emphasis may be more upon coordination and cooperation. That is, we should expect the relative emphasis upon negotiation tactics (the tactic mix) to vary as the negotiations progress. In the early stages the essentially competitive tactics of coercion and deception—tactics by means of which each party attempts to "move" his opponent's position in his own favor—will be relatively more prominent. In the predeadline stages, tactics of cooperation—tactical problems associated with mutual convergence upon an agreed position—will be relatively more prominent. In some circumstances during these stages, it would seem that each party seeks more for the agreed position which has by now become inherent in the negotiation picture than he attempts to influence that position in his favor.

We should recognize that the concept of a contract negotiation cycle may be misleading if pressed too far. For example, although the chapter organization takes account of such a cycle, it is not intended to imply that tactical problems discussed in Chapter VI may not sometimes be relevant to early stages of negotiation, or, for example, that tactics of coercion discussed in Chapter V may not be relevant to the later stages. In general, although we should expect the tactic mix to vary as the negotiations progress, most of the tactics and tactical problems discussed may appear at any stage of negotiation.

As a matter of empirical generalization, the negotiation-cycle hypothesis has some support. Further, analysis of the negotiation process suggests two theoretically significant distinctions between "early" and "later" stages of negotiation and suggests that a "divide" may be crossed during the negotiation process.

One aspect of this matter concerns the possibility of a manifest (or revealed) contract zone. The contract zone is a range of outcomes each of which is preferred by both parties to no contract. Whether a contract zone exists is of course critical to the outcome of the negotiations. If no contract zone exists (or if none can be brought into being by the exchange of information during negotiation) then the only possible outcome is "no agreement." However, for the analysis of choice behavior during negotiation, it is not only the existence or nonexistence of a contract zone that matters. How the parties perceive the contract zone is also critical. The analysis will differ greatly depending upon whether the parties are assumed to be certain or uncertain about the limits of the zone. Indeed, the whole character of the choice problem changes depending upon this assumption. Briefly, the proposition is this. If, during the course of negotiation, a contract zone becomes manifest, the character of the negotiation game will change; that is, revelation of the contract zone marks a sort of "divide"—the tactic mix and the important tactical problems shift toward cooperation and coordination.

The distinction between necessary and sufficient conditions for agreement in negotiation, developed in Chapter II in connection with the conflict-choice model, provides a second analytical source of distinction between "early" and "later" stages of the negotiation process. With this formulation, we may view the negotiator during the early stages as primarily concerned with the competitive tactical problem of moving his opponent's equilibrium position (the least favorable terms that the opponent is willing to agree to) as much as possible in his own behalf. Meanwhile, the negotiator occupies his own (as yet unannounced) equilibrium position, subject to the influence of his opponent's competitive tactics. The necessary condition for agreement will have been met when these equilibrium positions are consonant. The sufficient condition involves mutual awareness of this consonance. At some point, especially if there is a bargaining deadline, competitive attempts to influence the opponent will probably give way to the problem of "revealing" one's own equilibrium position—which may involve a delicate problem in communication. On this view, once the problem of revealing one's own equilibrium position has become the focus of attention, the later (coordinative) stages of negotiation have begun.

Mediation: Tactics and Functions

The final chapter focuses upon the mediation of industrial disputes. Mediation, concerned as it is with the "peaceful" resolution of industrial conflict, is of considerable significance and interest *per se* in a generally interdependent economy. Beyond this, it develops that a discussion of the functions and tactics of mediation affords an excellent way in which further to examine and tie together many of the results developed in the previous chapters.

Finally, it may be noted that the general subject matter of the appendices is discussed in various places in the preceding chapters. It is the function of the appendices to develop special topics related to this subject matter and to include some technical material which might have diverted attention from major themes had it been included in the main text.

CHAPTER II

Conflict-Choice Model of Negotiation[1]

The objective of a theory of negotiation is to achieve an analysis that will provide insight on the choice problem. One approach to such a theory would be a list of questions about negotiation which an adequate theory should answer, and which would serve as a guide in devising the theory. This approach has a number of disadvantages and has not been used here. Some such list of questions might, however, be helpful in appraising theory surveyed and developed in this inquiry.[2]

An alternative approach to a theory of negotiation would be to begin with certain theory elements which must be present—at least in a generic or categorical sense—in any adequate theory of negotiation. One, dealt with in this chapter, is the theory of individual-choice behavior which is supposed to characterize the actors. It is upon this theory element that the negotiation interaction is to be predicated.

CONFLICT VERSUS NONCONFLICT CHOICE

An actor, when confronted with a choice between goals, may behave in either of two distinctly different ways. We call them conflict choice and nonconflict choice. In nonconflict choice the actor immediately elects one or the other goal. In conflict choice, he elects neither goal. Rather, he is "conflicted," he remains uncertain for a period of time in a behavioral equilibrium between the two.

How is this difference in behaviors to be explained? In terms of economic-choice theory (modern utility theory), one might be tempted to suggest that in the conflict-choice situation the goals are equally preferred or indifferent, whereas in the nonconflict-choice situation the relative preference for one is greater.[3] Such an explanation is not, however, on any simple interpretation of it, adequate. Psychological-choice theory suggests that all nonconflict choices, will be made quickly, the matter of relative preference being manifest in the probability that one goal rather than the other will be elected. Thus, in the case of a nonconflict choice involving goals of equal preference, we should expect on a series of trials that each would be selected about half the time. (This is an operational significance that has been given the concept of "indifference" in experimental work on utility theory.) The conflict-choice situation is of a generically different sort to be explained by the conflict-choice model.

Utility theory is essentially a nonconflict theory of choice behavior. In some of its applications, as in the theory of consumers' behavior, this is appropriate because the analysis is concerned with (time) rates of performance of choice behavior, not with individual episodes of choice behavior in which the phenomena of conflict might be manifest. Utility theory is also used to analyze particular episodes of choice behavior. Perhaps because of his traditional concern with long-run rates of performance, when an economist does analyze an episode of choice behavior he does so in such a way as to suggest the absence of conflict. Suppose an actor is confronted with two goals. The economist would analyze the choice by supposing that the subject assigned some magnitude of utility to each of the options (perhaps weighted by a probability coefficient) and then would choose so as to maximize utility (or perhaps expected utility). Or the subject may be supposed to employ some equivalent prudential rule such as minimax. Whatever the postulate, the analysis implies no conflict.

In analyzing collective bargaining negotiations, we are not of course dealing simply with a problem in individual-choice behavior. Rather, we are dealing with an interpersonal conflict-choice problem. However, as has been pointed out, any theory of interpersonal conflict must be predicated upon some theory of individual-choice behavior. Analysis of interpersonal conflict choice as developed in economics generally, and as developed in game theory more particularly, is predicated upon modern utility theory. However, it may be argued that, partly, because of the kinds of opportunity functions (range-of-choice options) afforded the actors, analysis of interpersonal conflict-choice situations frequently might better be predicated upon a conflict theory of individual-choice behavior. One such model, developed in psychological theory, is surveyed in this chapter and its application to analysis of negotiation suggested.[4]

The Conflict-Choice Model [5]

The model here described bases the explanation of behavioral equilibrium in the conflict-choice situation upon the concepts of the "approach gradient" and the "avoidance gradient." Just as an individual may learn approach tendencies to rewarding (positive) goals, so also may he learn avoidance tendencies to goals such that to elect them involves an expectation of punishment or nonreward (negative goals). The approach gradient is a name given the hypothesis that the strength of an individual's tendency to approach a positive goal is a decreasing function of his distance from the goal. Analogously, the avoidance gradient is a name given the hypothesis that the strength of an individual's tendency to avoid a negative goal is a decreasing function of his distance from the goal. [6] A number of stable and unstable equilibrium-choice models can be constructed in terms of these gradients. This analysis will make use only of the avoidance gradients. That is, the choice-theory model employed is of the avoidance–avoidance type. This model is represented in Figure 1. [7] (At present, the reader should ignore the graph labels in brackets.) In Figure 1, view the goals A and B as negative goals. The function AA is an avoidance gradient for goal A, representing the increasing strength of the tendency to avoid goal A as the subject gets closer to it. Analogously, BB is the avoidance gradient for goal B. At a position such as D1, the strength of the tendency to avoid goal A is equal to the strength of the tendency to avoid goal B. At such a position, the individual is in a

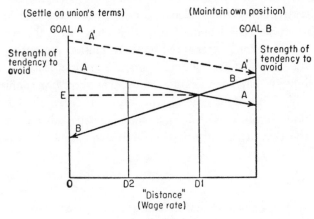

FIG. 1

stable equilibrium position. If, in this avoidance–avoidance situation, the individual be momentarily displaced from a position such as D_1 to D_2, he will tend to return to D_1. The reason for this is that in a position such as D_2, the strength of the tendency to avoid goal A is stronger than the strength of the tendency to avoid goal B. Hence there is a net avoidance tendency operating to drive the individual toward goal B—that is, back toward position D_1. An analogous argument applies to displacements on the other side of D_1, closer to goal B.[8]

Suppose the individual to be in equilibrium at position D_1. Further suppose that due to a change in environmental circumstances his avoidance gradient AA shifts upward to occupy the position A′A′ (the dotted line function). In this instance, the avoidance gradient to goal A lies everywhere above that to goal B, hence everywhere there is a net tendency to avoid A. In this circumstance, the individual will elect goal B. It is only in such a circumstance that in spite of the avoidance–avoidance nature of the choice one goal will be immediately elected.

It will be observed that the model determines two variables: (1) the distance of the subject from each goal in equilibrium; (2) the strength of the tendency to avoid both goals, which is the same for both goals in equilibrium. In Figure 1 and for position D_1 this is measured by OE. Regarding this latter variable, conflict-choice situations involving this kind of behavioral equilibrium are apt to be an uncomfortable experience for the individual. Such situations give rise to a drive stimulus commonly termed "tension" (or anxiety, and so forth). The level of tension experienced in such an equilibrium-choice situation is an increasing function of the strength of the tendency to avoid, which the individual feels in equilibrium, and the length of time the subject is in the equilibrium situation. High or long-experienced levels of tension are apt to be associated with a variety of aberrant behaviors like reduced learning capacity, reduced ability to pay attention, and so on. The theory of conflict choice involving this kind of behavioral equilibrium suggests that if there is available some compromise behavior—some strategy other than electing either of the two negative goals—the individual should be expected to choose it.

Why the Parties Negotiate

It is fair to say that the first task of a theory of collective bargaining negotiation is to explain why, in a choice situation such as this, the parties negotiate at all.[9] Negotiation is not after all the only way in which the transaction might be concluded. Why should the parties not elect some alternative method? Considering the collective bargaining situation in light of our conflict-choice model will help to supply an answer to this question.

Let us imagine a well-organized union whose members comprise the major portion of the company's work force. Further assume that the company would have extreme difficulty in replacing the union members should they strike and that the union members would experience extreme difficulty in finding alternative employment. Now assume the following market procedure: The union unilaterally states its terms (demand for a wage increase) on a take-it-or-leave-it basis, with no compromise possible and with the understanding that should the company choose to "leave" it, a strike would be a certainty.[10] In this situation, two strategies (choices) are available to the company: (1) refusing the union's demand —insisting upon maintenance of the prevailing terms of employment; (2) granting the union's demand—settling on the union's terms.

Economic-choice theory would suggest that the choice in this situation should turn simply upon the maximization of expected utility, taking into account such factors as the probability and cost of a strike on the one hand, and the cost of paying the rate increase on the other. However, this is a conflict-choice situation conforming to the avoidance–avoidance model. The company confronts two negative goals; that is, an expectation of cost consequent upon the election of either. Company choice 1 exposes the company to a strike and the costs associated therewith. Company choice 2 means, *ceteris paribus,* loss of profit due to paying the higher rate.[11] In consequence, one should expect the company to make neither choice immediately. Rather, the company will be conflicted, will remain uncertain in a behavioral equilibrium between the two. In such a choice situation the company should be expected to perform some alternative or compromise response, were such available. In avoidance–avoidance choices generally, one possibility is escape from the choice situation entirely. However, in this case the company is constrained in the choice situation (motivated to make the choice) by the symbiotic nature of the collective bargaining relationship—preservation of the employer–employee relationship is vital, in other words. Thus constrained to participate in the choice, the company might prefer that the rules of the market game permitted an additional strategy: (3) seeking a compromise via negotiation.

The market game here presented (the take-it-or-leave-it model in the market context of bilateral monopoly) is an example of what we shall term an unnatural purposive game. A purposive game is one in which the relation between the game and its associated, economic (or other) transaction is such that it makes the game a means to an end. This is in contrast to certain parlor games in which the relationship between the game and its associated economic transaction (wager) is the reverse of this. In these games, the game itself is the end, and the economic transaction a means to the end—to lend interest to the playing of the game. The distinction between purposive and nonpurposive games is important because the two classes may differ with respect to properties crucial to analysis. Thus, purposive games are more apt to create conflict-choice situations involving uncomfortable tensions. A game theory elaborated chiefly with respect to nonpurposive games might well neglect this possibility.

The take-it-or-leave-it game is considered unnatural in the avoidance-avoidance choice situation because, in this situation, the player is highly motivated (by tensions generated in the choice situation) to seek strategies in addition to those made available by the rules. Of course, in any game, increasing the number of opportunities available may, *ceteris paribus,* increase the value of the game. However, it is not argued here that, in the case of an unnatural game, the player seeks an additional strategy (negotiation) because he may thus be assured a more favorable outcome.[12] Rather, it is argued that the avoidance–avoidance conflict-choice situation is inherently and generically of such a nature that the game take-it-or-leave-it must create strong motivations to discover alternative responses. In this situation the individual cannot immediately make up his mind which goal to elect. He is in a behavioral equilibrium such that strategies other than those available in take-it-or-leave-it are psychologically necessary if the game is to be an appropriate (natural) one for resolving the transaction. The author concludes from the foregoing argument that in a bilateral monopoly situation such as that represented by collective bargaining, the parties would probably prefer to play the game negotiation rather than the game take-it-or-leave-it.

The Statutory Obligation to Negotiate

The National Labor Relations Act obligates the parties to collective bargaining to negotiate. Section 8 (a) (5) of the act provides: "It shall be an unfair labor practice for an employer to refuse to bargain collectively with the representatives of his employees." Section 8 (b) (3) lays down a similar prescription for labor organizations. Section 8 (d) then provides that "to bargain collectively is the performance of the mutual obligation of the employer and the representative of the employees to meet at reasonable times and confer in good faith with respect to wages, hours, and other terms and conditions of employment."

One may well inquire: If the parties would prefer to play the negotiation game, what is the point of legislation designed to constrain them so to do? That is, how does the fact of this statutory obligation fit into the burden of the present analysis?

From an over-all point of view, the statutory obligation to bargain collectively is primarily an obligation to "recognize" the union. From this point of view, refusal to bargain collectively is refusal to accord *de facto* recognition, an attempt not so much to deal with the union in a particular way as an attempt to be rid of it. In such cases, the parties may negotiate largely because one of them is constrained by law so to do, but such cases fall outside the scope of this analysis. It will be recalled from Chapter I that this inquiry is restricted to "mature" bargaining relationships. A company party to a mature bargaining relationship need not be fond of collective bargaining or unions. Indeed, as with the "armed truce" type of relationship, the company may feel that the union is at best a necessary evil. Note, however, that in this mature case the evil is viewed as necessary. We assume that in the mature bargaining relationship force of circumstances has caused the parties to accord each other "recognition," and these same circumstances set up a choice situation in which the parties would prefer to negotiate rather than play take-it-or-leave-it.

To the extent that the statutory obligation to negotiate has its bearing as an obligation to accord *de facto* recognition, it is not an important factor in this inquiry. From a more particular point of view, aspects of this statutory obligation are relevant in the context of this study and will be dealt with when appropriate.

Analysis of the Process

By way of initial characterization, we may say that during the negotiation process each party uses tactics to move the future agreement as much as possible in his own favor. We want now to consider how the use of tactics fits into analysis of negotiation in terms of the avoidance-avoidance model.

Assume for expositional simplicity that the sole bargaining issue is the wage rate and consider just one side of the situation—the choice problem as confronted by the employer and the negotiation task as seen by the union. (The principles involved will also apply to the situation seen from the other side.) Figure 1 now represents the employer's position, the goal A being "settle on union's terms," and the goal B being "maintain own position." Since this is a negotiation situation, the union's demand and the company's position must be viewed as bargaining positions—that is, ostensible prices leaving room for negotiation rather than final prices.

In order to depict the negotiation situation in terms of this model, we need an appropriate idea of the concept "distance" (from goal)—the horizontal axis in Figure 1. In some contexts in which the avoidance-avoidance model has been used, this distance can be interpreted in a spatial sense. In other contexts, it can be interpreted in some subjective sense—that is, as "nearness to having made up one's mind" to choose goal A or B. In our negotiation situation, the two goals represent certain wage rates (the then announced or ostensible positions of the parties), and hence the distance between these goals may be thought of as scaled in terms of such rates. For example, suppose the company's announced position to be $1.50 and the union's announced position to be $2. An equilibrium position halfway between the two announced positions would be represented by a rate of $1.75. The equilibrium position represents the least favorable terms to himself, characteristically less favorable to himself than his ostensible position, which a party is willing to accept. Further, the party in such an equilibrium position will be supposed ready to settle at that rate—if there were any way to do so, a point to be elaborated subsequently.

Returning to the negotiation task as seen by the union, one important aspect of it is to move the company's equilibrium position in a direction favorable to the union, that is (in terms of Figure 1), toward the company's goal A. This aspect of the negotiation task will be accomplished by the union's operating upon (shifting the locus of) the company avoidance functions, and, in the context of this model, this is one function of the tactics used during the negotiation process. That is, an analysis of the negotiation process in terms of this scheme is in large part an analysis of the shift parameters relevant to the avoidance functions, among such parameters being the tactics used during the course of negotiation. Two classes of union negotiation tactics which will have a favorable (from the union's point of view) impact upon the company's equilibrium position must be distinguished:

Class I: Tactics which will raise the company's avoidance gradient to the company's goal B—insisting upon its own position.

Class II: Tactics which will lower the company's avoidance gradient to the company's goal A—settling on the union's terms.

Subsequently, tactics of Class I will be referred to simply as raising the avoidance gradient, and tactics of Class II will be referred to as lowering the avoidance gradient—the goals of reference being understood.[13] The treatment of tactical moves within the context of this model can be made more definite by a generalized example. Again with reference to Figure 1, the goals confronting the company are negative. To elect goal B may result in a strike. The expected cost calculation on this score must presumably be compounded of two parts:

(1) an estimate of the probable cost to the company of a strike, should it occur;

(2) an estimate of the probability that the company's insisting upon its own position will indeed eventuate in a strike.

Goal A is also negative, the cost being lower profits in consequence of higher wage rates, *ceteris paribus*. The company may be viewed as initially in equilibrium at position D1. The union's negotiation task is to shift the company avoidance functions in such a way as to move that equilibrium position toward goal A, or, if possible, make it coincident with goal A. Anything that the union can do to make the company think a strike more probable and/or increase the company's notion of the cost of a strike should it eventuate will have a Class I tactical effect—increase the company's tendency to avoid insisting upon its own position. Also, for example, anything that the union can do to minimize the company's estimate of the labor-cost implications of higher wage rates will have a Class II tactical effect—decrease the company's tendency to avoid settling on the union's terms.[14]

Necessary and Sufficient Conditions for an Outcome by Agreement

Although we have thus far been looking at the negotiation process largely from one side of the table, it will be recalled that the analysis is intended to apply symmetrically to both sides. To complete the analysis, it is necessary to think in terms of two figures such as Figure 1, one representing the union's conflict-choice situation and equilibrium position and the other representing the company's conflict-choice situation and equilibrium position. The definition of equilibrium positions implies that it is a necessary condition for agreement that the equilibrium positions of the parties be brought to the same position. One definite task to be accomplished by the exchange of information in negotiation is to bring this consonance (necessary but not sufficient for agreement) about. Beyond this, the parties must somehow be mutually informed of the similarity of their equilibrium positions if the fact of this equality is to create a route to agreement. This is the second major function of the exchange of information during negotiation—it must be fulfilled before the conditions for an outcome by agreement are sufficient.[15] The question of precisely how such a communication may be accomplished is important and will be discussed later, especially in Chapter VI. One difficulty is the fact that a party's simple and direct announcement of his own equilibrium position may serve to stiffen his opponent's resistance and make him less ready to compromise—rather than serve to set up a route to agreement.

Theoretical Determinacy of the Outcome

May we say that analyzed in terms of the avoidance–avoidance model the outcome of collective bargaining negotiations is theoretically determinate? Without becoming involved in general discussion of the concept "determinacy" in this context, we may consider the following few points on this score.[16]

The avoidance–avoidance model is a stable equilibrium model. As applied to both sides of the bargaining table, it determines an equilibrium position for both parties—the least favorable terms upon which each is willing to settle. Analogously to comparative statics analysis generally, the model permits (at least in principle) prediction of the direction of shift of these equilibrium positions consequent, *ceteris paribus,* upon shifts in certain parameters of interest. Although consonance of these equilibrium positions is not sufficient for an outcome by agreement, it is a necessary condition for such an outcome, and, hence, shifts in either or both equilibrium positions have a predictable effect upon the locus of the outcome by agreement. Because it does exhibit equilibrium positions, there is a kind of technical determinacy in this analysis which brings a sense of order to analysis of the negotiation process.

Again analogously to comparative statics analysis generally, the avoidance–avoidance model "sets up" subsequent substantive analysis of negotiation by directing attention to presumably critical factors—namely, those which will shift the avoidance functions and hence the equilibrium positions of the parties. We have seen that among these factors are the negotiation tactics employed by the parties. Discussion in the following chapters of tactics like persuasion, rationalization, bluff, notbluff, commitment, and so on, is related to the avoidance–avoidance model and to the results of this chapter in the sense that these tactics may be viewed as shift parameters in the avoidance functions. Although these tactics might, for the most part, be discussed independently of the avoidance–avoidance model, such a discussion would be much less satisfactory. However, perhaps it should be noted that the tactics discussed are related to the formal theoretical structure of the model developed in this chapter in only a rather *ad hoc* fashion; that is, the various tactical entities are not formally incorporated into the avoidance functions as parameters. There is little in the way of formal theory which relates shifts in these functions to the tactics. These tactics can also be discussed in connection with other choice models like the game-theory matrix.

It should also be noted that a formal model structures the analysis of the choice problem involved in negotiation by suggesting those positions (for instance, various wage rates, where this is the sole bargaining issue) upon which the parties are supposed to focus during negotiation. The avoidance–avoidance format depicts the negotiator as concerned at each point during negotiation with four bargaining positions: his announced position, that of his opponent, his own equilibrium position, and that of his opponent.

Asymmetry in Negotiation Tactics and the Possibility of "Breakdown"

There is one implication of the avoidance–avoidance model which because it has a bearing upon negotiation tactics generally warrants attention here. This is the possibility of an important asymmetry in the two classes of negotiation tactics previously distinguished.

It will be recalled that the avoidance–avoidance model determined not only the party's equilibrium distance from the negative goals, but also the strength of the party's tendency to avoid these goals, which in equilibrium is the same for both goals. The possibility of the "breakdown" is suggested by the second of these two variables. Tension experienced in this choice situation, an increasing function of the strength of tendency to avoid experienced in equilibrium, provides a motivation for escape. The parties are initially constrained to participate in the choice situation by the symbiotic nature of their basic relationship. However, high and/or long-experienced levels of tension may lead to various forms of aberrant behavior, such as reduced learning capacity, reduced ability to pay attention, and so forth. Such behavior might *per se* reduce the chances of finding a compromise solution via negotiation. Beyond this, a part of such behavior might be simply to "bolt" the negotiation choice situation in a precipitate and nondeliberate fashion (unlike, for example, a calculated strike which is an integral part of the negotiation process). Such a termination of negotiations is what we here term a breakdown of the negotiation—to be distinguished from the outcome "no agreement." (It may be noted that the statutory obligation to negotiate may be a bar to escape from the choice situation.)

The argument here is not that collective bargaining negotiations will typically involve the kind of emotional content leading to breakdown.[17] Rather, the position is this: If the avoidance–avoidance paradigm is conceptually appropriate for analysis of the negotiation-choice problem, then the possibility of breakdown must be taken into account.

The above considerations suggest the possibility of an asymmetry in the effects of two classes of negotiation tactics. Class II tactics, as used by A, for example, serve to decrease B's tendency to avoid agreement with A on A's terms. Such an effect will drive B closer to A's position. It will also serve to decrease the amount of tension experienced by B in equilibrium. Class I tactics, on the other hand, serve to increase B's tendency to avoid his own position. Such an effect will also serve to drive B closer to A's position, and in this sense may be equally efficacious with the Class II tactics. Unlike the Class II tactics, however, the Class I tactics will increase the degree of tension experienced by B in equilibrium. On the basis of the earlier argument, then, negotiations featuring heavy emphasis upon Class I tactics should, *ceteris paribus,* be more apt to terminate in breakdown (rather than agreement or simple no agreement) than negotiations featuring relatively heavier emphasis upon Class II tactics.

THE THEORY OF GAME DESIGN

In undertaking to analyze, as we do in the following chapter, the rules for play of the collective bargaining negotiation game, we are concerned with the theory of game design. In emphasis, at least, this analytical concern is rather different from that characteristic of game-theory analysis. Game theory is largely concerned with efficient or optimal play of extant or specially contrived games. The rules defining such games are characteristically taken as given—not to be explained (as, for example, by analyzing the consequences of alternative rules). They owe their appearance in the game-theory literature to the fact that they are in some sense interesting; for example, they serve to illustrate a particular theoretical point.

De-emphasis of game design in the game-theory literature is quite understandable. For one thing, some of the game rules—for example, those characterizing the players as "rational"—must be accepted as a virtual *sine qua non* of the analysis. Beyond this, analysis in extensive form of any but the simplest games is not feasible. Analytical concern is with abstract games in normal form, game formats which somehow represent all possible (or a large sample of all possible) games rather than any particular games. In actual purposive social games, some of the most crucial rules concern the choices available to the players at each move of the game, but in analysis of abstract games in normal form, the domain of possible choices, rather than being explicated, is buried in the concept of a "strategy." [18] Further, perfect move symmetry is imposed upon the game by definition, and this leads to a loss of much that is interesting—for example, analysis of a variety of coercive tactics.[19]

Parlor games and simple games intended as examples of analytical points are designed as complete packages with an eye to the internal consistency of the rules. Social games usually are not contrived as complete, internally consistent packages. The rules for social games evolve via social interaction, an interaction in which the *de facto* constraints implicit in one stage, for instance, the way in which the game "gets started," may only subsequently be revealed to the parties. The rules which will ultimately govern a class of social interactions thus grow in the process of play and are not necessarily foreseen or anticipated in the beginning stages. Therefore, the rules of evolving social games may easily develop perplexing internal inconsistencies and may develop in such a way as to obstruct discharge of the functions for which the game is intended. With reference to collective bargaining, it has been observed that in the absence of deliberate attention to procedural questions, like selection of methods of negotiation, negotiation methods "just grow," and may grow in such a way as to obstruct the objective of obtaining agreement.[20]

In part for the above reasons, the understandable de-emphasis within the context of formal game theory of analysis of the rules for play of games, of game design, should certainly not be carried over into more general systematic approaches to the analysis of social games. Indeed, it may well be that from the point of view of purposive social games, emphasis upon game design is more important than emphasis upon the theory of optimal play of any particular social game.

The importance of attention to game design is further suggested by a concept developed in this chapter—that of "unnatural" purposive games. An unnatural game, it will be recalled, is one in which pressures generated in the choice situation it comprises impel the parties to seek strategies and tactics in addition to those made available by the existing rules for play. This concept is important in part because the players of purposive social games have some control over the rules for play of the games in which they participate. Confronted with rules for play which create an unnatural choice problem, they may be expected to respond not only by attempting optimal play of the extant game, but also by operations on the rules for play themselves. It may be argued that, since unnatural games may evoke responses designed to eliminate them, such games will tend to be transitory phenomena in an historical sense. In consequence, game analysis intended to bear on social games should perhaps concentrate on natural games. At least, such analysis should query with respect to the significance of game formats which appear to be unnatural in the above sense. The query should particularly be with respect to whether the response of operating upon the rules structure is not apt to be prepotent as contrasted with optimal play of the extant game.[21]

CHAPTER III

Rules for Play of the Negotiation Game

Certain customary features of collective bargaining negotiation may be assumed under the rubric "rules for play" of the collective bargaining negotiation game (or game-variant sequence). These are not for the most part rules in the formal sense. Rather, they are basic features characteristic of collective bargaining as it is conducted in this country. Although separated for analytical purposes, certain of the following rules are related. For example, the "large demand rule" is related to the "agenda rule" since it is the initial demand and counterdemand that usually set the negotiation agenda. Also, one cannot generally maintain a sharp distinction between rules for play and tactics used for subsequent play within the context of the rules framework. For instance, the "deadline rule" has important tactical implications during the later stages of negotiations. Certain of these rules will be discussed in following chapters where apropos.

In the initial statement of each of the following rules, characteristic practice will be adduced. Common exceptions and/or different procedures of analytical interest are considered later.

RULE FOR BEGINNING EACH PLAY OF THE NEGOTIATION GAME: IMPENDING EXPIRATION OF THE EXISTING COLLECTIVE AGREEMENT

Collective bargaining negotiation does not usually begin in desultory fashion, that is at any time at the option of either party. Each collective agreement carries a terminal date, the provisions having been agreed to for only a specific period of time. During its life, the agreement serves as a bar to further substantive negotiation. Impending expiration of the agreement permits reopening of negotiations.[1]

Historically, collective agreements of one-year duration have been the most popular. Beginning with the General Motors–United Automobile Workers agreement in 1948, there has been some trend toward longer contract periods—three or even five years. Such longer-duration contracts frequently provide for wage adjustments during the life of the agreement. Wage adjustment plans may be either permissive or automatic. Permissive plans permit the reopening of wage negotiations, either at stated intervals during the life of the agreement (for instance, thirty days prior to the anniversary date of the agreement) or when either party can demonstrate that changes in the economic environment may warrant a change in wages.[2] Wage reopening of a long-term contract at stated intervals means that if either party avails itself of the opportunity provided the period of time for which the wage terms have been agreed to can be shorter than that applicable to the other contract terms. (Generally speaking, not all provisions of a collective bargaining agreement need expire on the same date.) Permissive plans based on factors other than the elapse of time will be taken up further along.

Automatic wage adjustment plans, rather than providing opportunity for reopening negotiation, make wage changes compulsory. Some such plans involve step increases, payment of a negotiated wage increase in annual (or other) installments (perhaps rationalized in terms of a productivity-based "improvement" factor). Other contracts of the automatic-adjustment type base wage changes upon changes in the cost of living as measured by some agreed-upon index (escalator clauses). In recent years, as many as five million employees have been under this type of agreement.

In this country, a notable exception to the general rule that collective agreements carry terminal dates has been found in the railroad industry (the railroad agreements have in the past carried no fixed terminal date, and have been of indefinite duration with provision of notice of desire to change the agreement). In 1956, however, rail agreements were negotiated for a three-year period, the wage increase to be paid in three annual installments—and a three-year moratorium on new proposals to alter working rules was provided.[3] It is of interest that in Great Britain the great majority of collective agreements do not run for any stated period. In that country agreements usually remain in force until one party gives notice of a desire to modify, and, as a result, new negotiations can be started at any time.[4]

For a number of reasons (including the fact that the relative power positions of the parties may be influenced by the timing of negotiations), the rule for beginning each play of the negotiation game is a feature of collective bargaining which warrants attention.[5] There are a variety of possibilities in addition to that of beginning upon a date determined by the expiration of an existing agreement. Play might begin upon a signal originated by a third party or by "nature"—a change in a cost-of-living index. Play might begin whenever both parties agree to begin or at the option of either party. If there is to be a contract, this latter rule suggests one of indefinite duration. A contract of "indefinite" duration may also be one in which the provisions are intended, explicitly or by tacit agreement, to prevail in perpetuity.

There are economic reasons why the collective agreements which are binding for stated periods may be desirable.[6] Production processes require some minimum periods of stability in the basic terms governing the relationship between the parties. A contract of indefinite duration, one which may expire tomorrow, might result in frequent and unpredictable changes in these terms. Such a contract might involve the parties in more or less continuous substantive negotiations. Such continuous negotiation, or at least continuous uncertainty about the basic terms to govern the relationship between the parties, would disrupt production. Some minimum-length periods, free from changes in terms and free from industrial dispute, are if not a necessity certainly highly desirable.

These considerations suggest a basic reason (with strategic as well as substantive implications) why collective agreements are negotiated for stated periods of time. Negotiation is essentially prospective. It is very difficult to negotiate terms for the future without having in mind some minimum period of time during which they shall remain unchanged.[7]

In the context of the present inquiry, interest inheres in the rule for beginning each play of the negotiation game particularly because of its tactical significance; that is, for tactical reasons, the rule is not neutral with respect to the outcome of the negotiations. It has often been observed that the bargaining position of unions is relatively strong during periods of full employment, tight markets, and high profits—and relatively weak during periods of unemployment, and slack markets. The familiar reasons for this need only be suggested. During prosperity and full employment, union treasuries are usually larger, strikebreakers are harder to come by, alternative employment opportunities may be available for permanently replaced strikers, and so forth. The employer's will to resist is weakened by fear of loss of profits and profitable markets, by the relative ease with which increased labor costs may be passed on in the form of higher prices, by previously made contractual commitments to deliver output, and so on. Depression and dull trade seasons tend to reverse the positions.

Were negotiation to begin at any time at the option of either party, each one should be expected to exploit these environmental circumstances affecting his relative power position, and hence each party would live in fear of such exploitation.

In the early days of collective bargaining in this country, when collective agreements were not constrained by contracts of definite duration, precisely this kind of exploitation of the market situation took place, leading to alternating increases and decreases in the rate depending upon market conditions.[8] The seasonal factor was particularly important from this point of view. Local unions, particularly of those workers with little experience in unionism, were prone to strike at any time—dull season or no. Officials of national unions, however, were well aware that the timing element was critical and well aware of the strategic importance of the seasonal element. National officials urged the locals not to attempt strike activity during the dull market season or in more prolonged periods of generally depressed conditions, but to reserve such activity for periods of high demand. Some unions (bricklayers, cigar makers, sheet metal workers, piano workers, carpenters) passed laws providing that the national would not recognize, sanction, or give aid to strikes undertaken by locals during the dull trade season.

In time, employers attempted to forestall seasonal demands for wage increases and the strikes associated therewith by demanding annual contracts from their employees, and the national unions began to favor a policy of substituting the annual agreement for the short-run tug of war based upon alternating market conditions. Generally speaking, the tactical implications of the seasonal factor were a strong force working in the direction of annual agreements.

Another tactical aspect of the definite-duration agreement may be noted in this context. Prior to the negotiation of annual agreements, some emphasis was put upon the surprise element in strike activity. Officials of the molders and the carpenters, for instance, advocated giving employers no notice of intention to strike. Preparation for the possibility of overt industrial conflict is facilitated by definite contract terminal dates. Customers of firms which may be struck may accumulate inventories, firms may get orders completed, and, generally, the parties to the prospective conflict may put intraorganizational and extraorganizational fences in order.[9]

There are reasons such as those discussed above why collective bargaining contracts should serve as a bar to new negotiations for some minimum period of time, and why negotiations should not be begun at any time at the option of either party. However, there are problems in such an arrangement. Not only does the expiration of an existing contract permit the opening of negotiation, it also tends to "invite" the making of new demands. That is, the institution of terminal contract dates tends to make the institution of serving new and increased demands upon the bargaining opponent a frequent and quasi-automatic procedure. In part for the reason that collective bargaining negotiations always carry with them the possibility of overt industrial conflict, this frequency and quasi-automaticity in the serving of demands may be undesirable.

Such considerations suggest that perhaps some cue more clearly relevant than the mere passage of time should signal the opening of negotiations. Although a third party (a public authority) might provide such a cue at his discretion, the most logical candidate for this role would seem to be relevant aspects of the environment. For example, the union, rather than demanding a wage increase every October 20, might agree to a rule permitting such demands when the cost-of-living index had risen a certain amount, or when productivity (intraorganizational or national) had increased a certain amount, and so forth. With this approach, the basic criteria now adduced during wage negotiations might become the cues for beginning wage negotiations.

To some extent this kind of arrangement is currently used, not with respect to new contract negotiations, but with respect to wage adjustment plans operative during the life of an existing agreement. Permissive wage adjustment plans have based wage reopenings upon a variety of factors.[10] The most common factor specified in wage reopenings has been changes in the cost of living, either by some definite amount or by some more vaguely defined "substantial" or "decided" amount. (More popular than reopening on the basis of cost of living is the escalator clause which automatically changes the wage rate during the life of the agreement depending upon movement in a price index.) During the war years, when wages were controlled by stabilization regulations, reopening of wages was frequently based upon substantial changes in the national wage policy. Some contracts have based reopenings upon changes in general "economic conditions." Some wage adjustment plans have provided for reopening based upon changes in the company's competitive position or financial condition. Other reopenings have been based upon changes in industry or area wage levels and upon changes in the length of the workweek, and even sometimes upon changes in the price of the company's product.

Thinking in terms of the general problem of a rule for beginning each play of the negotiation game, it may be argued that such environmental clues might indeed be more relevant in beginning wage negotiations. However, numerous difficulties would seem to attend much extension of their use. Some of these would be the same difficulties of measurement (and, from a social point of view, of economic logic) which attend the usual use of these criteria during the course of negotiations.

If we extend cognizance beyond wage negotiation to contract negotiation generally, more difficulties arise. The wage rate is only one of the numerous items comprising the subject matter of collective bargaining. In addition, the parties bargain about such matters as seniority, other rules for the allocation of job opportunity, work schedules, vacations, pensions and health and welfare plans, union security provisions, the status of union representatives, the form of wage payment, supplemental unemployment pay, and so on. It might be argued that such environmental clues as an increase in a price index are relevant to opening negotiation about the wage rate. But what environmental clues are similarly relevant to the other subjects of collective bargaining? For such subject matter, the terminal contract date would seem to provide the best rule in a system such as ours for beginning a new play of the collective bargaining negotiation game.

THE "LARGE" INITIAL BARGAINING DEMAND RULE

It is difficult to maintain a sharp distinction between rules for play of the negotiation game on the one hand, and tactics utilized for subsequent play within the context of a rules framework on the other. It might be argued that the large demand belongs more properly in the latter category. The large demand will be discussed from this point of view in Chapter IV. In this chapter, however, the rule-like character of this institutional arrangement will be suggested. Attention will be directed to the consonance of the large demand with the requirements of the negotiation process as a whole.

The large-demand rule provides that the initial bargaining demand and counterdemand are in excess of the least favorable terms upon which each party is willing to settle, and in excess of what each expects the agreed-upon position to be. Both parties know this.

It has been observed that insight into bargaining demands is requisite to an understanding of the bargaining process.[11] Demands which are large in the above sense are an integral part of most collective bargaining negotiations. A few bargaining relationships, however, feature what may be termed the "minimum" demand (or "maximum" concession), which is an initial bargaining proposal virtually identical with the least favorable terms upon which a party is willing to settle.

A general explanation of large demands is that the rules for beginning an interaction have much to do with the kind of game that can subsequently be played to resolve that interaction. Or, put the other way around, once it has been decided that a certain kind of game is appropriate to the resolution of an interaction, then only certain rules for beginning that interaction are permissible. The opening move is dictated, within limits, by the properties of the game that is desired. For this reason, the beginning of a purposive social game such as collective bargaining negotiation is critical.

We saw in Chapter II that to resolve the collective bargaining interaction by playing take-it-or-leave-it results in what was termed an unnatural purposive game. It impels the parties to seek an alternative, to prefer to resolve their conflict via negotiation. At this general level, if one has in this fashion explained why the parties to collective bargaining elect to negotiate, one has also explained the institution of the large demand as a rule for beginning. This is because the only rule for beginning really consonant with subsequent negotiation is the initial large demand. If there is to be subsequent negotiation, initial demands must permit what is frequently termed "room for bargaining," and this the large demand does. Such demands set up a context in which information can be gained during the course of negotiation to elect a firm strategy. Initial uncertainty about the range in which an agreed position can lie makes the large demand prudent, that is, the large demand precludes the possibility of inadvertent commitment to a position either less favorable than that which might have been obtained or to a position sure (it develops) to result in an outcome "no agreement."

Another basic consonance of the large initial bargaining demand with the negotiation process is related to the fact that negotiations frequently

take considerable time, time during which conditions affecting the negotiations may change. This fact, coupled with the consideration that the
practice of adding to demands during the course of negotiation is not
itself compatible with the negotiation process, create pressures in favor
of large initial demands.

The Minimum Demand or Maximum Offer ("Boulwareism")

The major alternative to the large demand as a tactic for beginning
negotiation is the "minimum" demand or "maximum" offer, that is, an
initial bargaining proposal which is (virtually) identical with the least
favorable terms to himself upon which a party is willing to settle.[12] A
prominent case in point is the approach to collective bargaining commonly termed "Boulwareism" (after a chief proponent of the technique,
Lemuel Boulware of the General Electric Company).[13]

The central feature of this approach is to meet the union's initial bargaining demand with a single counterproposal to which the company
intends to adhere. That is, the union is told that it can accept or reject
the company proposal, but come what may, the company does not intend
to move from its announced position. With the Boulware approach, the
single counterproposal is carefully researched in an effort to come up
with an offer which is "right" by any reasonable standard, which is
"fair," and which will be considered fair by the employees. Once the
proposal is formulated, the technique is to stick to it, not to "haggle"
about it.

Although emphasis has been put upon the negotiation implications
of the Boulware approach, it is important to recognize that this approach
is much more than simply a negotiation technique. Actually, it is a whole
"philosophy" of labor-management relations. It involves not only carefully
researched proposals, but also continuing, year-round efforts to keep lines
of communication with employees open to insure that they are adequately apprised of the "fairness" of the proposals.[14]

In large measure, the maximum offer (or minimum demand) is not
just another way to begin a game of negotiation. It is a technique for
converting a would-be negotiation game into one of take-it-or-leave-it.
It may be argued that the maximum offer is basically inconsistent with
the collective bargaining relationship underlying negotiation. It may be
interpreted as an attempt to deny the function of the union as an organization which "gets something" for its members. It is, in a sense, an appeal
directly to the employees. The latter are told that they will get what is

"right" and "fair" because the company has decided to give it to them, not because the union has extracted it from the company. Kerr has noted that "to insist to the end on the original proposal is almost an unfair labor practice, under the rules of the game, for it denies the other party the opportunity of forcing some concession and thus claiming a victory of sorts." [15] Peters, having pointed out that "prestige is an inexorable regulator of the practices of collective bargaining, and will not be denied," noted that the prestige factor will not permit the parties to forego at least the semblance of bargaining. The difficulty is that if either side accepts a "one-shot" demand or proposal, in the eyes of the employees it might appear as if that side had surrendered. A bargaining technique which completely denies "victories" will invite interminable prestige fights.[16] It is this basic nonconsonance of the minimum demand with the negotiation game and with the bargaining relationship underlying negotiation which suggests treatment of the large demand as rule for play— rather than just as a tactic used during the early stages of negotiation.

It should be noted that not all evaluation of the Boulware approach is negative. For example, R. W. McMurray, having expressed the view that the key to power in labor relations is to be found in the allegiances of the workers, advises that management demonstrate by actions that it can be depended upon, without constant prodding by the union, to be concerned with the welfare of its employees. From this point of view, he feels that Boulwareism is "basically more realistic" than more conciliatory techniques, although he does note that Boulwareism may be "unnecessarily provocative." [17]

Further it may be contended that, in a bargaining situation such as that between the General Electric Company and the IUE, the union could develop an acceptable position (other than striking) in the face of what may be a reasonable, albeit take-it-or-leave-it offer. For example, if the union officials believe the offer to be reasonable, they might attempt to take credit for it by contending that the only reason the offer is satisfactory is because of pressure by the union.

The "Commitment"

Closely related to the maximum-offer approach to negotiation is a class of negotiation tactics to which T. C. Schelling has drawn attention, tactics which he considers "peculiarly appropriate to the logic of indeterminate situations. The essence of these tactics is some voluntary but irreversible sacrifice of freedom of choice." [18] By an indeterminate situation in this context is meant a bargaining situation featuring a manifest contract zone—a range of positions each of which is preferred by both parties to "no agreement," and both know this. He terms this class of tactics the "commitment." The essential thrust of this tactic is that it enables a player to convert the bargaining choice confronted by his adversary into one of the take-it-or-leave-it variety. For example, player A contrives to so bind himself to a position that B is convinced that A will not (cannot) make any concession. (A, having asserted that he will not remain up a tree, may issue irrevocable instructions to an accomplice to start sawing off the limb upon which he is sitting.) As we shall see, tactics such as bluff, notbluff, and threat, all involve a problem of (at least apparent) commitment—and means to such commitment will be discussed in conjunction with those tactics. The commitment itself, as a tactical entity, is to be distinguished as "a means of gaining first move in a game in which first move carries an advantage." This is in contrast to the threat which, although it involves a problem of commitment, is a commitment to a strategy for second move.[19] The maximum-offer tactic characteristic of the Boulware approach may not be literally considered a commitment in the sense that the company has made an "irreversible" sacrifice of freedom of choice. However, it may be argued that this approach is virtually autocommitting. It has been pointed out with respect to this approach that: "Failure is disastrous. . . . If a company can be made to back down from what is originally announced as an unalterable position, future unalterable positions will not be taken seriously. A substantial gamble is involved, and the penalty for losing is heavy—the loss of the ears and minds of the 'job customers.' " [20] In a continuing relationship such as collective bargaining in which negotiation occurs regularly, the minimum demand is autocommitting, that is, no special device is needed to bind the party to its position insofar as insuring its own performance is concerned.

Although Schelling has included wage negotiations among the economic interactions with which the subject of his bargaining essay is concerned,[21] we should not expect the commitment tactic, as a way to seize first move, to be of prime importance in many collective bargaining negotiations. We have seen that the structure of the choice situation created by the bargaining relationship underlying collective bargaining negotiation is such that the parties are impelled to choose to negotiate rather than to play take-it-or-leave-it. In consequence it would not seem plausible that a primary negotiation tactic should be an attempt immediately to convert the game negotiation into one of the take-it-or-leave-it variety. As pointed out, in some collective bargaining negotiation (Boulwareism, for example) what amounts to the commitment has played a significant role. Further tactical implications of this move will be discussed later.

The Statutory Obligation to Bargain Collectively as an Obligation to Listen

Although it conveys the essence of the matter, it is not quite correct to say that a maximum offer of the Boulwareism type literally converts a would-be negotiation game into take-it-or-leave-it. The parties to collective bargaining are obligated by law to bargain, which includes a requirement "to meet at reasonable times and confer in good faith . . ." (Section 8 [d], National Labor Relations Act). Bargaining under the minimum-demand approach in general and under Boulwareism in particular is no exception to this rule, and, indeed, in this case the company stands ready to meet the union (even though, at such a meeting, it may point out that it does not intend to budge from its announced position.)

Investigators who doubt the efficacy of the statutory bargaining obligation are apt to apply: "You can lead a horse to water but you can't make him drink." This evaluation misses an important part of the tactical picture, however, for if you can lead a party to the bargaining table you can at least make him listen—and this may be critical. This is because manipulation of the communications structure of a bargaining situation, including destruction of the possibility of communication, may have important tactical implications. Luce and Raiffa have pointed out that there are some games in which it is advantageous to one party if the rules do not provide for preplay communication, that is, do not provide for negotiation.[22] These are situations in which the game structure provides the opponent with a latent threat—a threat which can be exploited if preplay communication is permitted, but not otherwise. In general, a threat must remain latent, it is powerless, unless it can be communicated to the opposite number.[23] These considerations are related to the commitment tactic as a way to gain "first move," since one device for commitment is to destroy the possibility of communication immediately after having assumed a position. This possibility is not open to the parties to collective bargaining. This fact may reduce the tendency of the parties to resort to commitment as an opening tactic.

THE AGENDA RULE—AGENDA SET BY INITIAL DEMAND
AND COUNTERPROPOSAL

Characteristically in collective bargaining the initial demand and counterproposal set the agenda for each periodic agreement conference. That is, there is no systematic negotiation of the agenda prior to the beginning of substantive contract negotiations.

As with other rules for play of the negotiation game, there are possible alternatives to the agenda rule. In some international negotiations, for example, it is customary to decide upon the agenda itself by negotiation before the beginning of substantive negotiation. In some collective bargaining relationships there are preagreement-conference procedures which tend in the direction of agenda negotiation.

The problem of the tactical significance of agenda composition is related to the institution of the "large demand" since the agenda is brought into being by the bargaining demand and counterproposal. Nevertheless, these phenomena ought to be distinguished. Suppose that "n" items are to be negotiated by the parties in one or more plays—that is, in one or more separate forums. The tactics of agenda design are concerned with the distribution of these n items among the one or more plays. The large demand institution is more concerned with the number n itself. The above supposed demand would have been larger, for example, if we had supposed that $n + 1$ items were to be negotiated by the parties in one or more plays (but this need not affect the composition of the agenda pertaining to other than one play). Since the agenda for each play is brought into being by demand and counterdemand, a decision to increase the magnitude of a demand will alter the composition of the agenda pertaining to that play. However, in this case the alteration of the composition of the agenda is essentially a by-product of the initial bargaining demand decision, the latter made on grounds not peculiarly concerned with the tactics of agenda composition.

Interest in the agenda rule for collective bargaining negotiation inheres in the possibility that agenda composition has tactical significance. There is no *prima facie* case that agenda composition has significant tactical implications in collective bargaining negotiation. Nevertheless, this possibility should be explored. Schelling has expressed the opinion that whether two or more items are negotiated simultaneously or in separate forums may affect the outcome. For example, negotiating items simultaneously may facilitate the use of threat, by bringing to bear on one proposition the threat of adverse action on others. Also, multi-item negotiations may play a generally enabling role in cases where the principal means of compensation available to the parties is concession on some other item. In such a case, if two simultaneous negotiations can be brought into a contingent relationship, a means of compensation may be made available, where otherwise none might exist.[24] These suggestions are aspects of the proposition frequently encountered in the literature on collective bargaining that items may be included in bargaining demands because of their trading value.

It is sometimes suggested that in a bilateral-conflict relationship such as collective bargaining there may be a tactical advantage attached to "first move," especially if this can be seized by commitment. However, the above considerations suggest that there may be an offsetting asymmetry of tactical advantage stemming from agenda composition inherent in any procedure in which the demand and counterproposal are not presented simultaneously. For example, in a nonsimultaneous procedure, the party with "first move" may "waste" a potentially useful threat by attempting to exploit it in circumstances which turn out to be inappropriate in the light of the counterproposition. Suppose that a union, aiming for a substantial wage increase, thinks that the company will offer little or nothing. The union might include a union security demand in the agenda for this forum, hoping to trade it for a tolerable wage increase. If, however, the company's "real" position on the wage increase is much more generous than the union had expected (a fact which might have been inferred had the company made the initial proposal), the union security demand "turns out to have been" used in a context in which its trading value significance was not tactically required. The party with "second move" may be able to avoid such waste.[25] Moreover, the party with "second move" (the counterproposer) can judiciously avail himself of means to compensation and, thus perhaps induce agreements which would not otherwise be possible. A company, wishing to eliminate an objectionable clause from the collective agreement, might attach this demand to an agenda which contained union demands on which it is willing to make a concession. Thus, the company, in making its demand, does so in a context known to contain at least potential means of compensation. Were the demand and counterproposal procedure simultaneous, the company might attach its demand to an agenda which contained no other union propositions it was willing to concede and which therefore contained no means (agreeable to the company) for compensating the union for accepting its own demand.

Why do the parties to collective bargaining negotiation not engage in prenegotiation agenda negotiation rather than simply accept whatever agenda eventuates from the initial demand and counterproposal? One answer to this lies in the nature of the political relationship between the negotiators and their constituents, especially on the union side, a matter to be discussed subsequently. Another answer probably lies in the nature of those sanctions available to the parties which underlie their bargaining relationship; namely, the strike or lockout. Just as A's refusal to accept a given B demand may be backed if necessary by the strike, so A's refusal to admit a given B item to the agenda may be backed by the strike or lockout if this be necessary. What is to be gained by striking an opponent during prenegotiation if he may be struck as well during the course of substantive negotiations?

Another answer is that the continuing nature of the collective bargaining relationship may greatly attenuate the tactical implications of agenda composition. In a continuing relationship such as collective bargaining it may not be possible to achieve *de facto* isolation of the agenda for one play from the (anticipated) agendas for subsequent plays. Indeed, and this is another explanation of large initial bargaining proposals, some demands may be included in this year's agenda largely for "educational" purposes; that is, included not so much with the intention of obtaining them this year as with the intention of familiarizing the bargaining opponent with demands to be pursued in earnest at a future date. A recent case in point has been the guaranteed annual wage (GAW) demand. For many years before the UAW finally negotiated a GAW plan with the automobile industry in 1955, many major CIO unions made demands for the GAW, only to drop these in favor of other benefits more directly felt by their members. Hence, in the years just prior to 1955, a question existed as to the "seriousness" of the GAW demand.[26]

More generally, many demands and counterdemands tend to be in the air before they make a formal appearance at the bargaining table.[27] The mere exclusion of a pension demand, for example, from this year's agenda may not keep the expectation of such a demand on next year's agenda from having a strong influence upon this year's negotiation. Even if the agenda pertaining to any one play of the collective bargaining game is not neutral with respect to the outcome of that play, it would not be of great significance in collective bargaining if the agendas pertaining to a succession of plays were collectively neutral with respect to the grand total outcome. However, since some significance attaches to the order in which items are negotiated, nonneutrality of the agenda *vis-à-vis* the whole series of plays seems probable.

The Negotiation Agenda and the Law

It was pointed out earlier that in prescriptive principle, and to a large extent in practice, a distinction between periodic contract negotiation and day-to-day contract administration is recognized and accepted. However, this line is not always finely drawn, and the statutory obligation to bargain collectively may have important implications from this point of view. More particularly, if the statutory obligation to bargain collectively is interpreted as obligating the parties to bargain in good faith at any time on any issue, the distinction between contract negotiation and contract administration would tend to break down. This view, carried to an extreme, might involve the parties in continuous substantive negotiation. This is not the place to debate the merits of such an interpretation of the law.[28] However, of importance in this context is the fact that if the parties were to become involved in more or less continuous substantive negotiation, then the matter of agenda design for any one "play" of the negotiation game would become practically irrelevant.

It is of interest to note that the parties have attempted, by contract language, to avoid the implications of such a construction of the law. This has resulted in a situation in which the agenda rule adduced in this section is not only a "rule" by force of custom, but has found explicit expression in contract language:

The parties acknowledge that during the negotiations which resulted in this agreement, each had the unlimited right and opportunity to make demands and proposals with respect to any subject or matter not removed by law from the area of collective bargaining. [There follows a waiver of right, for the life of the agreement, to bargain about matters covered by the agreement, or upon matters upon which the agreement is silent.] [29]

The above contract language suggests another aspect of the law important from the point of view of agenda composition. Some provisions, such as the closed shop, have been removed by law from the area of collective bargaining. More important in this context, Section 8 (d) of the National Labor Relations Act obligated the parties to "confer in good faith with respect to wages, hours, and other terms and conditions of employment." In consequence, NLRB interpretation of the concept "conditions of employment" becomes important from an agenda point of view. Although the parties may agree to bargain about items outside the legally defined scope of the obligation, the board and the courts will rule when there is doubt that items fall within this scope. Thus, resisting any given demand by refusing to talk about it may be deemed an unfair labor practice if that demand falls within the statutory list of items as the law is interpreted. (Beyond this, while an NLRB ruling placing an item on the agenda does not preclude other kinds of resistance to that demand, this administrative ruling may tend to prejudice the case in favor of the demand thus included in the statutory list.)

Prenegotiation Conferences

Reason can be adduced for neglecting agenda negotiation in collective bargaining. Nevertheless, it may be argued that the efficiency of collective bargaining might be improved by a less carefree approach to agenda design. For example, suppose that an n-item agenda to be negotiated contains $n - 1$ negotiable items, and one item which is absolutely unacceptable to one side. So long as the rule for play obtains that all settlements are to be package settlements (a rule to be discussed later), inclusion of this one item in the agenda will preclude settlement of the other $n - 1$ items. This may be a tactically desirable circumstance from the point of view of the party with an interest in the critical item, but it may involve considerable loss of efficiency from another point of view.[30]

Some collective bargaining relationships feature a prenegotiation conference arrangement. Taylor cites as an outstanding example the National Agreement between the Federation of Hosiery Workers and the Full Fashioned Hosiery Manufacturers of America, Inc.[31] Under this arrangement, an impartial chairman made a "joint wage survey" for the guidance of the parties in formulating their initial demands and counterproposals. The advantage of this procedure is that the parties start their actual negotiations with agreed-upon facts about the earnings of employees in the industry. In addition, these conferences included some preliminary discussion of the general "state of the industry." In Taylor's view, tactics used in collective bargaining negotiation have tended to restrict the possibility of arriving at agreement. He feels that the institution of the prenegotiation conference, designed primarily to get agreement as to the "facts" before negotiation begins, is a step in the right direction—if understanding is to supplant tactical maneuvering.

Additions to Initial Demands

Another aspect of agenda composition is the proscription that, generally speaking, a party to collective bargaining negotiation does not during the course of negotiation make demands in excess of those contained in his initial proposal. This proscription applies both to increasing the magnitude of a given item and to adding additional items to those contained in the initial proposal.

Since negotiation sessions are frequent and the initial bargaining demands can be "large" in any event, there is no general necessity to provide for subsequent increases in demands. Moreover, the practice of adding to demands during the course of negotiation is not compatible with the negotiation process. How can a party really begin to negotiate until he knows what his opponent's maximum asking price will be? Certainly the basic bargaining processes of changing position, rewarding by concession, threatening by adherence, and so on, could scarcely begin until the total demands to be served during a given play of the negotiation game were on the table.

The above considerations do not rule out the possibility that certain special functions might be served by such subsequent changes in position. One such function, for example, would be the exploitation of information about one's opponent gained during the course of negotiations. The fact that negotiation sessions are frequent greatly reduces the importance of serving this function *vis-à-vis* any particular contract negotiations; that is, it can be served during the next contract negotiations. One legitimate aspect of this function *vis-à-vis* a particular set of negotiations is the case in which the initial demander gets new ideas from the counterproposal— ideas which suggest that some redesign of the initial demand would facilitate agreement.

Much more dubious is the practice whereby a party attempts during the final stages of negotiation to exploit the fact of near agreement by tacking a last-minute demand, as a sort of "rider," onto a virtually wrapped-up package. Such an attempt, even if successful, would surely degenerate the atmosphere prevailing during subsequent negotiation sessions. However, Peters, discussing "bad faith" on the part of negotiators, cites the case of a union negotiator who habitually uses this tactic. Peters classifies this tactic as, while not perhaps properly considered bad faith, a borderline case—certainly to be regarded as bad practice.[32]

"Package" Settlements (Tentative Proposals) Rule

The outcome of collective bargaining negotiation is by agreement. Characteristically, such agreement must be upon all the items comprising the agenda. Agreement upon all items is defined as mutual assent to a disposition for each of the agenda items. This may involve overt agreement in the sense of settling upon a wage rate somewhere between the initial demands of the parties. But it may also involve other kinds of disposition such as covert agreement in the sense of the parties' refraining from further mention of an agenda item. Or it may be agreement by the parties to submit a disputed item to arbitration. Such a provision for package settlements is fairly straightforward. The items comprising a package are to a considerable extent commensurable in terms of cost, and, to a considerable extent, it is the total cost of the package that matters. In consequence, agreement on all the items is what matters.

Discussion of the package settlement provision, relating as it does to termination of negotiations, should perhaps have been delayed till the end of this chapter (where we will deal more generally with the rule for termination). Nevertheless, an aspect of the package settlement relating to tentative proposals during the course of negotiation is involved with the matter of agenda composition, and, in consequence, it facilitates matters to bring it into the discussion at this juncture.

The agenda-related point of interest is that even though a number of items are on the "same" agenda, they may in a sense be accorded separate "forums." In some collective bargaining negotiation, a division is made between "cost" and "noncost" items, and an effort is made to get the latter out of the way first.[33] The union in particular is apt to favor seriatim treatment in an effort to wrap up fringe items before attention is given subjects of major importance. According to Peters, the motivation for this is the union's knowledge that the employer is aware that a strike is unlikely over subordinate differences. However, so long as the major issues have not been settled, the union exerts strike pressure in the negotiations.[34]

The significance of the attempt to distribute items on the "same" agenda among separate forums by pressing for seriatim treatment is conditioned by a provision strongly implied by the package settlement rule: Any agreements or proposals relating to individual items made during the course of negotiations are understood to be provisional and may be withdrawn (without prejudice) if final agreement upon all items in dispute is not reached prior to a strike or lockout. This tentative-proposals provision is not quite a necessary consequence of package settlements. Even with package settlements, it could be understood that all interim agreements and concessions were binding in the sense that they would comprise part of the final agreement if and when such was achieved.

Perhaps the most interesting aspect of the tentative-proposals provision is its ambiguous status as a "rule." Dunlop and Healy have observed that withdrawal of an offer is more a matter of ritual than of fact in the sense that, barring serious defeat of one side or the other in a strike or lockout, offers already made are seldom effectively withdrawn.[35] The ambiguous status of this "rule" would seem to reflect a basic institutional ambiguity in the negotiation situation. On the one hand, such a rule is very understandable. Agreements and concessions during the course of negotiations are expected to induce mutual agreement. These are made as "promises" against a *quid pro quo*—namely, concessions and agreement by the opposite number. If agreement is not reached prior to strike or lockout, earlier concessions have not served their function. They become essentially gratuitous. In such circumstances, it seems reasonable that they be withdrawn.

On the other hand, free withdrawal without prejudice of prior agreements and proposals in the event of strike or lockout would seem to decrease the efficiency of the negotiation process. If the parties characteristically returned to their initial positions in the event of a strike or lockout, whatever function the prestrike negotiations had served in bringing the "real" positions of the parties closer would be nullified; that is, the efficiency of the negotiation process as a whole will be enhanced if strike negotiations are concerned with settling a residual difference between the parties inherited from the prestrike negotiations, rather than with settling the entire initial difference between the parties.

THE BARGAINING STRIKE (LOCKOUT) DEADLINE RULE

Characteristically in collective bargaining negotiation there is a fixed deadline after which negotiations proceed under strike or lockout conditions. The deadline is more than just a "threat" to strike if some agreement is not reached by a certain time. It is also an (implied) promise not to strike prior to that time.[36] Thus the deadline gives the parties a known period in which to negotiate free of the fear of rupture of the basic relationship.

As with other rules for play of the collective bargaining negotiation game, there are possible alternatives to the deadline. There is no natural law which says that negotiations generally, or collective bargaining negotiations in particular, must feature a deadline. Indeed, in some instances of negotiation (for instance, certain international contexts), the suggestion that there be a deadline is received with protest. Partly in consequence of the fact that alternatives to the deadline procedure are available, the question arises: What are the consequences of the fact that collective bargaining negotiations feature a deadline? (In this section, the deadline will be discussed from the point of view of its status as a rule for play. Other aspects of the deadline such as its impact upon the agreement process will be discussed later.)

Although the statement of the rule makes provision for the lockout, the deadline is ordinarily a strike deadline. A major reason for this is simply that it is the employer who pays the wages. There is ordinarily no necessity for the employer to lockout his employees, since they are either satisfied with the terms and conditions of employment set by him or they are not. In the latter event, they will strike. However, in the case of multiemployer bargaining, if the union singles out one employer for attack, other employers in the alliance may resort to lockout (or some other form of strike aid) to forestall the union's divide-and-conquer tactic.

Although the statement of the rule and subsequent discussion of it contemplate a fixed deadline, it should be recognized that some collective bargaining negotiations feature a flexible or movable deadline—one not known at the outset of negotiations. As we noted earlier, the railroad industry is an example of this. Although under the Railway Labor Act there is a deadline, the essence of this legislation is to delay it, to make uncertain the time when a deadline might become operative. Even in industries in which the "no-contract, no-work" rule prevails, a deadline which would ordinarily occur in consequence of contract expiration may be made flexible on an *ad hoc* basis. The 1958 negotiations in the automobile industry provide a case in point. In this case, contract expirations came with the union having won no concessions. The companies refused contract extensions, whereupon the UAW urged its members to go on working without contracts. The union explanation of this move was that it would not allow the companies to provoke it into a strike and that it would not give the companies a reason to justify a lockout. Many observers (including the companies themselves) felt that the strike had been postponed because the deadline occurred at a time tactically inappropriate from the union's point of view. It was in the spring of 1958, which was near the end of a poor sales season with considerable unemployment in the industry and large inventories on hand. In September with work on the new models well under way, the union did set a strike deadline for ·Ford.[37]

Game-Variant Sequences

A bargaining strike occurring in consequence of a deadline is an integral part of the negotiation process—not an instance of the "breakdown" of that process. The deadline is not a particular "threat" in the sense that A's deadline makes an A strike contingent upon some particular B course of action. A's deadline makes an A strike contingent upon "no agreement" at a particular time.

From a general analytical point of view, the principal significance of the deadline is that it sets up a game-variant sequence. The deadline rule is essentially a rule for changing the type or variant of negotiation game to be played at a particular point in time. Either player can elect this new game-variant by simply refusing to agree during the original one.

Thus the deadline rule sets up this game-variant sequence: Game-Variant 1—negotiation under no strike conditions (deadline), Game-Variant 2—negotiation under strike conditions. Thinking of 12:00 as the "moment" the strike occurs, the deadline brings with it an 11:59—a predictable "last minute" before a strike. This is important. Without the institution of the deadline, there is only a 12:01, so to speak. With the deadline, the bargaining strike is provided for in the rules framework and is confronted by the parties at the outset of negotiations; it does not occur as an *ad hoc* tactical maneuver during the course of negotiation.

In analysis of game sequences generally, a critical aspect is the interaction between the games, that is, the mutual influence of each game upon the play and solutions of the others. If a party plans to elect game-variant 2, his play of 1 may be calculated more to influence a solution to be achieved via play of 2 than to achieve solution via play of 1. For example, prestrike negotiations may be used not to achieve agreement during this stage but rather to influence an outcome to be achieved during strike negotiations. Or, even if a party does not wish to elect game-variant 2, the possibility that it might be forced upon him may cause him during the play of 1 to be concerned about the *status quo* which game 2 will inherit from 1, if indeed a play of 2 should eventuate. For example, a party may enunciate as his "last" prestrike offer not his true equilibrium position, but terms somewhat more favorable to himself than the least favorable upon which he would be willing to settle rather than take a strike. Or if a game 2 has an unambiguous solution whereas 1 does not, the former may be adopted as the solution to 1; that is, without a play of 2. For example, a probable outcome were the parties to negotiate under strike conditions may be adopted as the outcome during prestrike negotiations—without playing the sequence through to strike.

Familiar aspects of collective bargaining negotiation have been adduced as "examples" of the mechanisms whereby the mutual influence of variants in a game sequence upon the play and solution of each game may be felt. Conceptualizing the deadline as essentially a rule for setting up a game-variant sequence generalizes this institutional arrangement by placing it in a framework pertinent to the analysis of game-like interactions involving strategy and conflict.[38]

The game-variant sequence concept can be extended to encompass additional collective bargaining institutions. For example, if, in a particular case, provision is made for the introduction of a third party into negotiation either before or after the strike deadline, an additional variant is added to the game-variant sequence. It is for this reason that the mediation process may be an integral part of negotiation whether it is employed in a particular instance or not. The parties may elect this game-variant, or it may be imposed upon them in the case of negotiation affected with the public interest, and these possibilities may influence the premediation play. The same may be said of arbitration or of the intervention of public bodies generally, such as fact finding, and so on. We find in these considerations an additional explanation for the "large" initial bargaining demand. Items and issues may be included in the initial demand not so much with the intention of securing these during normal negotiation as with an eye to their potential usefulness should arbitration, or the intervention of third parties, eventuate.

Relevance and Efficiency of Variants in a Social Game Sequence

There are some requirements upon the properties of variants in a social-game sequence if the sequence considered as a whole is to be satisfactory for resolving the interaction to which it belongs. Some of these may be assumed in the concepts "relevance" and "efficiency" of variants in a social-game sequence.

The "relevance" of variants in a game sequence involves the notion that if the rules provide that a game 2 is to follow a game 1, the two variants should be homogeneous with respect to the critical properties of the choice situation out of which play of the sequence arises. If for example the basic situation involves conflict choice, suggesting that the parties resolve their interaction by negotiation during game 1, then game 2 should be some variant on a negotiation game. Or for example a game 2 will be relevant in sequence with 1 if it brings on the pressures in the sanctions upon which the bargaining relationship was predicated in the first place. Thus it has frequently been observed that it is the possibility of boycott—of refusal to deal—that makes collective bargaining negotiations "meaningful." In our case, in game-variant 2—negotiation under strike conditions—the bargaining strike brings to bear pressures which reflect the basic sanctions underlying the whole relationship and which were operative during the play of variant 1—prestrike negotiations.

A game-variant sequence may be appraised in terms of its efficiency as a whole—in terms of the consequences to the parties (or to others) of the way in which the entire sequence resolves an interaction. The concept of the efficiency of variants in a game sequence does not, however, refer to the efficiency of the sequence as a whole. It refers to internal efficiency in the relations between the variants. For example, for a game 2 to be efficient as a sequel to game 1, it must not destroy the contribution of game 1 to the ultimate resolution of the interaction. A game 2 would be inefficient in sequence with a game 1 if the mere possibility of electing 2, or the mere anticipation that 2 might be played, led to virtual abandonment of 1. In such a case, 1 would make no contribution to the functioning of the sequence as a whole. The bargaining strike (negotiation under strike conditions) is efficient in the sense that it does not generally render game 1—prestrike negotiations—otiose.

The Problem of Historical Terminacy

The fact that the bargaining-strike deadline rule sets up a game-variant sequence in which variant 2 is both relevant and efficient as a sequel to variant 1 may be viewed as a permissive condition for the prevalence of this rule. But it is not enough by itself to explain the institution of the deadline. It is necessary to show why the negotiation game as a whole would tend at least to be significantly different without the deadline rule. Some such particular functions will be discussed in the following chapter.

One aspect of this matter, however, that relating to the problem of the terminacy, in an historical sense of a given play of the negotiation game, warrants attention here. What mechanism terminates the process of negotiation itself? Or why should a play of the negotiation game not go on forever. One function of the deadline is to hasten the termination of negotiations. There are reasons in the situation to suppose that collective bargaining negotiations might go on for a very long time under a guarantee of no strike. The occurrence of a strike on the other hand would certainly bring about pressures to hasten the termination of negotiation. The deadline rule brings about these same pressures—an 11:59.

The problem of terminacy of the negotiation process in an historical sense should be distinguished from that of theoretical "indeterminacy" of the outcome in the sense of comparative statics analysis. Allusion to the former problem is seldom encountered in the literature. The latter is frequently discussed, the prevailing view being that the price under bilateral monopoly generally (including collective bargaining) is theoretically indeterminate within the limits afforded by the contract zone.[39] A theory which did yield a determinate outcome for bilateral monopoly would not necessarily be very helpful in explaining historical terminacy. This is natural since comparative statics analysis is "timeless" not only in the sense of being nondynamic, but also in the sense of lack of historical-time significance. Nevertheless, the two problems are related. One might suppose that a process which was indeterminate as to outcome would tend to continue for an indefinite time, that is, the absence of a determinate solution would imply an absence of mechanism to resolve the forces giving rise to the process in the first place.

More important from the point of view of economic theory is influence in the other direction. If the parties to an interaction devise a mechanism to cope with the problem of historical terminacy of the process, this mechanism may be expected to affect the determinacy (location) of the outcome. This will particularly be the case if the termination device is, like the deadline, a rule setting up a game sequence. One aspect of the interaction between games in a sequence already remarked upon is the possibility that if, in such a sequence, a game 2 has an unambiguous solution whereas 1 does not, the former may be adopted as the solution to 1, that is, without a play of 2. For example, in this case if the outcome of strike negotiations is relatively unambiguous, this outcome may be adopted as the solution during prestrike negotiations without playing the sequence through to strike. In collective bargaining negotiation, influence upon the outcome tending toward determinacy may run from game 1 to game 2 as well. Negotiation under strike conditions from the outset may be "less determinate" than negotiations under strike conditions where these are a consequent of the deadline rule. That is, the limits within which an outcome to negotiation under strike conditions can lie will be considerably narrowed if such negotiations have been preceded by a period of prestrike negotiations. For in this case the parties have had a period of time free of fear of immediate strike in which to discharge the information giving and seeking function of negotiation, establish some notion of minimum asking prices, feel out the underlying power relationships, and so forth. If a strike does eventuate in consequence of a deadline, it begins on the basis of a *status quo* inherited from the prestrike negotiations—a *status quo* in which limits on an eventual outcome are narrower than they were initially. Indeed, once overt warfare has broken out it may be terminated on the basis of a solution developed (but not accepted) during prestrike negotiations.

No theory of the outcome under bilateral monopoly can afford to overlook the influence of a deadline (or other termination device) if such is provided for in the rules framework of the interaction. Pen, one of the few writers directly suggesting the problem of historical terminacy in collective bargaining negotiations, seems to overlook the deadline. He contends that if we assume perfect knowledge on the part of the negotiators so that the contract zone is known with certainty, threatening the opposite party with conflict will have no effect. That is, under these circumstances, unless a party can alter his opponent's preferences, "the contract is 'indeterminate' in the sense that negotiations can continue indefinitely without one party being able to compel the other to accept an unfavorable wage rate." This view would seem to overlook the possibility of eliminating the contract zone by "contrivance." One example of contrivance is the deadline rule.

The desirability of a deadline (or some other device for hastening the termination of negotiation) depends in part on the characteristics of the *status quo* from which negotiation has begun. In more recent years in collective bargaining there has been an asymmetry of advantage in favor of the employer in prenegotiation *status quo*. In an economy such as this, the fruits of increasing productivity have in large measure been passed on to wage earners in the form of higher money wages. For some years the trend of money wages has been steadily upward, and both parties expect this to be the case. Thus, the *status quo* contains an inherent advantage for the employer. (Here is a reason why negotiation might be long drawn out in the absence of a deadline rule.) Within limits imposed by the cost of the negotiation process itself, as long as the employer can hold the money-wage line by simply continuing to negotiate, he gains an advantage. From the union's point of view, the situation is reversed, and thus the union has a stronger interest in such an institution as the deadline. We would expect, again within limits imposed by the costs of the negotiation process, that employers would prefer no-deadline negotiation.

A device sometimes used for coping with the asymmetry of advantage in the prenegotiation *status quo* is that of "retroactivity." For example, it is sometimes agreed (the point is usually one for negotiation) when a new contract is being negotiated that any wage increase shall apply retroactively to the date of expiration of the existing contract.[40]

RULE FOR TERMINATION BY AGREEMENT

Characteristically, each play of the negotiation game terminates when there is agreement upon a position, that is, upon all the items comprising the agenda. Agreement upon all items was previously defined as mutual assent to a disposition for each of the agenda items.[41] Other rules for termination of a play of the negotiation game may be envisaged. For example, each play might terminate when public authority decided to blow a whistle. However, if a whistle were to end a play of the game prior to agreement, although the process of negotiation would terminate, there would be no "solution." In consequence, such a rule for termination would have to make auxiliary provision for a device alternative to agreement whereby a solution could be imposed upon the game such as an arbitration scheme.

Games generally have rules for termination of each play, and if collective bargaining negotiation is to be thought of as a game-like "model," it should be similarly provided. However allusion here to the rule for termination of the negotiation game has been included for additional reasons. There is a strong public interest in the rule for termination, of which the emergency strike problem is an excellent (and extreme) example.

Emergency Strike Solutions as Variants in a Game Sequence

Although this is not the place for extended discussion of the emergency strike problem, it is of interest to accord it brief attention. We have so far been concerned with the sequence—negotiation under no-strike conditions, deadline, negotiation under strike conditions. Proposed solutions to the emergency strike problem are properly viewed as efforts to append a game-variant 3 to this sequence, and one approach to appraisal of the adequacy of such proposed solutions is to view them in light of relevance and efficiency of game-variant sequences.

Consider, for example, compulsory arbitration—a frequently discussed solution for emergency strikes. Such a solution is strongly rejected by the parties, and it seems to run counter to the basic concepts of "voluntarism" and "self-determination" upon which our industrial relations system has been based.[42] From the analytical point of view here suggested, this solution seems neither relevant nor efficient as a component of the collective bargaining negotiation game-variant sequence. It was suggested earlier that if the basic choice situation impels the parties to resolve their interaction by negotiation during game-variant 1, then game 2 (probably) should be some variant on a negotiation game rather than take-it-or-leave-it.

The same line of reasoning can be extended to all the components of game-variant sequences generally. Compulsory arbitration is not relevant in these terms as a sequel to variants 1 and 2. Nor is compulsory arbitration (as ordinarily conceived) relevant in the sense that it adequately reflects the basic sanctions (pressures) underlying the whole negotiation relationship, which were operative during preceding play of the game.

Compulsory arbitration is not efficient in the sense that it tends to nullify the contribution of prearbitration play to the ultimate solution; that is, it is most likely that the parties will see advantage in waiting upon the expected award and will hence abandon negotiation pending that award.

A frequently suggested alternative to compulsory arbitration is that public authority be given a considerable arsenal of weapons to use in the event of an emergency strike. This approach has a number of merits. It might be deemed "fair" in the sense that although the eventual solution may seem unjust to one of the parties, the "gambling" situation confronted by the parties in facing the array of weapons may itself be deemed fair. It is probably efficient since the parties, uncertain about the game-variant 3 to follow, will not be led to pervert or abandon their negotiation in attempting to anticipate the action of public authority. However, the arsenal-of-weapons approach does not clear the relevance hurdle, for it seems difficult to find relevant weapons to put into the arsenal.

Finally, we may take note of a number of ingenious emergency-strike schemes known variously as the "statutory" or "nonstoppage" strike. These schemes do not depend upon substitution of some other procedure for that of agreement by negotiation but depend instead upon rigging the collective bargaining negotiation game to preserve the essential flow of goods and services.[43] The general idea is as follows: in case of an emergency strike the government would take control of the plant by one legal device or another. The government would actually run the plant; that is, it would not be a purely nominal "seizure" of the World War II type. Strikes or concerted walkouts would be prohibited, although individual voluntary departures would be permitted. What about the terms to be imposed during the period of governmental custody? The schemes differ somewhat in this regard. These terms must be sufficiently favorable to induce labor and management to continue production; at the same time, they must be onerous enough to bring real economic pressure on the parties and impel them to seek a solution via collective bargaining. It might be provided that some percentage of net revenues be diverted to the federal treasury for the duration of the seizure and that pre-existing terms of employment be frozen for the duration.[44] It might be provided that wages be reduced by some percentage and returns to the company reduced to variable costs plus some percentage of fixed costs. Whatever the detailed provisions, once agreement via collective bargaining had been reached, government control would cease, and the parties would continue under terms and conditions devised by themselves. In order that the statutory strike might bear upon the regular process of negotiation, either party should have the right to invoke such proceedings.

The nonstoppage strike differs from other proposed solutions in that it does not attempt to impose an outcome on the collective bargaining process. Instead, it defines a socially tolerable game-variant 3, the playing of which allows the parties to arrive at an outcome via agreement. The nonstoppage strike is a generally relevant game 3 in the same sense that the ordinary bargaining strike is a relevant game 2. Also, it is probably efficient. In other words, there would seem little point in abandoning all but nominal negotiation in anticipation of such a strike. However, it is probably not acceptable to the parties. The major difficulty is in finding suitable terms to impose upon the parties during the period of government custody—terms which would be deemed "fair" in the sense that they would not be thought to distort the basic power relationship underlying the bargaining relationship. This difficulty may be inherent in the scheme because the mutual boycott upon which the wielding of economic power ordinarily depends has been suspended in the social interest. It is true that substitute economic pressures are proposed, but these only partially reflect the basic economic power relationship. Since production is maintained, the company need not fear loss of customer allegiance and future markets —penalties perhaps greater than immediate loss of profits. And, since employment is maintained, the workers do not experience actual unemployment and are not in danger of permanent loss of their jobs to replacements. In spite of the difficulties adduced, some kind of statutory strike scheme has much to recommend it if one thinks about solution to the emergency strike problem in terms of the concepts of relevance and efficiency in game-variant sequences.

STATUTORY RULES FOR PLAY AND "GOOD FAITH"

The six rules for play discussed in this chapter are basic features of collective bargaining, common to many instances of such negotiations. Additional rules might have been included. A brief comment upon some of the exclusions is in order.

We have seen in this chapter and in the preceding chapters that the law regulates collective bargaining negotiation in various ways including here an obligation to meet at reasonable times and confer in "good faith." Administrative and judicial construction of this statutory obligation has resulted in a number of rules governing the negotiation process. For example, there is a proscription of unilateral action by either party during the course of negotiation—a unilateral grant of wage increase in excess of the terms being offered the union during negotiation. There are also rulings against a party's refusal to furnish certain kinds of information requested by the opposite number during the course of negotiation. Hence the question arises: Should not such statutory rules be here elaborated and included in the set of rules for play of the negotiation game? The orientation of this inquiry is set forth in Chapter I. This is that the decision to restrict the inquiry to "mature" bargaining relationships largely excludes those cases in which the statutory rules have an important bearing. That is, neglecting particulars, the statutory obligation to bargain collectively is essentially an obligation to deal with the opposite number. From this point of view, failure to meet the statutory requirements is essentially refusal to accord *de facto* recognition to the opposite number, an attempt not so much to deal with the opposite number as to be rid of him. However, as in the foregoing discussion, where the law does bear closely on the rules for play as here conceived, the relationship is discussed.

The concept of "good faith" in labor (and other) negotiations is by no means confined to legal constructions. Peters, noting the difficulty of distinguishing *bona fide* bad faith from what might be considered undesirable or bad collective bargaining practices, treats good faith as "some minimum standards of fair play which it behooves the parties to observe in their own self-interest, once there is a conflict." He further observes that: "The one basic criteria of good faith, recognized and accepted by the parties, is contained in the iron rule: *Preserve the sanctity of your lines of communication.*" [45] For example, do not imply that you have accepted a position which you subsequently repudiate—arguing that you did not technically commit yourself to the position in question. The question that arises in this context is: Should not some set of standards comprehended under the rubric "good faith" in labor negotiations be here elaborated and included among the rules for play of the negotiation game? Such standards are, of course, generally relevant to an analysis of collective bargaining negotiation. However, they are better treated as a part of the analysis of particular tactics used during the course of play (see Chapter VI) than as a part of the basic rules framework governing the negotiation relationship.

CHAPTER IV

Classification of Tactics, Early Stages of Negotiation, and Persuasion versus Rationalization

CLASSIFICATION OF TACTICS

To analyze the negotiation process, we need to classify tactics. Thus, we may say that in negotiating with B, A may:

(1) Represent his own preferences—the satisfactions A associates with various outcomes of the negotiation.

(2) Attempt to discover B's preferences.

(3) Attempt to alter B's preferences.

(4) Attempt to alter or establish B's expectations about B's negotiation and extranegotiation environment.

(5) Attempt to alter or establish B's expectations about A's intended courses of action. (For example, in what contingencies A will take a strike.) This will include A's representation, misrepresentation, and/or concealing of his own preferences since B's inferences about A's course of action will be based in part upon his perception of B's preferences.

(6) Attempt to alter or establish the preferences and courses of action of "third parties" where these may affect the outcome of the negotiations.

This working classification scheme is comprehensive. We now need a subaggregation of tactics within the framework of this scheme, one which will focus upon issues probably critical in the analysis of collective bargaining negotiation. Which particular classes of tactics an investigator of negotiation emphasizes in his analysis depends in large part on the basic postulates of the theory with which he is working. Considerations stemming from potentially fruitful theoretical approaches suggest the following distinctions.

Persuasion and Coercion

An actor's choice, B's in his interaction with A, may be conceptualized as a resultant of two sets of factors. One, B's preference function: the satisfactions he associates with various outcomes; two, B's opportunity function: the range of options (outcomes) available at each choice point. In a game-like interaction involving strategy such as collective bargaining, B's opportunity function will depend importantly upon A's course of action (choice of strategy). For example, in an abstract two-person game represented by a payoff matrix, the outcome associated with any B choice of row depends upon which column A elects. Or, in collective bargaining, an outcome—"agreed rate $2.00"—is not potentially available to B if A would prefer the strike to agreeing to the rate in question. B's opportunity function also depends upon the extranegotiation environment. (For example, a firm cannot offset a wage increase with a price increase if it is under severe price competition in output markets.)

We may distinguish persuasion as: A's attempts to control B's course of action by operations upon B's preference function and/or operations upon B's perception of the extranegotiation environment. Persuasion includes items (3) and (4) from the classification of tactics.

Coercion may be said to be: A's attempts to control B's course of action by operating upon B's opportunity function, the range of outcomes (at least apparently) available to B—as these depend upon A's own course of action, and/or the courses of action of "third parties." Coercion includes items (5) and (6) from the classification of tactics.

Persuasion versus Rationalization

Closely related to tactics of persuasion are those of rationalization. This distinction is elaborated in the final section of this chapter.

Bluff and Notbluff

Tactics of coercion may themselves be divided into two classes—bluff and notbluff. The distinction involves the question of an actor's intentions with respect to a subsequent course of action. If he does not intend to do what he asserts or implies he will do, he is engaged in bluff. If he does intend to do what he asserts or implies he will do, he is engaged in notbluff. In both cases he confronts tactical problems discussed in Chapter V.

EARLY STAGES OF NEGOTIATION

Allusion to "early" stages of negotiation implies that there are "later" stages and suggests the phenomenon of a negotiation "cycle." As pointed out in Chapter I, such a succession of stages is discernible in many negotiations, and the concept has proved a convenient device for organization of inquiry. Nevertheless, the warning should be repeated that this concept can be misleading unless one bears in mind that it represents an idealization of the actual process. More particularly, use of this idealization should not be taken to imply, for instance, that a tactical function or entity emphasized in discussion of one stage may not likewise be served or appear at other stages.

The Negotiators as Delegates

The negotiators who face each other over the bargaining table are delegates of an organization (or organizations) on each side of the bargaining relationship. Douglas has suggested that the early stages of the negotiation interaction are dominated by the negotiators' roles as delegates—that these stages emphasize interparty conflict, as contrasted with greater emphasis upon interpersonal (negotiators *qua* negotiators) interaction.

Characteristic features of the early stages may be viewed in this light. Thus there are frequently vigorous speeches in support of firm positions (the large demands) which, it is generally understood, will subsequently be abandoned. At this stage, each party may express surprise and consternation over the proposal advanced by his opposite number. Such manifestations of interparty conflict do not preclude good will and good feeling between the negotiators as individuals.[1] Although the term "grandstanding" is frequently used with reference to this stage of negotiations, such reference should not obscure the fact that performance during this stage is functional. For example, Stagner has pointed out that "ritualistic" attacks upon the employer during the course of negotiation may serve one of the functions of the union official in his role as leader. This function (more characteristic of the union leader than of management) is that involved in the official's "role of spokesman for feelings, demands, hostilities, and insecurities among the workers."[2] Beyond such functions, the early stages begin the job of blocking out the contract zone.

More About the "Large" (Initial Bargaining) Demand

In Chapter III the large demand was considered as a rule for play. Stress was upon consonance of the large demand with the whole negotiation process. However, a satisfactory treatment of initial bargaining proposals must go beyond this. The functions, in more particular terms, of the initial demand within the context of the ensuing negotiations it facilitates must be discussed. Further, the discussion should suggest some constraints upon the magnitude of initial proposals.

The fact that the negotiators are delegates has an important influence upon the size and composition of initial bargaining proposals.[3] Typically, such proposals are initiated by the suggestions of many people. (For this reason alone, demands may be large in the sense of the number of subjects.) Although some screening of suggestions takes place before initial demands are presented, the critical matter of negotiators' relative valuation of these demands, rating them and deciding upon the "trading value" of each in terms of the others, and so on, takes place in the course of the negotiations.

These considerations bear upon a question raised (and partially answered) in the preceding chapter: Why do the parties to collective bargaining not engage more frequently in prenegotiation agenda negotiation, rather than accept whatever agenda eventuates from the initial demand and counterproposal? Part of the answer lies in the nature of the political relationship between the negotiators and their constituents, especially on the union side.

Each of the various "interests" comprising the organization on each side will want his own demand taken into the substantive negotiations. Agenda negotiation would involve either: (a) formal intraorganizational negotiation to establish the package to be insisted upon for the agenda; or, (b) establishing that package by an exercise of discretion on the part of the officials who will do the negotiating. Formal intraorganizational negotiation would probably be very time consuming, would probably be internally disruptive, and would probably be embarrassing (and perhaps fraught with adverse political consequence) for the official who had to make his own relative valuation of the various demands known. The exercise of discretion in (b) might likewise be politically embarrassing. Many difficulties are avoided if any intraorganizational prenegotiation can be rather informal, and if the official can take into the substantive negotiations a rather large package. It is of course true that no particular demand may survive the negotiations, but at least the negotiator can point to the fact that he took that demand to the other side. Had he been forced to reject that demand by excluding it from the agenda, his position is rather more awkward.

Also, relative rating of demands in advance of negotiations may prove a tactical mistake since the party making such a rating does not know his opposite number's rating of these demands. This is another reason that discourages prenegotiation rating.

Whatever the advantages, an initial bargaining demand which has been subjected to very little screening also carries disadvantages. Principal among these is the fact that it may be difficult to avoid an appearance of defeat in the outcome of the negotiations. Also it may be argued that one of the important functions of a union official *vis-à-vis* collective bargaining negotiation is to set up effective procedures for intraunion bargaining and screening of proposals prior to formulation of the initial bargaining position.

Constraints Imposed by Information-Giving and -Seeking Functions of Initial Proposals. The important thing about periodic contract negotiations is their outcome. A party's initial demand and his opposite number's counterproposal are intended by each to influence that outcome from his own point of view. The question is: by what routes is this influence supposed to be operative?

We may begin an answer to this question by recalling the first two items in the previously developed working classification of tactics. Items (1) and (2) involve information-giving and -seeking functions, functions which are discharged, in part, by the initial bargaining proposals.

It has been suggested that an aspect of (1)—the security function—is a primary function of the large demand. That is, the large demand serves to shield one's own position while one seeks to determine the real position of one's opponent. Indeed, objections have been raised that the initial bargaining demand is too frequently "used solely as a screen for concealment—something behind which one can hide and play safe." If security were the sole consideration in the formulation of initial demands, the ordinary large demand would have to be deemed relatively inefficient. For example, a higher level of security could be achieved by employing some chance device. The negotiator could formulate six large demands and elect one of these at random. The negotiator would achieve some protection against an inadvertent signaling of his own intentions, and his opponent's knowledge that the plan was selected by chance would preclude his thinking that it was intended to convey the negotiator's actual preferences.

It may be noted parenthetically that a theoretical disadvantage of the security interpretation of the initial demand is that it puts very few constraints upon the magnitude of that demand. Given the negotiator's large demand, why could it not be of twice the magnitude?

Most participants in and investigators of collective bargaining negotiation would feel that an initial demand procedure based upon a chance device would be wholly inappropriate to such negotiations, however much such a device might facilitate the security function of the initial demand. This very fact suggests that security is surely not the sole (or even the primary) consideration in formulation of the initial demand.

The security function is, however, one of the considerations in formulation of the initial bargaining position. The other major function is no. (1) in the classification of tactics—representation of preferences. As summed up by Peters: "In skillful hands the bargaining position performs a double function. It conceals, and it reveals. The bargaining position is used to indicate—to unfold gradually, step by step—the maximum expectation of the negotiator, while at the same time concealing, for as long as necessary, his minimum expectation." In this context, a party's maximum expectation is the most favorable settlement he could hope for, his minimum expectation is the edge of the contract zone—he would rather take a strike than go lower. Peters continues that in operating with his bargaining position, the negotiator attempts by indirect means to convince his opposite number that his maximum expectation is really his breaking-off point.

The fact that the initial bargaining proposal serves the function of revealing preferences puts (indefinite) constraints upon the magnitude of that demand. At its largest, the large demand will be of the type that mirrors total constituents' demands (including, perhaps, some demands originated by the leaders and "sold" to the constituents), or at least all those demands which the negotiator feels he must take seriously enough to make a show of taking to the bargaining table. The process of revealing his maximum expectation will involve the negotiator's relative valuation of the items he initially carried to the table. If indirect means, such as the manner and timing of changes in position, are to reveal a maximum expectation, the initial position itself must be appropriate in the sense of credibility and feasibility. Suppose, for example, that in a given situation the area of hard bargaining is actually in the neighborhood of from five to ten cents, and that in this situation the union opens up with a demand for forty cents. Such an initial position is so far removed from the actual range of difference in the negotiations as to be virtually meaningless. In this context, a retreat to thirty-five cents will give no information about the maximum expectation and cannot be expected to invite the reciprocal concession necessary to begin narrowing the range between ostensible positions toward the area of hard bargaining.[4]

Typically, elements of bluff and deception will be involved in the early stage of negotiation. This consideration puts constraints upon the magnitude of the initial demand which are similar in nature to those just discussed. For if a negotiator's bargaining position is to serve as an effective bluff, it must be at least credible. Thus if a negotiator intends bluff, he will be dissuaded from asserting a "huge" demand.

The initial bargaining proposal is an information-seeking device. During the early stages of negotiation, each party, in addition to giving information about (and concealing) his own preferences, is attempting to discover the true preferences of his opponent. In part, the negotiator will infer these preferences from his opponent's bargaining position. He will also infer these from his opponent's reaction to his own bargaining position. The parties are at this stage attempting to demarcate the limits of the contract zone. The movement from initial bargaining positions to some fairly clear perception of the range within which (if any) an outcome by agreement can lie is devious. There is reliance upon ceremonial and semiritualistic modes and upon sign language as each side attempts to estimate the meaning of what is said by the other side. Peters has provided an excellent account of this aspect of the process and there is no need to elaborate upon it.

The fact that the initial bargaining proposal is an information-seeking device also imposes some constraints upon its magnitude. If the initial proposal is so far removed from any possible range of difference in the negotiations as to be virtually meaningless, then it will not invite a reaction or response which will itself be meaningful.

Shackle's Theory. The formal bargaining theory developed by G. L. S. Shackle includes the notion of restrictions upon the magnitude of the initial bargaining proposal. Shackle's point is best developed in his own terminology.[5] In his view, a party to bargaining will be concerned with the following prices:

m his absolute minimum price to accept which would leave him neither better nor worse off than to abandon the negotiation.

g his initial asking price.

j his effective minimum price, the least price permitted by some chosen policy.

v the price, unknown to either party until the completion of bargaining, which may ultimately be agreed on.

A bargaining plan consists in selecting a pair of values g and j. These values are related because retreat, in the process of bargaining, over the interval g-j involves more or less "loss of face" and consequent impairment of bargaining power in subsequent negotiations. Shackle identifies three bargaining policies based upon this consideration:

(1) Possible breakdown—choice of g and j such that conceding the whole difference will not involve loss of face.

(2) Possible loss of face—planning to retreat from g as far as m if necessary in order to achieve agreement.

(3) A combined policy—accepting some possibility of loss of face, but setting some j greater than m.

Shackle's theory postulates restrictions upon the interval g-j, rather than upon the value of g *per se*. Nevertheless, the general suggestion of this approach is that the magnitude of initial bargaining demands may be constrained by fear of loss of face and impairment of bargaining power associated with subsequent retreat from such demands. This will be particularly the case if j itself is constrained by considerations other than the g-j interval. For example, it may be constrained if considerations suggest that a party's effective minimum price should be near its absolute minimum price.[6] This will be true if a party will not risk a breakdown of negotiation over a rate considerably in excess of his absolute minimum price. If this be true, then the Shackle-type loss of face consideration could impose an important constraint upon the initial bargaining demand *per se*.

The "Swap" Theory. This view of the functions of the initial negotiation proposal is related to the matter of nonneutrality of the negotiation agenda (discussed in Chapter III). The notion is that a large initial bargaining demand may facilitate negotiation by providing something to "swap" during the course of negotiations. Dunlop and Healy have observed that: "More than one company has 'bought' the withdrawal of a union-shop demand for an additional nickel in a series of contract negotiations."[7]

What the "swap" theory seems to say, in effect, is that a party to collective bargaining negotiation may increase his negotiation power by increasing the magnitude of his initial demand. Put this way, the mechanism implied would seem to constitute something of a *tour de force,* and it is not immediately obvious how it can work. Why should a party to collective bargaining get more simply because he asks for more? One answer to this question is that such a party does not get more simply because he asks for more—that is, naively including in the package "demands" manufactured more or less out of thin air will be of no tactical avail. Actually, to be effective, the included items must represent genuine issues, must be "blue chips" (as the argot of the participants would have it). These are demands which the negotiator might (at least in principle) hope to achieve, demands which in this sense are within the range of expectations with respect to possible (not necessarily likely) outcomes of negotiation.[8]

Another answer to the above question is to be found in the uncertainty which pervades collective bargaining negotiation, and in the fact that there may be a range of positions within which the outcome may lie. A's larger demand may alter B's expectations about the least favorable terms upon which A is willing to settle, and, in consequence, may lead B to suppose that he must concede more to achieve agreement than would have been the case had A's demand been smaller. This is not a trading operation, however. It is use of the communications implications of the size and composition of the bargaining position to convey as high an impression as possible of the negotiator's absolute minimum price.

In any negotiation in which an initial multi-item proposal (demand) adds up as a "cost package" to more than the cost of the ultimately agreed-upon package, a trade of some sort will appear to have taken place. That is, some of the items in the initial demand will not appear in the settlement, and these neglected items will, in this sense, have been "traded" for the included items. This is not really the kind of trading operation envisaged by the swap theory of the bargaining position. It is more a case in which the range of alternatives in the bargaining demand has allowed the opponent a chance to pick his own poison. This itself may facilitate settlement, since concession on one group of items may be preferable to concession on some other group, even though as monetary cost packages they total the same.

But the swap theory implies more than just a range of options from which the opponent may choose. If the dropped demand is relatively unimportant, the mechanism at work is more essentially one of bluff than a trading operation *per se.* A contrives to make B think that, in dropping a demand, he has made a concession, when, in point of fact, the unimportance of the demand to A means that he has given up little. Here the essential feature of the tactic is not so much in the trading operation as in the bluff technique whereby the conceded demand was made to appear *bona fide*.

It may be necessary in this context to distinguish negotiators' preferences and constituents' preferences. The dropping of any demand may be a concession in the sense that some members of that side regard the demand as vital, even though it does not rank very high in the negotiator's relative valuation.

Trading Leverage of Demand for Change in the Rules of the Bargaining Game. Another aspect of the "trading" matter is the distinction between a demand for more within the context of an extant "game" and a demand for a change in the "rules" of the "game" itself. Consider, for instance, "buying" withdrawal of a union-shop demand for an additional nickel in a series of contract negotiations. Suppose that a company enters negotiations prepared to grant a ten-cent wage increase but concludes the negotiations by agreeing to a fifteen-cent wage increase in response to the union demand: demand type (1), twenty-cent wage increase and the union shop.

One may inquire whether the union might not have extracted the extra nickel as well by another demand—demand type (2), thirty-cent wage increase. In principle, these demands may be comparable in dollar and cents terms. Most employers believe that union security provisions strengthen unions and increase their bargaining power. In consequence, granting the union shop is costly, and this cost might be appraised as a present discounted value. (In practice, of course, any such estimate would be extraordinarily difficult.)

One suspects, however, that demand type (1) has greater negotiation leverage than demand type (2) for reasons other than relative "magnitude." Whatever its ultimate "cost," the union shop does alter important structural properties in the relationship between the parties. The matter of how the union shop may alter the structural properties of the labor-management relationship need not be elaborated here. The point is that demand (1) is a demand for a change in the structural properties of the collective bargaining "game," whereas demand (2) is a demand for more within the context of a given game. Demand (2) says, in effect: Give me more under the existing ground rules. Demand (1), assuming that the union shop demand is included for its trading value, says: Give me more under the existing ground rules, or I will insist upon a change of those rules. The suggestion here is that in increasing the size of a demand by increasing the number of items it comprises, where the items suggest structural changes in the interaction, may be especially valuable, even though the present cost of the items in discounted dollar and cents terms can be only vaguely appreciated.

PERSUASION VERSUS RATIONALIZATION

Persuasion

Persuasion has been defined as A's attempts to control B's course of action by operations upon B's preference function and/or operations upon B's expectations about the extranegotiation environment. Persuasion includes items (3) and (4) from the classification of tactics. An example of the distinction between persuasive tactics and coercive tactics may be helpful. The expected cost to A of a B strike is compounded of: (a) the cost of a strike if it occurs; (b) the probability that a strike will occur. B's tactical operations upon A's expectations regarding (a) are persuasive, whereas B's tactical operations upon A's expectations regarding (b) are coercive. Also, for example, arguments based upon the so-called "basic criteria" used in wage negotiations (comparison with rates in other labor markets, ability to pay, cost of living, productivity, and so forth) might be persuasive. Thus a union argument based upon comparison with other wage rates which convinced the company that paying a higher rate would not put it out of line with other firms in the industry would be persuasive. Or a company argument which convinced the union that the wage increase aimed for would result in increased product prices, decreased markets for output, and hence unemployment of union members would be persuasive.

Analysis of games of conflict has tended to deemphasize the tactical role of persuasion and to stress the significance of coercion.

In the game theory analytical context, stress upon coercion and neglect of persuasion is readily understandable. The rationality postulate of game theory means (in part) that the utility functions of all players are known to each player. Further, utility functions are generally supposed invariant under play (or preplay) of the game. In consequence, persuasion, as defined above, is ruled out by postulation, and insofar as tactical "moves" are admitted to the analysis at all, these focus upon coercion.

In nongame theory discussions of collective bargaining negotiation (and associated concepts such as bargaining power), the position is rather more equivocal. Nevertheless, one likewise finds deemphasis of persuasive tactics, but the reasons for this are less clear. Such discussion ordinarily postulates uncertainty with respect to knowledge of opponents' preferences, and does not postulate that preference functions are invariant under the negotiation process. Rather, it seems to be held as a matter of empirical generalization that preference functions are probably not significantly affected by the negotiation process and that an actor's perception of his extranegotiation environment is probably not significantly influenced. Consider, for example, the following remarks by Pen (which serve as one illustration of the tendency to deemphasize the role of persuasion in analysis of collective bargaining negotiation): "This influencing of the ophelimities [preferences] of the opposite party is perhaps not an unusual characteristic of bargaining, but in essence it is rather futile to try to do it when faced with a more sophisticated bargainer. For the attempts to influence the opposite party entail an endeavor to make it clear to the opposite party what is good for him. One tries to persuade him that he does not see his own interests clearly and that he should therefore listen to the well-meant advice of his opponent." [9]

Although the tendency among writers on collective bargaining seems to be to depreciate the importance and efficacy of persuasion as a negotiation tactic, not all opinion reflects this view. For example, Taylor includes "persuasiveness in argument" as important, along with tactical moves, in affecting the outcome of wage negotiations.[10] Also, Harbison and Coleman include among the attributes of negotiation procedures making for effective collective bargaining, "negotiators who are armed with the facts and briefed regarding the reasoning underlying the positions to be taken." [11] Professor John T. Dunlop has come to the conclusion that preferences are significantly altered in direct negotiations, and that a succession of game-variants in negotiations is often primarily concerned to change initial preferences.[12] In this view, facts pertaining to the firm and industry—facts about work schedules, technology, market conditions, and so on—have an important bearing upon the positions taken by the parties. Arguments are buttressed by appeal to such facts, and these arguments must be answered during the course of negotiation.

Different views regarding the efficacy of persuasion in collective bargaining may in part reflect a semantic confusion, failure to distinguish "persuasion" as a tactical entity from "persuasiveness in argument" used as an adjunct to other tactical entities. In this section, the concern has been with persuasion as a tactical entity. This tactical entity has been distinguished from coercion. Persuasiveness in argument may, of course, be an important adjunct to coercion, such as convincing the bargaining opponent that one will take a strike under certain circumstances. This is not, however, an instance of "persuasion" in the tactical entity sense.

Different views regarding the efficacy of persuasion in collective bargaining may also arise from different interpretations of the concept "preferences"—a point to be developed in the following section.

The Basic Criteria as Instruments of Persuasion. Among aspects of collective bargaining negotiation seemingly related to tactics of persuasion, the most prominent is widespread use of economic data in negotiation. These data relate to the basic criteria so frequently appealed to in negotiation, for example, ability to pay, comparisons with other rates, and so on. In many wage negotiations, the participants devote considerable time, energy, and other resources to gathering relevant data and debating the applicability of these standards. This circumstance would seem to constitute at least *prima facie* evidence that appeal to these standards must play some functionally important role in the negotiation process. Also relevant from this point of view is the heavy emphasis upon these criteria revealed in the decisions and recommendations of third parties to labor disputes (mediators, arbitrators, and fact-finding boards).[13]

The question in this section is: What is the role (if any) of appeals to these criteria as tactics of persuasion?[14] Referring to the classification of tactics, A's tactics of persuasion (in negotiation with B) were defined as: (3) Attempts to alter B's preferences; (4) Attempts to alter or establish B's perception of (expectations about) B's negotiation and extranegotiation environment.

Looking at appeals to the basic criteria as possible instruments of persuasion, whether these should be classified as tactics of class (3) or (4) depends in part on the actual circumstances of the case and in part on the reference subsumed in the concept "preferences." For example, suppose that in particular negotiations the issue is the wage rate. The company argues on the basis of other settlements that a smaller increase than the union demand will result in parity with gains achieved in other labor markets. From the point of view of effect, this might be just a class (4) tactic, altering the union's perception of the extranegotiation environment, but leaving union preferences unchanged. On the other hand, if the union's wage preferences are based in part upon parity of rates with rates in other labor markets, the argument might have a class

(3) effect. However, from the point of view of preferences associated with the objective of this particular wage policy—achieving parity—we would expect no effect from this argument. For example, we would not expect a result of this argument to be a revision by the union of its views regarding the desirability of parity.

With respect to the same hypothetical negotiations, the union might argue that expected increases in productivity (output per manhour) are significantly greater than contended by the company. Again, this argument might just have a class (4) effect of changing the company's perception of the negotiation environment. On the other hand, if the satisfaction the company associates with various rates depends in part upon their presumed labor cost implications, then this argument might alter these preferences. Again, from the point of view of preferences associated with the objective of this particular wage policy—preference for a particular level of profits—we would expect the argument to have no bearing. Unless arguments such as those based upon wage standards have at least some class (3) effect, they will not be useful as instruments of persuasion (although, as we shall see, they might be otherwise effective).

The considerations adduced in the preceding paragraph are important because they have a bearing upon the plausibility of *ad hoc* evaluations of persuasion's role in collective bargaining negotiation. As an *ad hoc* proposition, Pen's previously cited evaluation of the probable significance of persuasion in collective bargaining has appeal if one is thinking of preferences referred to the objectives of wage policy, for instance. It would indeed seem futile for the union to try to "make it clear" to the employer that higher labor costs are "good for him." The same may be said of company attempts to make it clear to the union that rates below those prevailing in other labor markets are good for it. However, there is a much less plausible *prima facie* case against the efficacy of persuasion if, as suggested in the previous paragraph, "preference" is taken to have a more proximate reference—evaluations of the wage rate which depend in part upon perceptions of the environment which might be influenced by argument. Thus, in the first example, persuasive argument might alter company satisfaction with a particular wage rate by altering expectations about labor costs implied by that rate.

Returning once more to the commonly used standards for wage determination, there seems to be some agreement on two points. Whatever else may be said about the data marshaled under these standards, these should not be thought of as sets of unequivocal "facts" which can be applied in semiautomatic fashion to the resolution of wage controversy. The position yielded by appeal to each of these standards can vary within wide limits depending upon time intervals selected for comparisons, geographical areas selected for comparisons, estimates of future market and technological conditions, and so on. Thus even should the parties agree that comparison with wage rates in other labor markets is relevant, there is ample room for difference of opinion (and hence for difference in result yielded by the standard) with respect to the occupational categories, geographical areas, time interval, and so forth, over which the comparisons should be made. Secondly, with respect to each of the criteria, rigid application may yield results which are from the point of view of economic principle perverse or even absurd.[15]

Beyond fairly general agreement upon the above two points, there is less consensus in evaluating the role of economic data in collective bargaining negotiation, and individual positions on this matter tend to be somewhat equivocal. Some opinions would lead to the conclusion that these principles play no substantively important role in negotiations. For example, Lindblom, viewing this matter from the point of view of union wage aims, deems these principles mere "window dressing" used by the union for "expediency's sake."[16] Reynolds, in discussing these standards, points to the importance of distinguishing between the reasons why a party adopts a position and the rationalization of this position. He contends that the general public often does not realize in appraising collective bargaining that arguments by the parties based upon the various wage standards "are merely rationalizations or public relations arguments. They are not the basic reasons for the positions adopted by the parties."[17] Ryder, on the other hand, takes a position which minimizes the public relations implications of publicized justification of proposals—a process which he terms "bargaining dressing." In his view, the real purpose of these tactics is to weaken the force of the opposite party, to soften and undermine the foundation upon which his major proposals are based, to promote self-questioning of his own logic, and generally to weaken his "demand resolve." He concludes that: "Any favorable impact on public opinion is merely a by-product."[18] Bloom and Northrup take the view that the basic criteria used in wage negotiation play an important role in narrowing the range of possibilities in wage negotiation. They then note, however, that in "many cases" the agreed-upon wage reflects sheer bargaining power, contending that in these cases argument based upon the wage standards "is mere rationalization pressed into service to support demands or concessions which need justification." [19]

Backman feels that: "The statistical facts are important primarily in providing a central area from which it is difficult to stray very far." [20] However, he emphasizes that these data cannot simply be fed into a computing machine which will then yield the "correct" answer. Each of the criteria can yield a different answer depending upon how it is applied, and the answer will depend upon the relative weight accorded each of the criteria, and so forth. On the other hand, Dunlop and Healy feel that the range of possible rates which would follow from possible applications of these criteria would generally be wider than the normal variance between the parties in collective bargaining. That is, given the diverse alternative meanings and measurements available in the case of each of these standards: "The range of disputed application of any of these principles is likely to be much wider than the normal range of disagreement between the parties." [21]

Opinions on the role of standards in collective bargaining negotiations could be widely quoted, but the sample presented is representative. While it is clear that there is no firm consensus on this matter, the essential thrust of these views as a whole is certainly to deemphasize the importance of persuasion as a tactic in collective bargaining negotiation—at least insofar as persuasion might be a function of the use of the commonly adduced wage standards.

Persuasion and Asymmetry in Effects of Tactics. The question of the significance of persuasion as a tactic in labor negotiation is in need of clarification at the empirical level. For example, are the basic criteria adduced in wage negotiations at all important as determinants of the outcome because of some persuasive impact? [22] The issue of persuasion as a negotiation tactic derives considerable importance from one result of the avoidance–avoidance conflict choice analysis presented in Chapter II—namely, the possibility of an important asymmetry in the effect of two classes of negotiation tactics. Tactics categorized as Class II were those which serve to decrease a party's tendency to avoid agreement with his opponent on his opponent's terms. Class I tactics, on the other hand, are those which tend to increase a party's tendency to avoid his own goal. Both classes of tactics may be efficacious in moving the equilibrium position of a party to negotiation. However, asymmetry of effect enters the picture because Class II tactics tend to decrease, whereas Class I tactics tend to increase the amount of tension experienced by a party to negotiation, and hence emphasis upon the former tends to decrease the probability of a breakdown of negotiations. Tactics of persuasion are prominent members of Class II and may on these grounds be held preferable to members of Class I—tactics of coercion.

Rationalization

Opinions regarding the role of the basic criteria used in wage negotiations suggest that rationalization is one primary function of argumentation based on these standards. If this view is to be accepted, then the prevalence of such argument certainly warrants attention to the question: What precisely is the role of rationalization as a negotiation tactic, and how significant is this tactic as a determinant of the outcome?

This question is closely related to that of persuasion and also needs clarification at the empirical level. In both cases, conceptual difficulties arise in attempting an answer. Since we do not intend a general examination of these difficulties, exposition will be facilitated by a simple example.

Suppose that the amount of satisfaction a union negotiator associates with possible wage outcomes of negotiation increases over a relevant range of potential outcomes—that is, over this range, higher rates are preferred to lower rates. Suppose further that the union demand within this range is based upon relative bargaining power—the union negotiator demands the highest rate within this range which he thinks his bargaining power *vis-à-vis* the company can secure. During the negotiations, he argues his case on the grounds of comparison with rates prevailing in other labor markets. From the point of view of the union's posture, at least, this example might roughly represent one of the "many cases" adduced by Bloom and Northrup in which the outcome reflects sheer bargaining power and in which argument based upon wage standards "is mere rationalization pressed into service to support a demand which needs justification." Let us suppose that the frequently expressed pessimism with respect to the efficacy of persuasion holds in this case, that, insofar as the bargaining opponent is concerned, the wage comparison argument is not at all effective as an instrument of persuasion—that is, company wage preferences are not at all affected by the substantive content of the argument. Let us further suppose that in the instant negotiations, the company negotiators exhibit a similar posture, that is, they too are "rationalizing" (in terms of various wage standards) a position adopted on the basis of notions about relative bargaining power, and so forth.

What does the rationalization tactic accomplish in such a situation? What functions does (or might) it serve? [23] Given the circumstances specified in the hypothetical (and neglecting for now certain tactical implications of such argumentation to be discussed in Chapters V and VI), one is tempted to conclude that if the "rationalization" tactic is to be effective at all, this will be because it bears upon some party or parties other than the bargaining opponent. Parties of potential importance from this point of view are the negotiators' constituents and the extranegotiation public. Regarding the former, any agreed-upon package must be "salable" to these constituents. Further, the negotiator will want strong support for his position during the course of negotiation, since if a strike should eventuate, such support will be essential to its success. Thus, in the example cited, the union argument based on wage comparisons may be effective as a rationalization tactic in winning the support of union members for the demand. It has frequently been suggested that an important key to power in labor relations is to be found in the allegiance of the workers. This applies to company and union alike, that is, from this point of view the company and the union share a common constituency in the work force, and company rationalization tactics may be similarly viewed as an element in this power competition. The rationalization tactic thus conceived is essentially a tactic of persuasion (albeit not *vis-à-vis* the bargaining opponent). That is, if the argument is to win the support of the union members, for example, then these must be persuaded.

In cases where the tactical impact of the wage standard argument is via the route illustrated, whether the standard is substantively important as a determinant of the outcome depends upon other circumstances. Let us suppose that in the bargaining relationship in question, if the wage comparison is actually to be effective in winning the membership's support, only particular labor markets can be selected for comparison. That is, from the membership point of view, only certain labor markets are considered relevant. In such a case, the union negotiator cannot be arbitrary in selecting labor markets upon which to base the wage comparison argument. If, further, the support among the membership that might be recruited by appeal to the wage comparison is vital to the outcome of the negotiations, then this criteria must be reckoned as substantively important as a determinant of the outcome.

Rationalization tactics may also be intended to bear upon an interested extranegotiation public. The 1959 negotiations in the steel industry are an excellent case in point. In this instance, there was public concern with economic implications of any agreement that might be reached—concern with the impact of an increase in wages upon the general price level. The companies' public posture, in resisting any wage increase, was in effect one of assuming private "social responsibility" for movements in the general price level by insisting upon a "noninflationary" settlement. Also, it was widely thought that a work stoppage in the steel industry would have disastrous consequences. This made public intervention in the event of a strike very likely. Particularly in negotiations affected with the public interest, and in those cases in which a strike seems likely,[24] prestrike negotiations may be intended not so much to achieve a solution during play of this variant as to influence a solution to be achieved under strike conditions, or under the aegis of public authority. In these circumstances, negotiation arguments in support of positions may be intended largely to rationalize these positions for the potentially affected public. The rationalization tactic in this context is, as in the context of the relationship of negotiators to their constituents, essentially a tactic of persuasion.

Rationalization of a position during a particular set of negotiations has implications broader than the pressures the public or government agencies may thereby be induced to bring to bear upon the outcome of these particular negotiations. Such rationalization may establish a general public attitude toward the positions of the parties and in this manner may have an indirect impact on the outcome of future negotiations by modifying the entire legislative and public-opinion climate in which such negotiations will take place.[25]

Recent developments in collective bargaining—for instance, the wide publicity given the work-rules ("featherbedding") issue in various negotiations—may be an example of this function of the rationalization tactic. This issue has been a prominent public feature of recent negotiations in a number of industries—steel, railroad, newspaper, glass, longshoremen, and so forth. If, due to the publicity the issue has been given, the public was convinced that "featherbedding" was a serious national problem, this might be expected to have repercussions on the legislative front.

As matters stand, there has been some institutional innovation with respect to this issue. This has taken the form of settlements which do not themselves resolve certain work-rules issues but rather constitute study groups and arbitration panels to discharge this function. For example, a recent settlement in the glass industry (February 16, 1959, between Pittsburgh Plate Glass Company and United Glass and Ceramic Workers AFL-CIO) constituted a three-man arbitration commission empowered to settle certain work-rules issues by final and binding decision.

The work-rules issue was particularly prominent in the 1959 steel negotiations. In this case, the Memorandum of Agreement (dated January 5, 1960) which settled the labor dispute provided for a "Human Relations Research Committee" and a "Local Working Conditions Committee" to study the problem and make recommendations to the parties.[26] Similarly, the issue has been very prominent in the 1959 railroad negotiations, with wide publicity given to management pronouncements on this issue. In this case the parties agreed to submit the work-rules dispute to a Presidential Commission for study, mediation, and recommendations, and a tripartite fifteen-man commission has been appointed.

There are probably special factors involved in each of these industry cases which help to account for resort to the commission and study-group approach. However, it might be argued that the widespread publicity in conjunction with the "rationalization" tactics of the parties helped to create a public-opinion and legislative climate which urged resort to this approach.

Providing Bargaining Opponent with Useful Arguments. In the context of the above hypothetical negotiation situation, we were "tempted to conclude" that if the rationalization tactic was to be effective at all, it would be because of its impact upon parties other than the bargaining opponent.

One should not push this conclusion too far, however, for it neglects one important aspect of the rationalization tactic. This concerns the role of one party's arguments in providing his opponent with a means for rationalizing a retreat from the opponent's position.[27] Suppose that during the course of negotiation a party decides that he must retreat from a previously held position. This retreat will have to be rationalized for his constituents. In such a case, his opponent's arguments may provide him with the material out of which such a rationalization can be constructed. Thus a party to negotiation should bear in mind, when constructing arguments in terms of which to rationalize his own position, that these same arguments may help to rationalize a retreat by his opponent.

CHAPTER V

Tactics of Coercion: Bluff and Notbluff

In a game-like interaction such as collective bargaining, the outcome realized by each party depends, in part, upon the course of action pursued by the other, and hence what each party does depends, in part, upon what he thinks his opposite number will do. These considerations of strategy underlie tactics of coercion, which were distinguished in Chapter IV as: A's attempts to control B's course of action by operating upon B's opportunity function (the range of outcomes at least apparently available to B) —as this depends upon A's own course of action, and/or the courses of action of "third parties." Coercion thus defined includes items (5) and (6). In negotiating with B, A may (5) attempt to alter or establish B's expectations about A's intended subsequent courses of action and (6) attempt to alter or establish the courses of action of "third parties" where these may affect the outcome of negotiations.

As we have discussed in Chapter IV, tactics of rationalization were deemed persuasive insofar as their impact on a "public" was concerned. At the same time these tactics are coercive insofar as the impact on the bargaining opponent is concerned.

Tactics of coercion may be divided into two classes—bluff and notbluff. On the subject of tactics of collective bargaining negotiation, one finds frequent reference to the bluff as an important instance of such tactics, and, in this literature emphasis generally tends to be put on the deception aspect of the problem.[1] In other analyses of interactions involving conflict, some of which are of at least potential interest in analysis of collective bargaining negotiation, emphasis tends to be on notbluff.

NOTBLUFF

Straightforward Notbluff

As we have defined it, a party to negotiation is engaged in notbluff when he asserts or implies that he will do what he intends to do at the time the assertion is made. We may call the notbluff "straightforward" if the party would prefer (in terms of the original, that is, pretactical play, payoffs) to do what he intends to do. One major problem confronted by the player of notbluff is conveying to his opposite number the truth regarding his intended course of action. Resolution of this problem may be technically difficult. A party to negotiation does not believe something to be true simply because his opponent asserts that it is true. In short, the player of notbluff may be in need of some device whereby he may pledge or commit himself, to the satisfaction of his opponent, to a course of action which he intends to pursue.[2]

As an illustration of this kind of problem, consider what we may term the "information" strike. Suppose that a party intends to take a strike unless his opponent concedes a particular position. How can he convince his opponent that these are the facts of the matter? He may assert that these are the facts of the matter, but this assertion may not be compelling. Another possibility is simply to take a strike. In this way, he avails himself of the information content of the strike.[3] Previously he had tried to establish as a fact his intention to take a strike rather than retreat from the position in question. The actual occurrence of the strike convinces his opponent that the threat was no mere bluff. If the opponent would have conceded the position had he made a correct prestrike estimate of the probability (namely, 1.0) that a strike would occur, only the information content component of the strike will have served a "legitimate" function.

In a case such as this we have a strike which is "unnecessary" in the sense that it occurs only because of an incorrect estimate of the probability that it would occur. It is undesirable, from the point of view of the parties and that of society generally, that strikes occur in these circumstances.[4] This suggests the desirability of an institutional substitute for the information strike, a device which would allow a party to negotiation to convince his opposite number of his serious intentions. For example, let it be provided at law that a party could enter into a binding contract with the NLRB to pay a stated sum (to be transferred to the U.S. Treasury) in the event he settled below (or above) stated terms without a strike. To prevent inept use of this contractual arrangement, it might be provided that such a contract be entered into only two days prior to a lawful bargaining strike or lockout deadline.

There may be reasons in practice not to advocate resort to this particular commitment arrangement, and it is intended in this context more as an illustration of a particular tactical problem than as a policy recommendation. Such a device would in any event eliminate only one very special kind of strike—the information strike.

It is worth noting that devices of this sort emphasize that function of the law concerned with provision of facilities (to aid resolution of social interaction) in contrast with prescriptive or "nay-saying" functions.[5] In applying the law to collective bargaining generally and to collective bargaining negotiation in particular, perhaps ingenuity could more fully exploit the provision-of-facilities function of the law.

The Game-Theory-Type Threat

Further consideration will be given to devices for commitment. First, however, additional aspects of the notbluff tactic may be developed by consideration of the "threat" tactic in a game-theory context. T. C. Schelling has provided a lucid discussion of the threat from this point of view, and the points at issue may be presented in his terms. "The distinctive character of a threat is that one asserts that he will do, in a contingency, what he would manifestly prefer not to do if the contingency occurred." [6] In these circumstances, the threatener has nothing to gain by actually carrying out the retaliation. Rather, retaliation is threatened in the hope that the risk will be sufficient to deter the act.

The circumstances supposed in this version of the threat can be made more definite in terms of one of Schelling's examples—Figure 2. This matrix represents, as do such matrices generally, the payoffs associated with strategies (rows and columns) available to each of two players, and may be viewed abstractly for purposes of illustrating the point in question. Row has two strategies, i and ii, with payoffs indicated in the lower-left corner of the cells. Column has two strategies, I and II, with payoffs indicated in the upper-right corner of the cells. (Thus, for example, an outcome [i,I] would yield payoffs of 9 and 10 to row and column respectively.) Let Column have first move. Barring an effective threat by Row, he has an easy win (in the sense that he can secure the highest payoff to himself available in the matrix). He plays Column I, leaving Row the choice Row i (9) versus Row ii (0). Row (assumed to be a fully informed maximizer) plays the former, yielding Column the winning payoff (10). However, an effective threat tactic by Row will permit him to win, that is, he convinces Column that in the event of Column I, he will play Row ii. This leaves Column the choice (and payoffs to himself), I, ii (8) versus II, i (9). He elects the latter, yielding Row the winning payoff (10.)

This example illustrates the distinctive character of the threat as suggested by Schelling. Should Column actually choose I, Row would prefer i—(in terms of the original matrix, a payoff of 9 as against 0)—that is, he would have nothing to gain and much to lose by carrying out the threat. However, Row has threatened to retaliate with ii against I in the hope (in the certain knowledge, in a game-theory context) that the risk thereby created will cause Column to elect II.

It should be observed that this kind of threat is a "particular" threat, to be distinguished from the kind of threat implied by the bargaining strike deadline rule. In the latter case, the strike threat is contingent upon a general state of affairs—"no agreement." In the present example, the threat is against a particular outcome (choice of strategy).

We may term threats of the kind just illustrated (elaborated as they are in a game theory context) "game-theory-type" threats. These threats involve operations on "manifest" preferences, conforming to the rationality postulate underlying the analysis. This postulate assumes that the payoffs to all the players are known to each, and that each will behave to maximize (the expected) payoff. The basic assumptions of the analysis give the game-theory-type threat certain rather special characteristics—properties that need not obtain for the threat tactic more generally defined. For one thing, in a game-theory context, this threat is perfectly safe. Row, having fully committed his threat ii against Column I need not worry, for Column, a fully informed maximizer, is sure to elect II (and hence 9), as against I (and 8). Under an assumption of uncertainty,

	I	II
i	10 / 9	9 / 10
ii	8 / 0	0 / 0

FIG. 2

perhaps more appropriate to analysis of collective bargaining, the threat illustrated may seem rather reckless.

The rationality (including extent of information) assumptions of game theory are not of course, generally speaking, appropriate to a description of collective bargaining negotiation. Nevertheless, the game-theory-type threat can be thought of as a tactical entity in terms of the threatener's actual preferences, manifest or not. The distinguishing characteristic in terms of preferences is that the actor asserts that he will do in some contingency what (in terms of the original, pretactical play payoffs) he would prefer not to do in the event of the contingency. For example, a party threatens to take a strike unless his demand is met, under circumstances such that he would actually prefer, in terms of the pretactical play payoffs, to concede the position rather than strike. This type of threat is notbluff to be distinguished from threats which are straightforward notbluffs—a party asserts that he will pursue a course of action which (without tactical contrivance) he would prefer to pursue should the contingency arise. For example, a party threatens to take a strike unless his demand is met, under circumstances such that he would actually prefer, in terms of the original payoffs, so to do.[7]

Bargaining Power vs. Negotiation Power

The distinction between the straightforward notbluff and the game-theory-type threat is of interest in analysis of collective bargaining for a number of reasons. One of these relates to the kind of power implied. The power behind the straightforward notbluff may be thought of as peculiarly "bargaining" power, that is, power which is fully inherent in the original (pretactical play) payoff matrix. In these cases, a party simply asserts that he will do what he would prefer to do, the power of the move being based upon preferences already available in the basic bargaining situation. On the other hand, the power behind the game-theory-type threat is not (fully) inherent in the original situation (payoff matrix). Rather, the power in this case is (in part) tactically contrived by "moves" which rig the game. For example, in terms of the matrix on page 80, the original payoffs do not give Row the power to threaten Row ii against Column I, for having actually to carry out the threat would yield Row a payoff of (0)—the least of those available. Nevertheless, if by tactical move, Row can contrive to bind himself irrevocably to ii, he may capitalize upon the bargaining power inherent in the choice Column II (9) against Column I (8).

Contrived power of this sort may be thought of as "negotiation" power, power which in some sense distorts the basic bargaining power underlying the interaction.

Commitment

The word "commitment" is used here in the sense of pledging or engaging oneself. In usual usage, this word is somewhat ambiguous as to whether the pledge is binding or irrevocable. Generally, one may think in terms of various "degrees" of commitment. The extreme case (no freedom of choice reserved) will generally be referred to with such modifiers as "binding" commitment or "fully" committed.

We have seen that a major tactical problem confronted by the player of straightforward notbluff is conveying to his opposite number the truth regarding a subsequent course of action. In this case, a negotiator has no need of devices for binding self-commitment in order to insure his own performance at the threat choice point, for he would prefer to do, at the choice point, what he has asserted he intends to do. If the negotiator's preferences in the straightforward notbluff situation are manifest, he may need no commitment to convey to the bargaining opponent the truth regarding his course of action. If this is not the case, some degree of commitment may be needed, even binding commitment—if it is necessary for credibility to leave no apparent discretion in actually carrying out the intended course of action.

The player of a game-theory-type threat has need for devices whereby he may commit himself to his intended course of action.[8] The essential problem is that of credibility. However, in this case, since the player would prefer, in terms of the original pretactical-play payoffs, not to do what he threatens, a full commitment leaving himself no discretion in carrying out the threat may be necessary to achieve credibility. Further, such a commitment may be necessary in order to insure his performance at the choice point. Otherwise a desire, at the choice point, to avoid the consequences of actually carrying out the threat may, because the bargaining opponent may anticipate that it will, nullify the threat.

To achieve "effective" commitment, the negotiator need not achieve full commitment in the extreme sense of no freedom of choice reserved. If, for example, the negotiator wishes to eschew strategy 1 (in favor of strategy 2), he may attach penalties of various magnitudes to his choice of 1. What is necessary is that the penalties be of sufficient magnitude to cause him in point of fact to elect (to prefer) strategy 2 should the contingency arise. In game theory, the penalty may be thought of as altering the original payoff matrix. Tactical moves are used to contrive a new matrix in terms of which a threatened course of action, manifestly not preferred in terms of the original matrix, is now manifestly preferred at the threat choice point.

How, in collective bargaining negotiation, might the player of a game-theory-type threat (or a straightforward notbluff) commit himself to his intended subsequent course of action? Among practices common in collective bargaining negotiation which warrant examination from this point of view is the device of nailing a particular demand to a general principle of presumed importance.[9] This tends to commit the negotiator because it puts the principle on the block along with the demand. One may view as an instance of such tactics the 1959 negotiations in the steel industry in which the companies nailed their demand for no wage increase to the principle of private responsibility for noninflationary wage settlements.

Other "principles" frequently invoked in collective bargaining may be considered from the point of view of their commitment potential. A union may nail a demand for a wage increase to the principle of private responsibility to sustain "purchasing power" and hence to promote a high level of economic activity. A company may resist a union shop on grounds that this contravenes a basic American "right to work." In such a case, the union may nail its demand for the union shop to the principle of eliminating the "free riders" who are shirking the responsibilities of industrial citizenship. Frequently, a company will resist a union demand on the grounds that to grant it would be to compromise "management prerogatives" and contravene management's "right to manage." Or a union may resist company modification of work rules procedures on the ground that this will substitute arbitrary unilateral authority for bilateral government in industry. Numerous such examples of the tactic of nailing demands to principles could be given.

Once a demand has been nailed to a principle, the issue has become transmuted. If the steel negotiations be so interpreted, the issue is no longer simply whether or not to grant a wage increase. Rather, this issue has become whether to abdicate "social responsibility" by taking an action which the bargainer himself has deemed perverse from a public policy point of view. The success of this tactic may be conditioned upon adequate publicity. If the negotiations are conducted in secrecy, a party may defect with relatively small penalty. If, however, adequate publicity has been given to the stand upon principle, matters are very different. By means of publicity, a party may pledge his reputation not only *vis-à-vis* his constituents, but before the general public as well. Under these circumstances, to make a settlement which can be interpreted as defection from principle involves severe penalties such as "loss of face" and possible degeneration of future negotiation power. A party may deem these penalties severe enough to achieve real commitment. In other words, carrying out the threat has now become virtually mandatory.[10]

It is interesting to observe, keeping in mind the distinction between "bargaining" power and "negotiation" power, that government by admonition (for example, dealing with inflation by appeal to private "social responsibility") may put tactical weapons into the hands of negotiators—weapons which enable them to distort the basic underlying power relationship (because of the commitment potential of nailing a demand to a principle).

In addition to the appeal to "principles," other practices common in collective bargaining negotiation warrant examination from the point of view of their commitment potential. For example, taking a strike vote may not only facilitate a strike, if this becomes necessary, but may also commit the union to a strike. In this case the negotiator may be (or may allege that he is) bound to a course of action by the will of his constituents. Similarly, on the management side, the negotiators may be (or may allege that they are) bound to a course of action by company officers to whom the union has no direct access. A local union may contend that it cannot make a settlement inconsistent with the "laws" of the international union. Or an individual plant negotiator may contend that he cannot make a settlement inconsistent with company-wide policy. In general, "pattern" bargaining of any kind may not only compel settlement on terms less favorable to one side than the *status quo,* but may also commit the negotiator from that side to these terms rather than terms more unfavorable to himself.

This is not intended as an exhaustive enumeration of collective bargaining practices with commitment potential, but merely as a suggestion of the practices which warrant examination from this point of view.

Reactions to Commitment Tactics in Collective Bargaining Negotiation. The game-theory-type threat and associated tactics of commitment involve "contrived" power. These tactics may be peculiarly appropriate to certain abstract game situations. That they may not be similarly appropriate to collective bargaining negotiation may be inferred from the reactions of participants in and students of this institution. For example, in such negotiation ultimatum is a "dirty" word, and the parties react emotionally against tactics of threat and commitment. This has tactical significance since the satisfaction associated with an outcome in collective bargaining negotiation is not independent of the tactics whereby it was achieved, and a threat tactic may be nullified by an adverse reaction of the bargaining opponent to the tactic itself, as well as to the result it is intended to secure.[11] More generally, Peters contends that "threats are not only the most dangerous, but usually the least effective form of indicating strength.[12] There is a presumption that if one has the strength one does not need to threaten." Such a reaction to threats increases the problem of making them credible. The practice of tying demands to general principles tends to be discredited by investigators as a naive confusion of the real issues or a perverse refusal to negotiate at all. Publicity in labor negotiations is not favored by many investigators partly because of the commitment potential. For example, Jackson, having noted that public debate may occasionally be of some aid in mobilizing the public interest for a peaceful settlement, points out that: "Extended public debate by the parties in conflict tends, however, to harden them in their respective points of view."[13] He also points out that the Federal Mediation and Conciliation Service, realizing the adverse implications of public discussion, advises the parties in its cases not to discuss the case with reporters. Taylor, taking note of the practice of public announcements of positions even before the parties have met, says that differences between the parties are made less negotiable when the "fanfare departments" get to work. He concludes: "As if the actual problems weren't bad enough, artificial ones are created. Smart tactics of the kind under discussion have brought about many an impasse and many a strike."[14]

Although it is suggestive, the fact that participants and students of labor negotiation deemphasize and react negatively to tactics of threat and coercive commitment does not establish the case that these are generally inappropriate. Perhaps the power of these tactics has been not sufficiently appreciated, and their disabilities tend to be given too much weight. There are, however, good reasons in the logic of the collective bargaining situation for supposing that the game-theory-type threat may not be generally appropriate. In Chapter III's discussion of the large initial bargaining demand rule, we saw that the commitment as a means for seizing "first move" was not consonant with the requirements of the bargaining relationship underlying labor negotiations. We noted earlier in this chapter that in simple abstract games in which each actor may assume that his opponent is a fully informed maximizer, the game-theory-type threat has an element of safety which is denied under the more realistic assumption of uncertainty.

Failure Due to Simultaneous Commitment. There is another aspect of collective bargaining negotiation which bears upon the appropriateness of tactics of commitment. Unlike some simple abstract games, collective bargaining negotiation does not feature a well-defined succession of alternating "moves."

It would not be quite correct to say that all such negotiation is completely "moveless." For example, in negotiation the parties show or imply strength by the way in which they retreat from initial bargaining positions. The process is frequently one of alternating concessions. A concession by one party is expected to call forth some concession from the bargaining opponent before any additional concession is forthcoming from the first party.[15] This procedure in a sense involves alternating "moves"; that is, the parties maintain an awareness of whose turn it is to act.[16]

Nevertheless, the situation is not one in which a well-defined first move is assigned to one party, second move to his opponent, and so on. Further, if there is to be a process of commitment, it is apt to be progressive.[17] The commitment will be built up by a whole sequence of events in the interaction of the parties, events which do not assume the format of well-defined alternating moves.

These considerations suggest the possibility, perhaps even the probability, that if tactics of commitment are tried they will result in simultaneous commitment—a situation in which the commitment tactics of each party perforce fail, and in which both are worse off. In a game with a well-defined first and second move, and a suitable payoff matrix, he who seizes first move by commitment or who commits himself to a strategy for second move wins. In collective bargaining negotiation, a party contemplating tactics of commitment confronts the possibility that a sort of "race" to coercive commitment will eventuate. Neither party may be convinced that the other is committed in time to stop short of disaster for both. In a game-like interaction such as collective bargaining negotiation, tactics of commitment may indeed be reckless. This does not mean that in some instances of such negotiation the parties may not have resort to such tactics. Indeed, the deadlock in the 1959 steel industry negotiations may be viewed as failure due to simultaneous commitment.[18]

The Strike Over a Few Cents. Often a strike takes place when only a small difference separates the parties. It has frequently been observed that it seems "irrational" to take a long and costly strike to gain an additional few cents in the wage rate.

The commonest explanation of this phenomenon is a forward-looking one, emphasizing that collective bargaining is a continuing relationship. It is argued that if a party says he will strike but does not, he will decrease his future bargaining power by reducing the credibility of his strike threats in future negotiations. In this view, if the impact on long-run bargaining power is taken into account, such a strike is rational.

Such considerations may be relevant in explaining strikes of this sort. They emphasize the nonindependence of each "play" of the negotiation game in a continuing relationship. This suggests that analysis of tactics and strategy during any one play cannot be based solely upon scrutiny of events pertaining to that play, but must take into account the impact of past, and anticipated effects of future events. We have observed that the process of commitment is apt to be progressive during each play of the game, built up by a whole sequence of events. This point should be extended to encompass progressive build-up of a "posture" of commitment over a whole sequence of plays.

Consideration of the commitment tactic suggests an explanation for this type of strike alternative to the forward-looking one. This explanation is essentially backward-looking. The long and costly strike to gain a few cents may take place because, at the choice point, the striker had no option but to strike, that is, he had arranged to leave himself no discretion in the matter. He had so arranged in order to make his strike threat credible and thereby deter opponent's action upon which the threat was conditioned. The threat having failed in its deterrent mission, the strike takes place even though the present discounted value of future benefits from the strike is less than its cost.[19]

The "Hurt-More" Criterion for Feasibility of Threats

An interpersonal utility comparison issue is involved in the game-theory treatment of the threat tactic. Luce and Raiffa, for example, make the threat turn on such a comparison in the sense that A's threat *vis-à-vis* B is deemed acceptable or plausible only if A can assert that "this will hurt you more than it will me." [20] In Schelling's view, on the other hand, the threat involves essentially a commitment problem, not an interpersonal utility problem. Once A's threat is committed, B chooses from among his remaining options in accordance with his own maximizing interests. The threat works by constraining B's available options, and the interpersonal utility comparison is irrelevant.

The matrix on page 80 illustrates this point. In the event of Column's choice I, Row's actual choice ii (carrying out the threat) would cost Row (9); that is, with ii his payoff is (0) rather than (9) to be had by choice i. For Column, the cost of Row's carrying out the threat is only (2); in other words, he receives (8) rather than the (10) he would have had with Row choice i. Thus, as an interpersonal utility comparison, carrying out the threat hurts Row "more" than it does Column. Nevertheless, with fully informed maximizers, the threat should be both plausible and effective. Schelling recognizes that certain circumstances (such as the possibility of simultaneous commitment discussed in the last section) might suggest modification of the threat concept in the direction of the "hurt-more" criterion. However, he feels that "game theory adds more insight into the strategy of bargaining by emphasizing the striking truth that the threat does *not* depend on the threatener's having less to suffer than the threatened party if the threat had to be carried out" rather than by emphasizing the possible truth contained in the other position.[21]

The essential problem involved with the "hurt-more" criterion may be one of credibility under conditions of some uncertainty. It is true that in a game-theory context a threat that is assumed to be fully committed can be effective because of the constraints it imposes, quite apart from the matter of interpersonal utility comparison. However, in many negotiation contexts it may be difficult to commit a threat fully. It may be especially difficult to find means of commitment sufficient to make nonhurt-more-type threats sufficiently credible. If as a matter of cultural convention, such threats are not considered "plausible," they will be harder to commit. The issue here is one of empirical generalization: Do parties to negotiation characteristically deem nonhurt-more-type threats not plausible? Returning to the example matrix, these considerations might well allow the configuration of payoffs confronted by each of the players to defeat the threat. Suppose that Column is not fully convinced (for the reason given) that Row will play this threat of Row ii against Column I. He may consider Column I a good "gamble"; that is, even if Row does carry out the threat, Column stands to lose only (2).

More probably, however, the intuitive appeal of the hurt-more criterion inheres in the fact that it is actually an oblique way of saying something quite different, namely: "If the threat is carried out, you will be forced to capitulate before I am forced so to do, that is, although there is pressure on both, that on you is greater relative to your ability to withstand it." To put this another way, define A's bargaining power *vis-à-vis* B as the ratio: the cost to B of disagreeing with A on A's terms/the cost to B of agreeing with A on A's terms. B's bargaining power is similarly defined.[22] The hurt-more criterion may now be put: "My bargaining power will increase relative to yours." This does not involve an interpersonal utility comparison in the usual (dimensional) sense. It does, however, involve an interpersonal comparison of utility ratios pertaining to each party—cost of disagreement/cost of agreement.

This significance of the hurt-more criterion in collective bargaining negotiation is suggested by the fact that the typical threat—namely, to take a strike—is a threat not so much to insure a particular outcome as to set up a state of affairs under which an outcome will be achieved. In the concept of game-variant sequences, to take a strike is to elect a game-variant. The credibility of A's strike threat depends upon B's expectations about who would "win" the strike. The hurt-more criterion may be viewed as a somewhat oblique way of supplying an answer to this question.

BLUFF

A party to negotiation is engaged in bluff when he asserts or implies that he will do what he does not intend to do at the time the assertion is made.

In analysis predicated upon a perfect knowledge postulate (as in game theory), tactics of bluff are essentially inappropriate.[23] For one thing, the circumstance in game theory that the payoff matrix is out on the bargaining table for all to see precludes certain kinds of bluffing, notably that based upon misrepresentation of preferences. If, according to the original (pretactical play) payoff matrix, A's strategy 1 is preferred to his strategy 2, A cannot "pretend to prefer" strategy 2. If A cannot resort to bluff based upon such pretension, how can he convince B that he will elect strategy 2? One answer is to employ commitment tactics, "moves" which appropriately rig the (payoff) structure of the game so that strategy 2 is in point of fact preferred. Further, the analytical context of game theory strongly suggests that if commitments are employed, they must be binding if they are to be effective (and hence not consonant with bluff via the sham-commitment route).[24]

We noted at the outset of this chapter that in discussions of the tactics of collective bargaining there are frequent references to bluff as an important negotiation tactic. This is partly because the assumption characterizing the actors is one of uncertainty (rather than perfect knowledge) about opponent's preferences and intentions. Since a bluff which is thought by the bargaining opponent to be a *mere* bluff will not be effective, the player of a bluff confronts what may be a difficult tactical problem, that of establishing the credibility of his bluff. This tactical problem, although recognized in the collective bargaining literature, is seldom discussed. A's bluff tactics are intended to alter or establish B's expectations regarding A's subsequent course of action. During the negotiation, B may attach a probability from 0.0 to 1.0 to the fact that A's bluff will be carried through. A's tactical problem is how to raise this probability as near to 1.0 as possible without binding himself to the course of action in question (since bluff is involved, A wants ultimately to be able to withdraw if this proves necessary).

Bluff may not be as important a negotiation tactic as much discussion would imply. For one thing, the institution of the bargaining strike deadline does much to squeeze elements of bluff out of at least the later pre-deadline stages of negotiation. As the deadline approaches, there is considerable pressure on each negotiator to "come clean" in the hope that knowledge of the true positions (usually less favorable to each than his ostensible position) will preclude the strike. Further, collective bargaining is a continuing, year-in-year-out (and day-in-day-out) relationship. The negotiators on each side may get to know each other quite well. This personal familiarity considerably decreases the scope for bluff and deception.[25] In notbluff, it may be observed that the kind of familiarity which develops in continuing interactions also simplifies the problem of conveying the truth with respect to an intended course of action; that is, it may simplify the commitment problem. Generally speaking, tactics appropriate to the one-shot type of negotiation situation may not be similarly appropriate to a continuing relationship. In consequence, care is needed in transferring notions about negotiation tactics developed with reference to the first kind of situation to analysis of situations of the second kind.

Bluff through Misrepresentation of Preferences and Another Function of Rationalization

A primary bluff tactic in negotiation seems to be the negotiator's misrepresentation of his preferences with respect to potential outcomes of the negotiation, as a way to establish expectations about his intended course of action. That is, since it is generally assumed that an actor will elect courses of action which will attain his preferred position, a negotiator may imply a course of action by giving his opposite number information about his preferences. This is a matter of implication because there is some obliqueness here. Thus, the negotiator, rather than asserting that he will take a strike if his opponent sticks at $2.00, may simply express his extreme dissatisfaction with $2.00, implying that he will take a strike if the bargaining opponent sticks at $2.00.[26]

A position that a given wage rate is not acceptable is more credible if it is somehow rationalized, and hence one function of a negotiator's rationalization tactics is to support his assertions about his preferences. If an actor can show that a given course of action is consonant with his goal, and can show how it will lead to that goal, we are more apt to believe that he will adopt that course of action than we would be in the absence of such a showing.

To take an example, suppose that a union rationalizes a demand for a wage increase by appealing to comparison with other rates. From the tactical point of view here under consideration, the important function of the union's comparative-rates argument is less to communicate information to the company about its wage rate environment (and in consequence to achieve persuasion) than to communicate information about the union's beliefs on this matter.[27] That is, the argument may serve to convince the company that the union believes itself to be correct in asserting its demands to be minimal in accordance with the comparative rates criterion. This "information about own-beliefs" function of rationalization will have an impact if the company believes that to the union officials, because of their status as elected officials who must satisfy the membership, comparative rates parity is extremely important. To sum up, this function of rationalization is more to convince the bargaining opponent what one believes to be the case than to convince him what is in point of fact the case. Thus an appearance of "commitment" can be achieved by operating upon opponent's perception of one's own preferences—leaving him to make inferences about the course of action implied by those preferences.

The Inadvertent Strike. An important tactical problem associated with bluff is the danger that a sham commitment will be inadvertently converted into a *bona fide* commitment. That is, at some point in the prosecution of tactics of bluff and sham commitment, a strike may be begun less because, at that choice point, the negotiator ′ wants a strike than because at that point, the situation has gotten out of hand—real freedom of choice has been lost, and whether or not the strike occurs is a matter of "chance" insofar as the negotiator's relation to it is concerned.

The possibility that some strikes may be "accidental" in this sense does not seem remote. One possibility for inadvertent conversion of a sham commitment to a real one hinges on the consideration that it may be easier to "prove" the truth of something that is true than of something false.[28] Thus, the more (palpable) discretion an actor leaves himself with respect to carrying out his assertion that he will pursue a given course of action, the less credible the assertion may be to his opponent. This suggests that to make a bluff credible, it may be necessary to make it so nearly true that it turns out to be true.

The whole negotiation process suggests the possibility that inadvertent strikes may occur. We observed in the last section that the process of commitment—and we may add now, of sham commitment—in collective bargaining is apt to be progressive, built up by a whole sequence of events in the interaction between the parties. These events will include the negotiation sessions themselves, during which iteration of positions may slowly harden each party in his position. Speeches and advertisements addressed to the general public and to constituents may create a situation in which there is a sanction for failure to carry through on a threat. A party, in attempting to make a bluff credible by pursuit of such tactics, may likewise maneuver himself into a position where, for reasons of prestige, he does not possess the flexibility to withdraw (what were) sham demands.[29] Preparations necessary if there is to be a strike (taking a strike vote, organizing picketing and financial support, accumulating inventories and advising customers to do likewise, deciding what to do about unfilled orders and new orders, and so forth) may tend to increase its likelihood. During the whole cumulative process, emotions may build up, experience in the conflict-choice situation may engender anxiety and tension, which in turn may promote nondeliberate behavior.

In sum, tactics of bluff and the associated process of sham commitment comprise a chain of events which, once set in motion, carry with it some risk of an inadvertent strike, and this risk increases as time passes and events are added to the chain.

The Intentional "Inadvertent" Strike. From one point of view, the inadvertent strike is a danger to be guarded against when engaged in tactics of bluff. From another point of view, the possibility of such an "accidental" strike has a deterrent potential upon which the negotiator might hope to capitalize. This threat mechanism (which T. C. Schelling terms "the threat that leaves something to chance") is not bluff.[30]

To suggest the central features of this tactic, we start with the described notion that the actual initiation of a strike may be inadvertent, and, hence, these tactics themselves carry a threat which may be effective. That is, the negotiator may feel pressured to make a concession—not because he is convinced that otherwise his bargaining opponent will deliberately elect to strike, but rather in order to abort a chain of events which carries with it some chance of a strike over which neither party has precise control.

If such a strike does take place, it is "intentional" in the sense that the negotiator who sets the chain of events in motion is aware that it carries with it some "chance" of a strike—indeed this is the rationale of the tactical sequence elected. At the same time, such a strike is "inadvertent" precisely because of the "chance" element.

Not-Commitment

The effort to make a bluff credible is complicated by factors involved with the circumstance that in collective bargaining negotiation ultimatum tends to be a "dirty" word. Thus the parties face the problem of making a demand while at the same time avoiding even the appearance of commitment—avoiding being deemed by the opposite number to have "issued an ultimatum." This is a most interesting problem. If collective bargaining negotiation requires, as has been frequently suggested, an atmosphere in which the appearance of "ultimatum" is to be studiously avoided, how then can a party's "demand" carry any conviction whatsoever?

The answer to this question probably lies in the rather indirect modes employed in such negotiation. More particularly, the kind of obliqueness involved in bluff via misrepresentation of preferences seems peculiarly adapted to the discharge of this tactical function. Because of the deadline rule, a sort of "generalized" strike threat is in the air, and the question in each party's mind is how far he must retreat in order to avoid this. A party need not "threaten" in the sense of making a strike contingent upon some particular outcome. This would be an ultimatum. Rather, A may let B infer from A's actions and pronouncements where the breaking-off point is. Of particular importance here will be B's estimate of the satisfactions A associates with various outcomes. Negotiator A may attempt favorably to influence this estimate by representing (or misrepresenting) his own preferences, while studiously avoiding even an appearance of commitment.

Undoing a Commitment

The possibility of a failure of negotiations due to both simultaneous intentional commitment and inadvertent commitment suggests that the tactics of releasing an opponent from a commitment may be important in collective bargaining negotiations.[31] It may be in the interests of one or both parties to prevent an opponent from achieving commitment or to release him from it. The extent to which the parties recognize the release of an opponent from a commitment to be an important tactical problem, and what devices are employed for this purpose, are questions which need clarification. Here once again we find potential tactical functions for rationalization. From this point of view, A's argument in terms of wage criteria, for instance, are intended not so much to "justify" A's position as to provide B with a basis for contriving and justifying his retreat from his own position. If A's rationalizations are deliberately undertaken with this in mind, they will be designed with an eye to their potential appeal to B's constituents, and whatever "public" is relevant from B's point of view.

It warrants noting that this is the third distinct tactical function thus far assigned to tactics of rationalization. In addition, rationalization has been viewed as a way in which to consolidate the support of constituents and perhaps a "public." It has also been regarded as a way in which the negotiator can convince his bargaining opponent that he does in point of fact hold certain beliefs. These functions may be conflicting in the sense that argumentation best calculated to serve one of these functions may not be similarly optimal from the other points of view. Herein lies a good bit of the interest and complexity inherent in tactics of "mere" rationalization.

Incentive Effect

Coercive tactics may also be distinguished in terms of incentive effect. This is the distinction between Class I tactics and Class II tactics developed in Chapter II. A's tactics of the former class operate upon B by increasing B's tendency to avoid his own position—by increasing B's apparent cost of disagreement with A on A's terms. The latter class of tactics operates upon B by decreasing B's tendency to avoid A's position

—by decreasing the apparent cost to B of agreeing with A on A's terms. In Chapter II it was argued that there may be an analytically important asymmetry between tactics of Class I and II; emphasis upon Class I tactics may, *ceteris paribus,* increase the probability of a breakdown of the negotiation process as contrasted with emphasis upon Class II tactics.

The term "promise," although associated with a specified course of action, does not properly connote so much a particular class of courses of action as it does a means to commitment to a course of action. However, the term is frequently used as if it did connote a class of action, and, from this point of view, the matter of incentive effect is probably at the heart of the conventional distinction between the threat and the promise. That is, A's "threat" is thought of as potentially punishing to B, something which he does not welcome—which increases the cost of disagreement with A; whereas A's "promise" is thought of as potentially rewarding to B, something which he does welcome—which decreases the cost of agreement with A. It has been observed that considerations of this sort, relating to "the second party's interest," do not provide an analytically tight distinction between the "threat" and the "promise." [32] Nevertheless, it is an implication of intrapersonal conflict-choice theory that incentive effect does provide an analytically significant way in which to distinguish negotiation tactics generally (whether this be made the basis for distinguishing the "threat" and the "promise" or not).

A question arises: Should we view the existence of these two classes of tactics (distinguished in terms of incentive effect) as providing two distinct bases or sources of economic power? The usual view of economic power stresses the power to withhold, to refuse to deal (boycott). However, Chamberlain, in discussing the manipulation of bargaining power, has observed: "Such efforts involve two fundamentally different methods, one of limiting the alternatives which are available to others, the second of extending the alternatives which are available to others." [33] One method might be identified with threat—increasing cost of disagreement. The other with the promise of a *quid pro quo*—reducing the cost of agreement.

However, the power to promise a *quid pro quo* implies the power to withhold it, and, hence, the possibility of boycott is central to both methods. Perhaps the considerations here are best put in terms of movement from a *status quo,* defined as some collection of potential outcomes. Starting from such a *status quo,* a party might concentrate upon boycott in these terms, that is, upon limiting the alternatives available to others. Or, as a matter of basic strategy, a party might attempt to enlarge the range of strategies (and hence potential outcomes) over which he has control in order that he might operate by extending the alternatives available to others.

CHAPTER VI

The Later (Predeadline) Stages of Negotiation

An analysis of the later (predeadline) stages of collective bargaining negotiation focuses upon the process whereby agreement is or is not achieved. A thorough appraisal of these stages is one of the most important and most difficult problems in the development of a general theory of negotiation.

As we have pointed out, the concept of a negotiation cycle, a succession of stages of negotiation—from early to later—may be appropriate to the analysis of many contract negotiations. A consideration of the process suggests two theoretically significant distinctions between early and later stages and suggests that a "divide" may be crossed during negotiation.

The first of these distinctions is between necessary and sufficient conditions for agreement in negotiation—developed earlier in connection with the conflict-choice model. We shall return to this conceptualization of the negotiation process, consider implications of the deadline in the context of this analysis, and discuss the tactics of changing ostensible position.

The second involves the possibility that during the course of negotiation a contract zone becomes manifest, and, in consequence, the character of the negotiation game changes. In other words, revelation of the contract zone marks a sort of divide—the tactic mix and the important tactical problems shift toward cooperation and coordination. In this context, we shall discuss the implications of the "pure"-bargaining-game model.

In addition, certain agreement problems which might be relevant in either analytical context will be discussed.

The analysis in this chapter is not presented as a comprehensive portrayal of the later stages of negotiation. It is hoped that elements contained in the analysis may comprise at least a part of those characteristic of the later stages.

Considerations of the process whereby agreement is or is not achieved are also directly related to the function of mediation in the settlement of collective bargaining disputes. Consequently, certain of the points made in this chapter will be further developed in Chapter VII which is directly concerned with mediation.

THE AVOIDANCE–AVOIDANCE MODEL AND FURTHER FUNCTIONS OF THE DEADLINE

At this point we return to the avoidance–avoidance model. Figure 1 in Chapter II depicted one party's (the company's) equilibrium position. The analysis, however, applies symmetrically to both sides of the bargaining table. In discussing the predeadline stages of negotiation and the problem of agreement, we must think in terms of two figures like Figure 1, one depicting the company's equilibrium position and one depicting the union's equilibrium position. In these terms, the status of any particular collective bargaining negotiations at any particular time may be presented by the values assembled in Table 1. At each choice

Table 1. Illustrative configurations of collective bargaining negotiation.
(hourly rates)

Bargaining positions	Status 1	Status 2	Status 3	Status 4
Company's announced position	$3.00	$3.00	$3.00	$3.00
Company's equilibrium position	3.05	3.12	3.05	3.15
Union's equilibrium position	3.20	3.12	3.12	3.10
Union's announced position	3.25	3.25	3.25	3.25

point in the negotiation, each party knows these positions: his own announced position, the announced position of his opponent, and his own equilibrium position (which, it will be recalled represents those terms least favorable to himself he would at that choice point be willing to accept and is the position he would be willing to agree to were there some way to do it).

Retreat as a Sign of Weakness

The analysis in Chapter II led to a distinction between necessary and sufficient conditions for reaching agreement in negotiation. The necessary condition was that the equilibrium positions occupied by the parties be brought into consonance. Referring to Table 1, in Status 2 the conditions necessary for agreement have been met. This is the first task of the negotiation process. It was argued that by itself consonance of equilibrium positions is a necessary but not a sufficient condition for agreement. The parties must somehow mutually be informed of the fact of this consonance if it is to constitute a route to actual agreement. This latter task, the second major function of the negotiation process, may be difficult. It has frequently been pointed out that making an ostensible concession during the course of negotiation may be tricky since revising a demand downward may be interpreted by the opponent as a sign of weakness or even as a sign of impending collapse and capitulation.

This suggests that the fundamental tactical problem confronted by a party during the later stages of negotiation is not so much one of bluff, deception, or of coercive commitment, as it is how to reveal to the bargaining opponent one's own equilibrium position. The aspect of this tactical problem here suggested (other aspects will be discussed subsequently) is how to inform an opponent of the least favorable terms upon which one is willing to settle without, at the same time, implying weakness or even impending collapse—and thereby compromising negotiation power by the very process of the communication.

In a subsequent section of this chapter, we shall give some attention to how such a communication might be accomplished. Here, it is interesting to note that if these conjectures are correct, they have the most important consequences for the later predeadline stages of negotiation and for the mechanism whereby agreement is reached. For one thing, they suggest that negotiations may fail to terminate with overt agreement even though the parties are in covert agreement in the sense that the necessary conditions have been met. Further, they suggest that conditions necessary for agreement may be destroyed by the parties in their mutual efforts to inform each other of the fact of their existence. Referring once more to Table 1, suppose that the parties occupy Status 2 (necessary conditions for agreement met) and that, for example, the union simply announces its equilibrium position 3.12. This announcement, if interpreted as a sign of weakness by the opponent, rather than resulting in immediate agreement, may result in a situation such as Status 3—one in which the necessary conditions are no longer met: that is, the company, interpreting the union's downward revision of ostensible position as a sign of weakness, in turn revises its own equilibrium position downward (from 3.12 to 3.05).

The Deadline and Asymmetry of Tactical Advantage

The concepts of necessary and sufficient conditions for agreement and the tactical problems associated therewith have been discussed without reference to the institution of the bargaining-strike deadline. It is both necessary and illuminating to examine the implications of the deadline in this context.

Generally speaking, the deadline fits into this model via its effect upon the expected probability of a strike or lockout. We saw in Chapter II that if the company revises upward its estimate of the probability that adhering to its own position will eventuate in a strike, the effect of this is to increase the tendency to avoid such adherence—shift the avoidance-gradient to that goal upward. This means that the company's equilibrium position shifts in the direction of the union's announced position. The approach of the deadline revises upward each party's estimate of the probability that a strike or lockout will be consequent upon adherence to his own position. An approaching deadline puts pressure on the parties to state their true positions and thus does much to squeeze elements of bluff out of the later stages of negotiation. However, an approaching deadline does much more than simply squeeze elements of bluff and deception out of the negotiation process. It brings pressures to bear which actually change the least favorable terms upon which each party is willing to settle.[1] Thus it operates as a force tending to bring about conditions necessary for agreement.

It will help to spell out this argument. The deadline makes a strike contingent upon no agreement. Assuming that both parties intend to observe the deadline and that both know this, *this* contingent probability of a strike is zero up to the deadline and 1.0 thereafter. But it is not this contingent probability upon which the parties are supposed to focus during the negotiation process. At a particular choice point during the process each party is supposed to be concerned with the probability that a strike will occur at the deadline if he continues (at the deadline) to adhere to his announced position as of the choice point in question. It is argued that each party's estimate of this latter contingent probability of a strike gradually increases as the deadline draws nearer, and, as a result, the equilibrium position occupied by each party shifts in the direction of his opponent's position. In terms of Table 1, the positions occupied by the parties might shift from those depicted in Status 1 to those depicted in Status 2 or Status 4. Thus, once the institution of a deadline is admitted to the analysis, positions representing any given status of the negotiations must be supposed to pertain to some particular time relative to the deadline.

It may be argued that the deadline helps to preclude the before-mentioned possibility that negotiations may fail to terminate with overt agreement even though the parties are in covert agreement in the sense that the necessary conditions for agreement have been met. Let us suppose that the deadline has been set for 12:00, and that it is now 11:59. However hesitant the union may have been to announce its equilibrium position, now there is no choice. If upon that announcement the parties occupy Status 2, there will be agreement. It might still be true that were this yesterday, such an announcement would convert Status 2 into Status 3, thereby destroying the conditions necessary for agreement. However, if the parties occupy Status 2 at 11:59 today, there is no time for this to occur. The company has the option of agreeing to the union's proposal of 3.12, which is coincident with its own equilibrium position, or taking a strike—and presumably it will elect the former. Thus, however reluctant each may be, the pressures created by the deadline force them to reveal their equilibrium positions in such a way that if the necessary conditions for agreement have been met, overt agreement will follow. It is the deadline in particular, not just some arrangement for initiation of a strike, which achieves this result. The important thing about the deadline is that it brings with itself an 11:59. Without a manifest and predictable deadline, there would only be a 12:00, and then it would be too late.

Status 2 in Table 1—depicting a precise equality of equilibrium positions—is a special case of that consonance of equilibrium positions necessary for agreement.[2] Status 4 also represents a situation in which the necessary conditions are met. If at 11:59 the parties occupy Status 4 positions, and if the union announces its equilibrium position, there will also be agreement.

Although agreement is reached in both cases, there are important differences. In Status 2 the contract zone contains only one value. In Status 4 the equilibrium positions overlap, and the contract zone contains a range of values. In the conventional approach to price determination under bilateral monopoly, the contract zone is manifest to the parties, and the outcome is held to be theoretically "indeterminate" within the limits imposed by the contract zone. With the avoidance–avoidance paradigm conceptualization of the negotiation process, the contract zone (if such exists) is not manifest to the parties. That is, the analysis does not suppose that each party confronts a range of values known to constitute a contract zone. Rather, each party focuses upon his own equilibrium position. This model, if it incorporates the institution of a deadline, results in a "determinate" solution. The solution is the equilibrium position occupied by the party who announces it at 11:59.

This solution emphasizes an important asymmetry of tactical advantage in this model of negotiation. At 11:59 the time has come for "last" proposals. In the nature of the case, one of these proposals is an offer; the other, if there is a contract zone, is agreement. If the parties operate out of a situation such as that depicted in Status 4, the advantage will have gone to the one who waited. Thus, with reference to Status 4, if at 11:59 the union announces its equilibrium position (3.10), the outcome is more favorable to the company than the least favorable terms it would have been willing to accept (3.15), and vice versa.[3]

One may inquire: Why does one party, aware of the implications of the asymmetry in the situation, announce his equilibrium position at 11:59? The answer is because he is convinced that 11:59 has indeed arrived. That is, the party announces his position because he does not think that the other party will announce its own position in time to allow him to agree to it prior to the deadline, or, in the event he would not accept it, in time to allow him then to announce his equilibrium position and get the other party's reactions to it prior to the deadline.

One may further inquire: Why is the announcing party of this opinion? An answer to this question involves a modification of the deadline concept as developed. The critical predeadline moment of choice has been characterized as 11:59, implying that the deadline is a knife-edge phenomenon. Actually, this is not the case. For one thing, one important function served by the deadline is to facilitate the parties' making preparation for a strike or lockout.[4] If there is to be a strike, the parties must make a number of technical and organizational preparations, for example, equipment may have to be put in standby condition, customers and suppliers informed, pickets organized, information about the strike prepared, and so on. If the deadline is set for 12:00, these preparations will have to be begun some time prior to 11:59 so that the deadline is more a zone of increasing commitment to a strike. It seems plausible that the preparations themselves would assume the status of "moves" in the negotiation game, each successive move implying in-creasing commitment to taking a strike unless the opponent yields some ground. At some point during the process, one party will be convinced that 11:59 has arrived.[5]

Anticipating a Strike

We saw in Chapter III that the bargaining-strike deadline rule sets up a game-variant sequence in the analysis of which one critical aspect is the possibility of interaction between the variants. This aspect should now be considered in visualizing the choice problem confronted by the negotiator at 11:59. The negotiator, having decided that it is 11:59, can choose to: (1) stand pat and take a strike or (2) announce the least favorable terms which he is willing to settle (more favorable to his op-ponent than his then announced position) and perhaps achieve agree-ment. The contention was that he would elect (2). But what about the consideration that if a strike does eventuate, it will begin on the basis of a *status quo* inherited from the prestrike negotiation, that is, the "final" proposals as of the deadline? [6]

To the extent that this kind of anticipation plays a part in collective bargaining negotiations, it can mean that the final proposal enunciated by the party who believes it is 11:59 is, not the least favorable terms upon which he is willing to settle, but terms somewhat more favorable to him-self than these least favorable terms. That is, the negotiator may feel constrained to "save something" in case of a strike. This implies an element of inefficiency in the negotiation process, for it might be that the terms actually announced at 11:59 are not in the contract zone, whereas the least favorable terms would have been. In such a case, an "unnecessary" strike takes place, that is, a strike which occurs because the probability that it might occur prompted a higher (lower) "final" offer than was either acceptable or necessary.

The Problem of "Coming Clean" Without Prejudice

The model of the negotiation process developed so far in this chapter constitutes something of an "unnatural" game in the sense discussed in Chapter II. The game depicted would seem to generate psychological pressures similar to those in the game of "chicken," esteemed by the hotrod fraternity, in which the players speed head-on toward each other. He who turns aside first loses. Otherwise they both lose. The logic of the negotiation situation and such an institutional phenomenon as the photo-finish suggest that there are important elements of this sort in the negotiation process. However, one would anticipate that the psychological pressures generated in this game would motivate parties' negotiating on a year-in-and-year-out basis to contrive techniques to reduce such pressures. This consideration leads to the problem of the function of changes in ostensible (as distinguished from equilibrium) positions.

The discussion has proceeded as if, although the equilibrium positions of the parties do in point of fact change during the course of negotiation, the "announced" positions are not altered. This is not, of course, characteristic of collective bargaining negotiation. The announced positions themselves may be altered, and concessions will be made—particularly during the predeadline stages of negotiation. The question now is: What principles guide the formulation of such concessions during the course of negotiation?

The principles involved must take into account the fundamental tactical problem elaborated in this chapter: How may a party announce his equilibrium position without prejudice? In the interest of clarity, we may sum up the various reasons why such an announcement may be prejudicial:

(1) It involves a retreat from the ostensible position, a retreat which may be interpreted by the opposite number as a sign of weakness, or even as a sign of impending collapse and capitulation.

(2) Operating under the deadline rule, the solution of the negotiation game is the equilibrium position occupied by the party who "gives" at 11:59. This solution emphasizes an important asymmetry inherent in the end stages of collective bargaining negotiation. At 11:59 the time has come for "last" proposals. In the nature of the case, one of these proposals is an offer; the other, if there is a contract zone, is agreement. The advantage may well have gone to the one who waited.

(3) Operating under the deadline rule, either party may elect game-variant 2—negotiation under strike conditions. Even though a party does not wish to play game 2, it may be forced upon him, and this consideration may cause him to be concerned about the *status quo* which, if it does eventuate, game 2 will inherit from game 1. These considerations may create pressures for a party to enunciate, as his "last" offer, terms somewhat more favorable to himself than the least favorable upon which he is willing to settle.

The problem of how to "come clean" without prejudice would lead one to expect that, as is the case, eleventh-hour or even last-minute agreements would be common in collective bargaining negotiations.[7] Agreement well before the deadline would be expected only in those cases in which one party has succeeded in committing himself to a position which is preferred by his opponent to no agreement, or in those cases in which for some other reason both parties expect the same outcome early in the game, and expect it with such a high degree of certainty that the disutility of continued negotiation outweighs any small chance of additional gain to be had thereby. Perhaps a case in point is the pattern follower in industries in which bargaining is paced by "key" bargains.

The problems comprehended under the rubric "how to come clean without prejudice" suggest that changing an ostensible position, with the intention of conveying information to one's opposite number about one's equilibrium position, involves a rather delicate problem. Precisely how such communication may be accomplished is an important question in analysis of negotiation.

Widespread resort to the use of "sign language" is perhaps best interpreted as an attempt to resolve this problem. For example, Peters has suggested that sign language is an essential ingredient of this communications procedure. "Sign language is a protective device. You want to offer a concession, but you want to protect yourself against a rejection. You want to protect your strength even as you indicate a concession . . . Sign language enables you to offer concessions without having your actions interpreted as weakness. It gives you the flexibility to move in the direction of peace—or to *move back* to a position of strength." [8]

Peters notes that the use of sign language requires skill and experience. Unskilled negotiators do not frequently have resort to symbolic modes of communication. Further, the precise forms such communications take tend to be peculiar to particular contexts; in other words, what may be considered meaningful in one situation may not carry significance in another.

A few illustrations of what is meant by the use of sign language will help to make this notion more definite.[9] In some situations, silence may convey a concession. This may be the case, for example, if a negotiator who has frequently and firmly rejected a proposal simply maintains silence the next time the proposal is made. The degree of emphasis with which the negotiator expresses himself on various issues may be an important indication. The suggestion that the parties pass over a given item for the present, on the grounds that it probably will not be an important obstacle to eventual settlement, may be a covert way of setting up a trade on this item for some other. The negotiator may appear to act upon his own initiative without the authority of his committee or principals—taking the position that if he can get some concession along the lines indicated he will attempt to "sell" it to his principals. The parties may quote statistics (fictitious if need be) as a covert way of suggesting a position, or they may convey a position by discussing a settlement made in an unrelated industry.

This communications procedure should help to cope with one of the problems involved in "coming clean" without prejudice; namely, taking into account the fact that if a strike should eventuate, it will begin on the basis of a *status quo* inherited from the prestrike negotiations. This is so because with this procedure the *status quo* is not clearly delineated. More particularly, the final positions implied by the use of sign language are not made a matter of public record.

It is less clear how the use of sign language copes with the problem of allowing a party to make ostensible concessions without having his actions interpreted as a sign of weakness. The key to this seems to be that use of sign language is a device for breaking concession down into a number of small, revocable steps—each one of which invites reciprocal concession before the next step is taken. By the use of sign language, a party signals the direction in which he wants to go, and then waits for some answering signal. Either the parties go arm-in-arm, as it were, or they do not go at all. In some negotiations the parties maintain an awareness of whose "move" it is, and such a convention with respect to reciprocity affords each protection.[10] Along with this, because of the oblique modes in terms of which these communications are cast, each next step is revocable. If the procedure is to work, however, the whole series of past steps cannot be considered freely revocable. To communicate successfully by means of signs and symbols, the negotiator must be willing to take some chances.[11] Thus, he should not be so generally suspicious and fearful of a double-cross that he ignores a "smoke signal."

The negotiators are also afforded some protection by conventions with respect to "good faith" in bargaining. Peters has stressed that the basic criteria of good faith in negotiation, recognized and accepted by the parties, is contained in the rule: "Preserve the sanctity of your lines of communication." For example, do not abuse accepted symbolic modes of communication, that is, do not thereby imply that you have accepted a position which you subsequently repudiate—arguing that you did not "really" (technically) commit yourself to the position in question.

If the parties are deadlocked, cannot converge upon a solution by use of indirection and sign language, other communication devices may be pressed into service. It has been observed that in much negotiation, and in spite of the symbolism of the "bargaining table," initial agreement frequently is not reached at the bargaining table but elsewhere—for example, an informal-off-the-record meeting between two influential individuals, one from each side.[12] At an informal meeting, the parties will not have formal power to settle, but each as a recognized leader from his side may be assumed by the other to be able to indicate what would be practicable by way of settlement.

A MANIFEST CONTRACT ZONE AND
THE "PURE"-BARGAINING GAME

During the early stages of negotiation, uncertainty prevails with respect to the locus of the contract zone. Party A does not know, for example, the limits B intends setting for him, nor can he feel sure that B discerns the limits which A intends to impose. Hence, in these early stages, the relative emphasis is upon the giving and seeking of information and clarification of the meaning and significance of demands. Each party is concerned with setting up outer limits for his opposite number and with discerning the limits that the other is marking out for him.[13]

Also during the early stages, there will be relative emphasis upon "competitive" tactics—tactics of bluff and coercion.

As the negotiations proceed, the information picture clears and the contract zone, if one exists, becomes manifest—becomes demarcated and known (to some close degree of approximation). Also, as the negotiations proceed, the "competitive" tactics available to each side will tend to be "used up." For example, threats will have been tried and the results will be pretty well determined. The approach of the deadline will squeeze elements of bluff out of the tactical mix.

It was suggested in Chapter I that, as a consequence of these events during the negotiation process, the character of the negotiation game will change, that a sort of "divide" between "early" and "later" stages of negotiation will be crossed—that the tactic mix and the important tactical problems may shift toward coordination.[14]

If the foregoing characterization of a progression of events in collective bargaining negotiation is correct, then the later predeadline stages of negotiation approximate what has been termed the "pure"-bargaining game. Although it is plausible that the conditions of the pure-bargaining game situation may be approximated during the predeadline stages, the potential relevance of these suggestions does not depend upon any very precise analogue between the two situations.

T. C. Schelling has provided discussion at some length of what he terms the "pure"-bargaining game, and of the problem of coordination of expectations in this game context.[15] His abstract representation of the pure-bargaining game is one in which the parties must agree upon a division of a sum of gains, or else forego these gains altogether. In this division, more for one party means less for the other. The parties have freedom of communication, but tactical "moves" such as the bluff, not-bluff, commitment, and so forth, are not available to them. In this situation, any outcome (except that including zero gains for either party) is preferred by both parties to no agreement. In consequence, any such outcome is a position from which at least one party would be willing to retreat for the sake of agreement, and this the other party knows. In such a situation, to insist upon any position other than that most favored by one's opponent is "pure" bargaining in the sense that one would retreat if this were necessary to agreement. In Schelling's view, the only reason in a situation such as this for A to accept any position short of his own most favored is his conviction that B will concede no more, and there is no reason in the logic of the situation to support this expectation other than A's expectations about what is expected of himself, namely, that he will concede that much. That is, if A expects B to concede a position, this must be because A expects B to expect that A will concede no more. In answer to the question why A expects B to expect that A will not concede more, we must suppose that this is because A expects B to expect A to expect B to expect that A, and so on. In short, we run into an awkward regress in the description of the response sequence. To avoid this regress, Schelling suggests that we put it that both A and B share an expectation of an outcome—behave as if the game dictates its own solution.[16]

The critical questions then become: What, in an "indeterminate" type of situation such as this, causes the expectations of the parties to converge upon some particular solution? What makes both parties recognize that some particular outcome is indeed the solution? Suggesting that the subjective phenomena present in tactic bargaining (bargaining without communication) may also play an important role in explicit negotiation, Schelling has argued that the "intrinsic magnetism" of particular outcomes may serve this coordination function.[17] We need not be detained at this point over the definition of "intrinsic magnetism." It is intended to connote such properties of an outcome as prominence, uniqueness, simplicity, precedent, and so on—properties which an outcome might acquire in a number of ways, for example, via the power of suggestion from a mutually perceived analogue.

The question we intend to explore is whether any such mechanism might play a significant role in agreements achieved in collective bargaining negotiations.

Coercive Convergence of Expectations

To avoid possible confusion, it warrants parenthetical emphasis that in this section we are concerned with the phenomenon of coordination or convergence of expectations in the context of the pure-bargaining situation. Generally speaking, the phenomenon of convergence of expectations occurs in other contexts too—commitment tactics. But it is important to distinguish convergence of expectations in such a context from the phenomenon of concern in this section. That is, if A commits himself to a position within the contract zone with the intention of making this position the outcome, he expects that this position will be the outcome. If the commitment is successful in that B accedes to the position because of A's commitment to it, it must be that B also expected that no other position could be the outcome. In this sense, coordination of expectations has been achieved, but it has been achieved by a coercive device. This is not the kind of convergence of expectations of interest in the case of pure bargaining. In this case, with the absence of moves in general and coercive commitments in particular, the coordination of expectations must be achieved by other means, and it is upon such other means that we focus in this section.

"Pattern" Bargaining as a Convergence Mechanism

In solution by agreement in a situation indeterminate in the pure-bargaining-game sense, both the extranegotiation environment and the negotiation process itself may play a role in ascribing the properties of prominence or uniqueness to a particular position which make it the target for convergence of expectations.

In thinking about cases in which the extranegotiation environment plays the predominant role, the collective bargaining institution of wage leadership or "pattern" bargaining comes immediately to mind. This is the situation in which that settlement achieved by an industry "leader" (the United States Steel Corporation, General Motors Corporation, and so forth) in his negotiations with the union is subsequently adopted by the "followers" as the terms of their own settlements. Insofar as the negotiations of the followers are concerned, as a convergence phenomenon, these cases are relatively easy to "explain" in the sense of adducing the origin and nature of the properties of the position which made it a focus for the convergence of expectations about what the outcome of the (followers') negotiations would be.

From the more general point of view of a theory of bargaining or bargaining power, of the economic logic of the situation, the phenomenon of pattern following itself is less easy to explain. Reder has explained it in terms of "imitation," arguing the economic logic or rationale of imitation in the collective bargaining context.[18] He argues that principal problems confronted by an employer in selecting a wage rate are to select one high enough to insure recruitment of an adequate labor force without undue difficulty, and at the same time low enough not to put him at significant disadvantage *vis-à-vis* his competitors. He contends that imitation of a wage leader is a "logical" way to achieve this economic objective. This may well be the case. However, the matter of the economic logic of pattern bargaining is not the issue of primary interest in this immediate context.

What is of primary interest here is that the concepts discussed suggest that considerably more than economic logic may be involved in the institution of pattern bargaining. This "something more" has to do with resolution of indeterminacy in negotiation situations by convergence of expectations about the outcome upon prominent positions. That is, to the extent that negotiators throughout the system confront manifest contract zones, for the system of collective bargaining negotiation as a whole the institution of pattern bargaining may be especially valuable in resolving what would otherwise be a large amount of indeterminacy in that system as a whole.

For pattern bargaining to serve this function, the economic logic must be permissive, but, at the same time, considerations of economic logic may not really get at the peculiar genius of the institution. Suppose, for example, that the "pattern" is a rate increase of ten cents, and one inquires with respect to a particular follower why, in terms of the economic logic adduced above, a change in the neighborhood of ten cents, say, six cents or thirteen cents, would not have done as well? From the point of view of the economic logic of the situation, such alternative rates might indeed have done as well. From the point of view of the negotiation problem, however, it is clear why just any rate change in the neighborhood of ten cents would not do as well or do at all. To focus the convergence of expectations in indeterminate situations, we may require positions which are in some sense prominent or unique, and, in the pattern-bargaining case, the extranegotiation environment lends these attributes to precisely the rate change ten cents.

Pattern bargaining is often decried because of the presumed adverse economic implications of this institution. This sort of argument assumes that the rate structure that would be achieved in the absence of pattern bargaining would be substantially different. This issue is arguable, and we do not wish to pass judgment upon it in this context. However, as the above discussion suggests, from the point of view of the negotiation problems involved in a system of collective bargaining, pattern bargaining may carry desirable social connotations. This would be true, for example, if good substitute ways to focus expectations in essentially indeterminate situations could not be devised and, hence, the system of collective bargaining negotiation involved a larger expenditure of time and effort, more frequent conflict, and so forth, than is the case with pattern bargaining.

The Basic Criteria

In the case of pattern following, the negotiation process itself would seem to play a relatively simple role in ascription of properties of prominence or uniqueness to a particular position. That is, once the basic formula has been "agreed" upon, the extranegotiation environment provides a relatively unambiguous clue as to the outcome.

In other cases, the negotiation process itself must play a relatively larger and more complex role. In these cases, no basic formula has been agreed upon in terms of which the extranegotiation environment is unambiguous in the above sense. The parties organize their perception of an ambiguous environment by the way they impose their negotiation categories upon that environment. This process must "create" and ascribe to a particular position those properties of prominence, uniqueness, and so on, which constitute it a likely candidate for the convergence of expectations and hence solution. Cases of this kind are possibly of more interest from the point of view of a theory of negotiation than are cases in which the role of the extranegotiation environment is predominant.

In this context, it is of considerable interest to consider the role of the so-called basic criteria used in wage negotiations. The principal of these criteria are: (a) changes in the cost of living; (b) ability to pay; (c) changes in "productivity" (output per man-hour) in the firm or industry in question, or, sometimes, national average; (d) comparison with wage rates in a comparable labor market. As pointed out earlier, much discussion of the use of these criteria would lead to the conclusion that they play no important role in the negotiation process. The question here is: What role, if any, might the basic criteria play from the point of view of the solution problems discussed in this chapter?

We are here concerned with situations, unlike that of the pattern follower, in which no basic formula has been agreed upon which renders the extranegotiation environment at once unambiguous in pointing to an outcome. In these cases of interest, if the extranegotiation environment is to provide a clue to a solution, it will do so or fail to do so by virtue of the imposition of the negotiation categories upon it. That is, by arguing the case in terms of these basic criteria, the parties organize their perception of the relevant extranegotiation environment in the same terms. Once the record is in, will it suggest a solution in the sense that a particular rate now has "prominence," that the rate focuses attention and expectations about the outcome, and does so by virtue of the record?

One's first conclusion is that any negotiation procedure which involves appeal to a set of diverse standards each of which may be differently applied by each party must surely destroy agreement in a situation where it depends upon expectations on the outcome converging upon some particular position because it is prominent or unique. This may be correct as an appraisal of resort to the basic criteria in some cases. It may be noted that the fact that this is a negative conclusion does not mean that it is unimportant. In this interpretation, considerations adduced in this section of this chapter would show why resort to the basic criteria may tend to preclude agreement—thereby ascribing an important, albeit unfortunate, role to the institution.

However, one's second disposition is to lead away from this negative conclusion. For another thing, it somewhat misrepresents the situation to suppose that each of these criteria is given equal (or the same kind of) weight in each case. For example, in a particular case, the cost-of-living argument may be readily conceded, and ability to pay may play only a limited role (important only if the union can be convinced that the desired increase really means a substantial decrease in output and in employment opportunities for members). In such a case, some one other criterion like comparisons with rates in comparable labor markets might serve to focus expectations about the outcome upon a particular position.

But even in cases in which each of the criteria plays a somewhat similar role (that is, so that no one of them dominates the coordination function) there is another possibility. It is that on the basis of the record built up by these diverse wage standards, a particular position will acquire the prominence necessary to recommend it as solution by virtue of the fact that it measures a central tendency among the conflicting claims. In such a case, the very diffuseness of the record may be a source of strength. It will tend to divert attention from the relative merits of a pair of conflicting claims and force attention in the direction of some concept of centrality with respect to the record as a whole.

An example will help to make the above discussion more definite. This example involves a public utility, and hence a somewhat atypical context, especially for application of the ability-to-pay criterion.[19] The union's demand was for a general wage increase of 0.30 per hour; the company's counterproposal was no increase. The parties failed to reach agreement, and the dispute went to arbitration. Each side argued its case in terms of the wage criteria here under discussion, applying each of the criteria in such a way as to yield different answers. The arbitration board indicated that it would supply no new criteria or standards of its own but would sit in judgment upon the record built up by the parties. Table 2 summarizes the negotiation record as the arbitration board saw it.[20]

Table 2. Sample negotiation record.

Criteria	Wage increase yielded by application of the criteria	
	Company	Union
Changes in cost of living	0.00	0.13
Rate levels other companies	0.05	0.14
Rate increases other companies	0.00	0.09
Productivity increase ("normal" for American industry)	rejects standard	0.22
Ability to pay	0.00	rejects standard

It is true that in this case the parties failed to reach agreement and went to arbitration. But this does not by itself mean that the record built up in the course of negotiation had no "power of suggestion" that could have focused expectations about an outcome. For one thing, in a case like this (utility negotiations where arbitration is expected), one party may have forced the case to arbitration with the hope of obtaining more than he could via negotiation.

In this particular case, the arbitration board awarded a wage increase of 0.10. Why? The analysis of the arbitration board does not supply an answer, indicating only that, in addition to these five standards, certain other considerations were taken into account.[21] One suspects that in terms of economic logic and/or principles of equity, it might be difficult to build up a firm case for the award of 0.10 as contrasted with 0.05 or 0.15. On the other hand, as contrasted with 0.05 or 0.15, the position 0.10 does enjoy a certain suggestive "prominence," stemming, one suspects, from the fact that it is a "simple" representation of the central tendency inherent in this matrix of numbers. Although the expectations of the parties did not converge upon the position 0.10 as a solution during their own negotiations, one doubts that the award of 0.10 surprised either party very much. (This may be an operational definition of a "good" arbitration award.)

In this section of this chapter we have been concerned with the "pure"-bargaining game, and the problems of coordination of expectations (about an outcome) inherent in such a game. This example simply suggests that such considerations may help to explain or elucidate the role played in collective bargaining negotiation by the so-called basic criteria. The "pure"-bargaining problem has implications for the institution of mediation which will be discussed in Chapter VII.

SPECIAL AGREEMENT PROBLEMS

In this chapter we have looked at the predeadline stages of collective bargaining negotiation from two points of view: (1) in terms of the avoidance–avoidance conflict-choice paradigm and the implications of the deadline in this context; (2) the manifest contract zone and the pure-bargaining-game model.

We now consider certain special agreement problems. These may be considered pertinent in both the above analytical contexts.

Definition of Equilibrium Positions in Institutional Terms

The avoidance–avoidance conflict-choice model of collective bargaining negotiation has been discussed so far as if the wage rate were the only item in dispute. In these terms, the model featured an equilibrium rate for each party, that rate (different from the announced position of each party) which each would be willing to accept were there some way to do it.

Since a party would be willing to settle at his equilibrium wage if there were some way to do so, he remains in this conflict-choice situation because of the nonavailability of his equilibrium rate in his (effective) opportunity function. His equilibrium rate will be nonavailable if the necessary conditions for agreement have not been met, that is, if the rate is not consonant with the equilibrium rate of his opposite number. Even if the necessary conditions have been met, the parties may be unable to surmount the obstacles involved in "coming clean" without prejudice.

It is important to note that in the situation depicted the nonavailability of the equilibrium position is a result of the structure of choice situation, of the fact that the interaction is resolved via negotiation rather than because of something inherent in the variable in question. In a more general sense, the opportunity function (in terms of wage rates) is "continuous" (contains a variety of intermediate positions) and the equilibrium rate is defined and is available in the opportunity function in this sense.[22] However, in a negotiated interaction, the outcome is by agreement, and the effective opportunity function is constrained by the necessity of achieving the necessary and sufficient conditions. The effective opportunity function is, in this sense, characterized by uniqueness of goals. These considerations lie behind the previous assertion that partly because of the kinds of opportunity functions afforded the actors, analysis of interpersonal conflict-choice situations might better be predicated upon a conflict theory of individual-choice behavior.

An extension of the conflict model to certain nonwage issues in collective bargaining brings to light another bar to agreement with implications for cooperative behavior in the later stages of negotiation. Let us suppose that the negotiation issue is the kind of union security clause to include in the collective agreement. In terms of the model, negotiation over this issue proceeds analogously to the discussion in Chapter II. Looking at the matter from the company's point of view, we have two goals, say, (1) the open shop (company's announced position); (2) the union shop (union's announced position). The company negotiator is conflicted, occupying position D1, Figure 1, Chapter II. That is, he is unwilling to settle on the union's terms. At the same time, he is unwilling to "insist" upon his own announced position. Indeed, he is ready to accept his equilibrium position D1 if, as in the wage example developed, there were some way to do it. The position D1 may be unavailable in the effective opportunity function for the same reasons adduced in the wage-negotiation example.

However, an additional bar to agreement is revealed as soon as we ask the question: How, in this context, are we to interpret the concept "distance"—the horizontal axis in Figure 1? Where the negotiation issue was the wage rate (and the announced positions particular rates) it was natural to scale the horizontal axis in terms of such rates. Where the issue is union security, no simple metric is evident to the investigator. Scrutiny of Figure 1 reveals that position D1 is about one-third of the way from an open shop to a closed shop. But what particular institutional arrangement (the "X" shop) represents a position one-third of the way from an open shop to a closed shop?

These difficulties confronted by the investigator in analysis of this case may be precisely the same as the difficulties confronted by the actors in this negotiation game. In a situation such as this, the actor is ready to compromise (on position D1). However, he may be unable to do so because of inability to define his equilibrium position in institutional terms. We should emphasize that even though the equilibrium position is not defined in institutional terms, it is not "nonexistent" in the general sense. It exists as a position some "distance" from the other positions (announced positions of the parties) which are perfectly definite in institutional terms, and it is occupied.[23] Further, as in the avoidance–avoidance analysis of wage rate negotiation, operations by A upon B may move the latter's equilibrium position, and vice versa.

The earlier discussed bars to agreement may of course also operate *vis-à-vis* a nonwage issue such as the union security issue. That is, even if clearly definable in institutional terms, the position D1 will not be available to the company unless the union's equilibrium position is consonant with it. Similarly, the tactical implications of overt communication about the equilibrium position may pose problems for agreement. However, in cases such as this, this hazard is greatly reduced by the very indefiniteness in institutional terms of the concept "distance" from the announced positions. That is, ostensible concession of the form: "some arrangement which would provide . . . ," although it may represent retreat from an announced position, does not represent retreat to a definite position in institutional terms, and hence concession without prejudice should be considerably easier. Also, suggestions made by each negotiator in pursuit of his own position may help his opposite number resolve his own conflict-choice problem. In general, in cases such as this, one might expect more overt attempts to convert latent agreement into actual agreement and a more cooperative orientation and posture on the part of the negotiators.

These conclusions stem directly from a conceptualization of the negotiation process in terms of an intrapersonal conflict-choice model. Analysis in terms of nonconflict individual-choice theory, such as modern utility theory, would not yield these conclusions, at least not as inferences from the theory employed.

Problems of Dimensionality and Measurement

Intrapersonal conflict in the choice situation may constitute a barrier to agreement and may give rise to a more cooperative posture and orientation during the later stages of the negotiation process. There are potential sources of such conflict in collective bargaining negotiations in addition to the avoidance–avoidance nature of the choice problem already covered.

Some of these may involve problems of dimensionality (of choice objects), or at least problems of measurement. This rather equivocal way of putting the matter reflects certain technical difficulties with the construct "dimensionality." Nevertheless, it warrants attention in this context. The central theoretical point may be stated briefly to be followed by suggestions with respect to institutional analogues. Some theories of individual-choice behavior suppose that an actor makes his choice by ranking all pertinent options and choosing the option with the highest rank. This implies a unidimensional continuum—a common denominator—on the basis of which the ranking can be performed. The empirical generality of such an assumption may be questioned.[24] Psychologists frequently emphasize the multiplicity of ends, motives, or values confronted by the human actor. Intrapersonal conflict in a choice situation may arise from the circumstances of disparate objectives, if this gives rise to a conflict of basic values. That is, in terms of basic values, the options presented in a choice may be incommensurable; there may exist no unidimensional scale in terms of which these may be ranked. In such a case, an actor may have difficulty in establishing a relative preference because of the absence of a common denominator. The question of interest here is whether the phenomenon of nonunidimensionality of choice may be pertinent to the analysis of collective bargaining negotiations, particularly to analysis of the process by which agreement (or nonagreement) is achieved.[25]

A *prima facie* case for the possible importance of nonunidimensionality as a source of conflict in collective bargaining inheres in the fact that collective bargaining negotiations are concerned with a large variety of issues. A typical instance of collective bargaining negotiation will be concerned with a multi-item package. This fact does not by itself mean that nonunidimensionality will constitute a problem. It could be that all the items are commensurable in terms of some common denominator, like dollars and cents. Many of the items are commensurable in these terms, and one frequently sees reference to the "total cost" of a multi-item package which is comprised of nonwage as well as wage items. Even an issue such as the union shop might be made commensurable with other items in dollars-and-cents terms. Most employers believe that union security provisions strengthen unions, and, in consequence, granting the union shop might be reckoned as costly in the conventional sense. In principle, this cost might be estimated as a present discounted value in dollars-and-cents terms, however difficult such an estimate would be as a matter of practicability.

Actually, although union security issues may carry monetary implications, such issues are not really bargained over in cost terms. This is for reasons beyond the impracticability of an estimate of the implications in these terms. Union security and certain other collective bargaining issues involve other dimensions (at least in any proximate sense). The concept of "the union challenge to management control" is illustrative of one such additional dimension. Managements may see such collective bargaining subjects as work rules and schedules, seniority and other job allocation schemes, and so forth, in the light of this "challenge." Involved here are issues related to the status of actors in an industrial society, the legitimacy of "rights" based upon property concepts, and the opposition of these to "rights" predicated upon concepts of "industrial democracy" and the right of free men to have a significant voice in the determination of their terms and conditions of employment.[26] Involved with the union shop issue are considerations relating to industrial democracy in the most general sense. Arguments against union security may stress the rights of individuals in a democratic society. No man, it is argued, should be obligated to join a labor organization as a condition of employment. Enjoyment of the privileges of individualism must be protected by law. Proponents of union security may counter such arguments by pointing out that only because of collective bargaining, something approaching democracy in employer–employee relationships has been achieved. In this view, nonmembers are merely "free riders" shirking their responsibilities as "citizens" of the industrial "government." [27]

Or consider the "guaranteed annual wage" (supplemental unemployment compensation) issue. This clearly involves dollars and cents in a rather direct way, but much more besides. There are broad issues of the status of actors in an industrial society involved here, as well as issues relating to proper spheres of responsibility between the private and the government sector. Illustrations of the involvement of collective bargaining with a number of dimensions or value systems could be multiplied.

The phenomenon of nonunidimensionality of issues in collective bargaining does not by itself mean that conflict will arise on this score. What is peculiarly required for conflict is that noncommensurable items be incorporated in a given choice between them, and that they be competitive. It is the kind of case in which a union (or a management) must weigh the value of a concession on work rules, for example, or on the role of seniority in job allocation, against a change in the wage rate. Conflict may arise because of dimensional barriers to evaluation of the "package" as a whole. A variant of this situation is that in which a given issue is susceptible to evaluation in terms of either or both dimensions; (1) implications for unit labor costs; (2) implications for management versus union control of the work force, "proper" sphere for joint as opposed to unilateral determination, and so on. The issue might be debated and compromise achieved in terms of either (1) or (2). However, if one party emphasized (1) and his opposite number (2), the very concept of "a compromise" loses definiteness because of the noncommensurability of the positions. The meeting of two minds at an intermediate position is difficult if they do not even slide along a common continuum for evaluation purposes.

It should be noted that even if multi-item packages do not imply difficulties stemming from disparate dimensionality, such packages certainly involve difficult problems of measurement. In such cases, settlements are package settlements, and it is the total cost of the package that matters. But this total cost may be very difficult to calculate, and, by the same token, even more difficult to agree upon.

It should also be noted that collective bargaining issues involving some of the dimensions above may be more difficult to settle than the issue of a change in the wage rate, for reasons other than noncommensurability with other items. This is particularly apt to be the case when a proposal represents a departure from traditional modes, so that accustomed standards of evaluation are not at hand. A good case in point is the UAW-CIO demand for a "guaranteed annual wage" (which the companies preferred to term a "supplemental unemployment compensation plan"). Ford Motor Company negotiators in commenting upon the underlying philosophy of the proposal indicated that "we are entering upon an entirely uncharted course" and that "the area is entirely new and untried," and so on.[28]

It is useful in analysis of the agreement process in collective bargaining to think of collective bargaining demands or issues as falling into either of two categories:

(1) What are essentially alterations in the terms of trade within the context of a given collective bargaining "game," that constituted by the bargaining relationship in question. A change in the wage rate is a case in point.

(2) What are essentially alterations in the basic ground rules of the collective bargaining game itself, in the definition of the role relationships of the parties. Demands which are perceived as a union challenge to management control are of this variety.

Issues in category (2) may pose special problems for agreement. This is because all the problems discussed in this section may arise with respect to such issues. The parties may be willing to compromise but may have difficulty in defining their own equilibrium positions in institutional terms. Problems of nonunidimensionality may arise. This will be particularly the case if giving more under the rules of the existing game is seen as a possible alternative to a change in the rules of the bargaining game itself. Finally, even if problems on this score are resolved, difficult problems of measurement in terms of a common denominator—dollars and cents, for example—may arise.

The Negotiators as Delegates

In discussing initial bargaining demands, it was pointed out that one reason such demands are "large" is that they are ordinarily initiated by the constituents of the negotiators. The negotiators are in fact the delegates of the parties (organizations) who send them to the bargaining table. We saw that in the early stages of negotiation the delegate role of the negotiators may tend to be emphasized, that the conflict in these stages may be essentially interorganizational in nature.

The fact that the negotiators are in fact delegates of organizations may also importantly influence the later stages of bargaining, particularly if during these stages the conditions approximating those of a pure-bargaining situation are established. During these stages, the fact that the negotiators must ultimately return to their organizations with an acceptable package is an influence impelling them to a cooperative orientation and posture.

The institution of "large" initial demands and counterdemands and an agenda "rule" providing for no prenegotiation agenda negotiation facilitate matters in the early stages of negotiation from the negotiator's own point of view. Because of these institutions, formal intraorganizational negotiation can be minimized, and the negotiator is not forced to make his own relative valuations of the agenda items urged upon him by his constituents very clear. Ultimately these problems must be faced, and in a sense this means that in the later stages of negotiation the negotiators share a common problem. They must come up with a common package which is as "salable" as possible to their respective constituents. Thus, the end stages of the negotiation may become more a cooperative exercise in ingenious package design than an effort to make the opposite number give a final few inches.

The above considerations put the problem of "indeterminacy" in a bargaining situation in which a contract zone has become manifest in a somewhat different light. That is, determinacy in such situations may be effected by the requirements of intraorganizational bargaining and the fact of a common problem faced by the negotiators in the light of such bargaining problems on both sides.

CHAPTER VII

Mediation: Functions and Tactics

INTRODUCTION

It is appropriate that this final chapter focus upon the mediation of industrial disputes. Mediation, concerned as it is with the "peaceful" resolution of industrial conflict, is of considerable significance and interest *per se* in a generally interdependent economy. Beyond this, a discussion of the functions of mediation affords an excellent way to examine further and to tie together many of the results developed earlier.

As we have pointed out, collective bargaining negotiation is a social control technique for reflecting and transmuting the basic power relationships which underlie the conflict inherent in an industrial relations system. It is also a technique for containing this conflict, for resolving it short of overt trials of industrial warfare if this be possible. In consequence, peace—agreement without overt warfare—is from a conceptual and theoretical point of view of central interest. (Although the warning may be repeated that preoccupation with industrial peace for the sake of peace will obscure analysis of negotiation.)

Because of the strategic position occupied by the third party to an industrial dispute, and because of his relatively "neutral" orientation *vis-à-vis* the parties, an experienced mediator is an excellent source of information not only about the mediation aspects of collective bargaining negotiation, but about such negotiation as a whole.

Although one finds frequent reference to mediation in industrial relations literature, theoretical analysis of mediation is infrequent. The past two decades have seen a great proliferation of collective bargaining and of the mediation of industrial disputes. Shister, surveying recent collective bargaining research, has expressed the opinion that in the light of this practical development one might reasonably assume that studies of the dynamics of the mediation process would be most plentiful. He notes that the exact opposite is true.[1] Stark has deemed mediation the least-studied subject in the field of labor relations and observes that participants in discussions of mediation have for many years decried "the startling lack of information in this field."[2] Cole comments, in discussing the nature and function of mediation, that there is no clear agreement as to its nature and function. He continues: "As I see it, thus far mediation has been helpful in a haphazard way largely because of the talents of certain individuals who themselves would find it difficult to say why they had been successful."[3] Leiserson adds that what is "vague and uncertain" is what constitutes the work of mediating.[4]

In other words, there is relatively little theoretical analysis of the mediation process and even fewer results and conclusions in consequence of such analysis. A prevalent agnosticism toward analysis in this area may in part account for (and may in part be accounted for by) this phenomenon. This agnosticism takes the form of assertions that, for one reason or another, the institution of mediation is not susceptible to systematic analysis. Some views take the position that a mediator does little in any event—he simply gets the parties together—and anybody can do that. Mediation agencies themselves are apt to feel that there are "no set rules," that different mediators get equally good results by different methods. It may be contended that each case is a law unto itself, that the very "nature" of the mediation process does not permit generalization. Frequently, agnosticism is the result of emphasis upon the personal role of the mediator himself—the notion that mediation technique is so highly individual, so much a matter of the individual personal qualities of the mediator himself, that the process is not analyzable in general terms.

We may start with the assumption that mediation, like other social phenomena, is susceptible to systematic analysis.[5] The key to analysis is in recognizing that where mediation is employed it is an integral part of the collective bargaining process. If collective bargaining negotiation can be analyzed, so can mediation. By the same token, an analysis of mediation is not possible except in the context of a general analysis of collective bargaining negotiation. That is, unless the investigator has some theories about the agreement process in negotiation, about why and in what ways the parties do (or do not) reach agreement, it is difficult to see how he can analyze the contribution of the mediator to the resolution of conflict.[6]

Strictly speaking, mediation is an integral part of collective bargaining negotiation whether it is employed or not. We saw that the deadline rule sets up a negotiation game-variant sequence: negotiation with the assurance of no strike or lockout—deadline, negotiation under strike or lockout conditions. The introduction of a third party, the mediator, either before or after the deadline, constitutes an additional game-variant. Analytically, this game-variant is to be distinguished from the others in terms of the functions and tactics of the mediator. As earlier stressed, in the analysis of game sequences generally, a critical aspect is the interaction between games, the mutual influence of each game upon the play and solution of the others in the sequence. What is important is the sequence confronted by the parties at the inception of the negotiation. The parties may elect the mediation game variant, or it may be imposed upon them in the case of negotiations affected with the public interest.

Although we shall be concerned in this chapter with instances in which mediation is employed, it is of some importance to be clear that the above reasons explain why mediation is an integral part of negotiation whether employed or not in a particular instance. The influence of mediation upon premediation negotiation can be felt in various ways. For example, it has been recognized that if access to mediation is made too easy, then some of the pressure of responsibility for achieving settlement is removed from the negotiating parties. This would suggest that a mediator should be free to send the case back to the parties if he finds that they have not exhausted all possible resources.[7] Another influence upon premediation negotiation stemming from anticipating the possibility of mediation is suggested by the rule: "Always save something for the mediator."[8] That is, a party, anticipating that mediation may be necessary to resolve a dispute, may be dissuaded from making his "final" offer during premediation negotiation in order to have something left once the mediator is in the picture.

What Institutional Arrangements Constitute Mediation?

Leiserson has observed that there is some confusion in answer to this question.[9] For example, is a third party who simply "observes" negotiations—sitting in on but not participating—properly said to be mediating? Also, as he observes, mediation agencies as often intervene after as before a strike or lockout, and whether they are settling strikes or disputes, both efforts are called mediation—as if a strike were the same thing as a dispute. Is the locked-door technique, whereby the parties are confined to a room for extended periods until through sheer ennui they can easily be brought to agreement without being too finicky about what they agree to, properly called mediation? Is a publicly constituted third party with the power to make public recommendations really mediating or arbitrating?

For the present, a simple definition of mediation which is silent on most questions such as the above will suffice. Mediation is the intervention (the institution of mediation includes the prospect of, as well as actual, intervention) of a third party in collective bargaining negotiation before or after a strike or lockout. The objective of this party is to secure agreement. He does not have the power to make a binding award, although he may be able to bring "pressure" to bear in favor of a recommended settlement. The interest is in the functions a third party so motivated might serve, what tactics he might employ. The "efficiency" of such functions and tactics is of interest, but the question of whether these are in some sense really mediation is not.

In the ensuing analysis, certain factors which may impede the agreement process, and the mediator functions associated with these factors, will be neglected. Some of these are involved with what Kerr has termed "the case of awkwardness"—the case in which the mediator supplies the negotiation skills which the parties themselves lack.[10] We might include here various kinds of "ludic" complications such as vindictiveness, bitterness, unreasoning obstinacy, and bad manners. These factors have been neglected in our decision to deal primarily with the "mature" collective bargaining relationship. This in no way implies that these factors are not frequently encountered in the mediation of industrial disputes. Indeed, Cole lists them as the "principal problems" of the mediator.[11] Kerr includes the case of awkwardness as among the most common from a mediation point of view.

For the same reasons, we shall neglect the case in which two parties would prefer open economic warfare, parties who do not wish to mediate but have been constrained by public authority, or perhaps the demands of constituents to do so. Involved with this kind of situation are two more cases distinguished by Kerr, "The case of the hoodwinked membership": here the mediator helps the negotiators to fool the ignorant constituents into thinking that a real effort is being made to settle the dispute, whereas the leaders really want a strike for their own purposes. "The case of the impotent members": the members have no control over their leaders and hence nothing is to be gained by pretense to a real effort at settlement through mediation.[12]

We also assume in this section that the mediator is essentially the servant of the parties rather than the servant of public or of political authority. Finally, we assume that although the mediator may bring "pressure" to bear upon the parties by manipulating pressures naturally present in the situation, he does not attempt to use essentially extrasituational pressures contrived by himself—a threat to "put the parties on the spot" by publicly attesting to their incompetence and lack of good faith, and so forth.

The Personal Factor in Mediation

There has been frequent emphasis on the personal qualities of the mediator in discussions of the mediation process. In the extreme, this emphasis leads to "agnosticism" with respect to analysis of the mediation process. A less exaggerated view permits analysis of the process, but still gives considerable weight to the personal factor. Wilson, for example, "makes clear" at the outset of an analysis of mediation techniques, that such discussion cannot get very far without extensive reference to the "ideal mediator," his personal qualities, qualifications, personality, and so forth. He observes that: "While experts are not in agreement as to the weight of the personal factor, it cannot be denied, I think, that the process of mediation is largely a personal function of the mediator . . ." [13]

Emphasis upon the personal factor has produced some research upon and analysis of mediators themselves. A technically excellent and carefully done example of such a study is that of Landsberger.[14] The main question he sets out to answer is whether psychological tests are capable of predicting the parties' reaction to a mediator, that is, of distinguishing those mediators who will be deemed "good" by the parties. On the basis of interviews with persons who had considerable first-hand experience with collective bargaining and mediation, Landsberger built up a set of ten criteria—"areas of mediator behavior"—which seemed to be the ones to which the parties had most frequent reference when describing a mediator and attempting to evaluate him:[15]

(a) originality of ideas
(b) a sense of appropriate humor
(c) ability to act unobtrusively
(d) the mediator as "one of us"
(e) the mediator as a respected authority[16]
(f) willingness to be a vigorous salesman when the situation requires it
(g) control over feelings

(h) attitudes toward, and persistence and patient effort invested in the work of mediation

(i) ability to understand quickly the complexities of a dispute

(j) accumulated knowledge of labor relations.

This list of "areas of mediator behavior" is of considerable interest. Even by itself it says a little, by inference, about the tactics of mediation. That is, the fact that a "good" mediator quickly understands the complexities of a dispute, has original ideas, and is willing to be a vigorous salesman when the situation requires, suggests that mediation is not, as is often supposed, essentially passive. Beyond this, scrutiny of the list suggests in a very definite way the permissive aspect of the personal factor. One can well imagine that a person with a low score in these terms would enjoy little success as a mediator (or in many other endeavors). Except in this permissive sense, no such study by itself casts light on the question of the "weight" of the personal factor (as opposed to tactical factors, for example) in mediation.

Discussion Organized Around Bars to Agreement

An attempt has been made to organize this discussion around a number of different bars to agreement—the characteristics of the negotiation status confronted by the mediator which account for the inability of the parties to agree, or which describe the kind of tactical situation in which the failure to agree is manifest. There is no implied weighting of these bars with respect to relative importance. With respect to each, an attempt is made to emphasize those tactics and functions of mediation which are of primary importance in resolving that particular situation. This does not mean that other tactics and functions may not also be involved. For example, with respect to a particular bar, some aspect of the mediator's control over the communications structure in the negotiations may be of peculiar importance and in consequence will be emphasized. This does not imply that some other mediator function such as removing nonrationality from the situation may not also be efficacious *vis-à-vis* other aspects of the situation containing the bar in question.

NO CONTRACT ZONE THE MAJOR PROBLEM: THE STRAIGHTFORWARD CASE

No contract zone is the situation in which the least favorable terms upon which the parties are willing to settle do not overlap. Using our previous terminology, this is the situation in which the necessary conditions for agreement have not been met, and the equilibrium positions of the parties are not consonant.

Within this category it is helpful to distinguish two subcategories. One, the case in which the absence of a contract zone reflects the basic situation and the parties' perception of that situation rather than being the result of tactical maneuver. We deal with this case in this section. Two, the case in which a contract zone was inherent in the situation (at least if it were perceived rationally by both parties), but now there is none by virtue of the tactical maneuvering of the parties. We deal with case two in the next section.

If there is to be agreement in this first case, one or both parties must change equilibrium position, revise the terms upon which he is willing to settle. The mediator's role here may involve him in all the tactics by means of which each party attempts to control the other's course of action. More particularly, the mediator may engage in tactics of persuasion, rationalization, and coercion.

Persuasion and Rationalization

It will be recalled that tactics of persuasion are B's attempts to control A's course of action by operations upon A's preferences and/or operations upon A's perception of the extranegotiation environment. Just as the parties A and B may operate upon each other by persuasion, so may the mediator operate upon one or both of them by persuasion. The parties, particularly if they are relatively new to collective bargaining, may underestimate the cost of a strike or lockout, or overestimate the cost of agreement with the opponent upon the opponent's terms. In such a situation, the mediator may abet the agreement process by assisting them to see the realities of the situation.[17] If the parties would agree in the light of this realistic appraisal of the costs and gains associated with alternative courses of action, the mediator may serve a real function, and this may be one of the more important functions served by mediators generally.

If a mediator is resorting to persuasive tactics in an effort to induce the parties to change position, he should bear in mind the important asymmetry in the effects of what were previously termed Class I and Class II tactics. For example, in an attempt to move A's equilibrium position toward that of B, the mediator may attempt to increase A's estimate of the cost of disagreement with B on B's terms. Or he may attempt to decrease A's estimate of the cost of agreement with B on B's terms. Both classes of tactics may be effective in moving A's position toward B.

However, emphasis upon tactics of the first class will, in contrast with emphasis upon tactics of the second class, tend to increase the level of tension and anxiety in the negotiation situation, and hence increase the chances of a breakdown. To be more definite, suppose that the mediator is attempting to induce the parties to agree to a certain "package." He might emphasize to both that if a strike takes place it will be long and bitter, involving a major loss of markets and profits for the company and probably a destruction of the organizational integrity of the union. Conversely, he might emphasize to the company that the package in question will by no means put it at a competitive disadvantage *vis-à-vis* the firms in its market area. He might emphasize to the union that the package in question is "salable" to its constituency. It is an implication of conflict-choice theory that emphasis upon tactics of the first sort will increase the likelihood of a breakdown of the mediated negotiations, that is, it may precipitate attempts to "escape" from the negotiation situation. Of course, the mediator may have no option (if he is bent upon persuasion) but resort to tactics of the first sort. In this case, he had best contrive so far as possible to prevent the parties escaping from the mediated negotiation situation.

A delicate problem may arise if the mediator has resorted to persuasion. The mediator does not have a direct interest in bringing the parties to a realistic appraisal of the situation. His objective is to induce them to agree. Bringing them to a realistic appraisal of the situation may be a means to this end. However, bringing them to a nonrealistic appraisal may also be a means to this end. That is, it might be the case that a party could be brought to agreement if he overestimated the cost of a strike, underestimated the gains to be had thereby, and underestimated the cost of agreement with his opponent upon his opponent's terms. In this case, the mediator might abet the agreement process by deliberate deception.

The possible utility of deceptive tactics may arise in ways rather more subtle. From an analytical point of view, one of the most important aspects of the mediation process is the mediator's control over the communications structure in the negotiation situation.[18] Control of the communications structure generally facilitates attempts at persuasion and also coercion. The mediation tactic which has been described as one of "unselling" and "selling" is an example.[19] Suppose that the mediator has separated the parties and is conveying offers between them. He may, in talking to the party making the offer, minimize the possibility that it will be accepted—in favor of something else—while a few minutes later "across the hall" he may be maximizing the desirability of accepting the offer. He may in this way draw forth further offers and counteroffers which will more nearly coincide.

Generally speaking, control of the communications structure may enable the mediator to bring pressures to bear upon the parties which involve an element of deception. An interesting case in point is an example given by Lovell.[20] In this case, the union suspected that the company was involved in important defense contracts, and that this circumstance would create considerable difficulty in the event of a strike. The union asked the mediator to check this. Upon interrogation, the company testified with apparent sincerity that indeed this was the case, that there was much important and secret work in progress. The mediator suspected that the company's view might have stemmed from an exaggerated idea of the importance of the work on the part of the local defense authorities. A call to the Defense Department confirmed this, indicating that the department was not at all concerned about a strike in this company. The mediator so advised the company, thereby depriving it of what it had thought was a major defense weapon. The mediator did not, however, simultaneously inform the union. He let it continue for some days (until the next conference) under the pressure created by its suspicions.

We have been concerned with that aspect of persuasion as a mediation tactic involving operations upon the parties' perception of the negotiation environment. The mediator might also attempt by persuasion to alter their preferences, *per se*. One doubts, however, that this aspect of the persuasion tactic would be very effective in the typical bargaining context.

Closely related to persuasion are the tactics of rationalization. The implications of tactics of rationalization for mediation functions are quite straightforward, and much of the discussion in Chapter IV can be taken as directly applicable in this context. For example, the mediator may supply a party with arguments which the party may in turn use to rationalize a position (or retreat from a position) *vis-à-vis* his own constituents. This may be a potentially important mediation tactic.

Beyond this, it should be recognized that the mere fact of a mediator's entrance into a dispute provides the parties with a means for rationalizing retreats from previously held positions, particularly if the mediator can be made to appear to take a part of the "responsibility" for any settlement.

Coercion

Tactics of coercion are B's attempts to control A's behavior by operating upon the range of outcomes available to A as these outcomes depend upon B's own course of action. Tactics of coercion are frequently based upon bluff, and mediation tactics may involve the relationship of the mediator to the bluff tactics of the parties.

If either party is bluffing about his own course of action, the mediator may be able to abet agreement by removing the elements of bluff from the situation. That is, suppose that agreement is impeded, for example, because A believes that his bluff about willingness to take a strike (or to continue a strike indefinitely) will prevail, will bring B to terms. He would make a concession if he did not believe in the strength of his bluff weapon. The mediator may be able to diagnose A's true intentions, so advise B, and then advise A that the bluff is no longer effective. It would seem, however, that a mediator involved in a bluff situation would have to be on guard against becoming an unwitting tool of either (or both) of the parties. A party may have only partially succeeded in an effort to make its bluff fully convincing to the opposite number. If, however, that party can successfully bluff the mediator, he may enlist the mediator as an unwitting ally in his deception. For example, A may not quite believe B's assertion that he will strike, but he might believe the mediator's assertion that B will strike. The mediator's assertion is apt to be much more creditable, for A has reason to believe that B may be attempting to fool him, whereas his presumption will be that the mediator is not. Further, he may have confidence in the mediator's ability to "see through" B—if there is anything to be seen.

At this juncture the problem of deception as a mediation tactic arises once more. The mediator does not have a direct interest in eliminating bluff from negotiations. His objective is agreement. Elimination of bluff may be a means to this end. However, it might be that conniving in a bluff will be a means to this end. Thus, for example, A might capitulate if he did not suspect that B was bluffing. The mediator, aware that B was bluffing, might nevertheless convince A that he was not. It would not be appropriate to become involved here in the issue of whether a mediator, in pursuit of his objective of bringing the parties to agreement, "should" use deceptive tactics in conjunction with the persuasive and coercive tactics of the parties. One point should be made in this connection, however.

Ann Douglas, in discussing the invention of "fictions" with respect to the mediation process has observed that the claim of "neutrality" enjoys such widespread credence among mediators that it could almost be said to be universal in the profession.[21] In her view, the essential function of this fiction is to shield the mediator from responsibility for the outcome of mediated negotiations, to "purge the mediator of liability for the course of treatment, regardless whether the patient gets well or succumbs." This function is in turn necessitated by the ambiguous status in our culture of peace-making via the intervention of third parties into disputes. Whether the notion of the mediator's neutrality serves this social function is not critical in this context.

However, other aspects of the notion may be critical. If the claim to mediators' neutrality is read as a disclaim to any influence on the direction and shape of the outcome, then this claim is indeed a fiction. However, the concept of mediators' neutrality can be much more narrowly construed. It can imply that the mediator, in pursuit of his objective of bringing the parties to agreement, does not (even though it might be tactically efficacious in the light of his basic objective) connive in bluff and deception and/or deliberately distort the realities of the negotiation and extranegotiation environment as he sees them. Abjuring these tactics still leaves plenty of scope for him to be an active and inventive agent in the negotiations and to focus "pressures" upon the parties. One may inquire what the significance of neutrality is in this sense. One significance is the matter of acceptability of the institution of mediation by the parties. If the mediator were nonneutral in the sense that he connived in bluff tactics, he would in effect conspire with one party against the other. It seems doubtful that both parties to a dispute would desire to admit a third known to include conspiracy in his kit of tools.

A second significance has to do with the mediator's neutral posture towards "nature"—the extranegotiation context of the dispute. Within some limits for variation, the basic determinants of the outcome of collective bargaining negotiation are the determinants of the basic power relationships which underlie the conflict in an industrial relations system. Negotiation is a social control technique for reflecting and transmuting these basic determinants, while at the same time containing the conflict short, of overt trials of industrial warfare. The mediator's primary function is to abet the containment function of negotiation. In any particular case, there would be a kind of fortuitous conspiracy (distinguish systematic interparty discrimination) involved if the mediator were "nonneutral" in the sense that he deliberately distorted the realities of the negotiation and extranegotiation environment as he saw these. But the important nonneutrality here would be that *vis-à-vis* the "system," that is, it would involve a distortion of "legitimate" determinants of the outcome. In a continuing negotiation process such as collective bargaining, solutions achieved in this way would be spurious and transitory, would subsequently be undone, and would generally reduce the efficiency of mediated negotiation as a social control technique.

The final point to be considered under the straightforward case of no contract zone is the function of mediation as a substitute for the "information strike." As we discussed earlier, an important coercive tactic in negotiation is the notbluff. The principal tactical problem associated with notbluff is conveying the truth of the intended course of action. For example, how does A convince B that he will take a strike unless B makes a concession? One possibility is simply to let the deadline expire and in consequence of that expiration to take a strike. If, in such a case, B would have conceded the position had he made a correct estimate of the probability (1.0) that a strike would occur, only the information content component of the strike has served a legitimate function. Such a strike should not, perhaps, be considered strictly "unnecessary," for the institutional arrangements may not have permitted A to lay hold of a device (short of actually taking the strike) which would get his point across to B. Nevertheless, one may argue that it is socially undesirable that strikes should occur in circumstances such as these. One function of mediation is as a substitute for this kind of strike. That is, the mediator is in a position to testify to B regarding A's intentions, and this testimony may be compelling even though A's own assertions regarding his intentions were not.

NO CONTRACT ZONE THE MAJOR PROBLEM: FAILURE OF COERCIVE COMMITMENT

Negotiations may fail to reach agreement in a tactical situation in which a contract zone, initially inherent in the negotiation situation, has been eliminated by tactical contrivance. This will be the case, for example, if game-theory-type threats assayed by the parties result in simultaneous commitment. It will be recalled from Chapter V that the distinctive character of this threat is that a party asserts that he will pursue, in a contingency, a course of action which he would (in terms of the pretactical play payoffs) manifestly prefer not to pursue should the contingency arise. For example, a party asserts that he will take a strike unless the position is conceded, under circumstances such that he would actually prefer, in terms of the original payoff matrix, not to take a strike in this contingency. This threat is a notbluff under circumstances which suggest that it must be fully committed in order to be effective. The difficulty of particular interest in this context is that if both parties attempt this tactic, the race to commitment may end in a dead heat; both parties become committed to taking a strike unless the other concedes, and now agreement without a strike is impossible. This is the situation previously referred to as the failure of coercive commitment.

The mediator has a very clear, albeit difficult, function to serve in this kind of situation. Agreement may be possible in terms of the original payoff matrix—in terms of the payoffs prevailing before the commitment tactics altered the situation. Hence, the mediator's problem is somehow to assist in the undoing of the commitment. He is engaged in the tactics of retreat.[22] A particular kind of retreat is involved in this no-agreement situation. Other kinds of retreat might be distinguished, for example, that involved in changing ostensible position from an announced position to an equilibrium position. The retreat here under discussion is peculiarly the retreat involved in the undoing of a tactically contrived commitment.

One function that the mediator can serve in this kind of situation is to help "save face." As Kerr has pointed out, the mere entrance of a mediator into a dispute is in some ways a face-saving device.[23] Although there are no accurate tests of the performance of a negotiator, his constituents attempt to measure that performance, and he attempts to justify this aspect of his stewardship. In an ambiguous situation, the implication that the battle was so hard fought that a mediator had to be brought in may be helpful. More important, the mediator may share some of the responsibility for the outcome and thereby decrease the responsibility of the parties. In this way, the posture in retreat is more comfortable. The party has been constrained by the mediator, not by his opponent, and he lives to fight again without what might otherwise be significant impairment of his status. Public recommendations by the mediator may be particularly helpful in this situation. It has often been argued that public recommendations by fact-finding boards in emergency disputes may help to resolve the conflict because of the pressure of public opinion that can thereby be marshaled against the parties. In the context of no agreement because of a failure of coercive commitment, such recommendations may be efficacious not so much because of the pressures thereby created as because they provide the parties with a badly needed face-saving device, a device they may be eager to avail themselves of.

It is evident that a concept of mediator "neutrality," read to mean a disclaimer of any influence upon the direction of the outcome, is wholly inconsistent with the face-saving function of mediation. This function also suggests that there may be an important place in collective bargaining for the mediator who is not overly concerned with his own viability —the "one-shot" mediator. Making a recommendation, patently shouldering responsibility for the outcome, is hazardous for the mediator—it exposes him to the risk of the disaffection of one side or the other, and may decrease his popularity as a candidate for subsequent mediations. Nevertheless, if failure to agree is because of failure of coercive commitment, face-saving may be an essential ingredient in resolution of the dispute.

The face-saving device may nullify a commitment as a bar to agreement in a particular case. It is in a sense, however, essentially a device for "running around" the commitment while leaving it intact. A more subtle function of the mediator in a "no agreement" because of failure of coercive commitment is to attempt literally to undo the commitment. Thus, if a party has committed a position by nailing a demand to a principle, the mediator might attempt to cut the demand loose, show that the demand is not a case in point of the principle, and hence demonstrate to the party that he is not committed to a particular demand. Also, Schelling has suggested that a party, in attempting to release an opponent from a commitment, might confuse the commitment so that the party's principals cannot identify compliance with it.[24] The mediator can use these same tactics. Thus the mediator might show that a given standard (cost of living, ability to pay, productivity, comparative rates, and so on) is ambiguous. Or he might show, for example, that a given "package" is not really inflationary, providing the party taking the stand against the package on these grounds with a set of arguments he can use to show that he miscalculated his commitment.

NO CONTRACT ZONE NOT THE MAJOR PROBLEM

The parties may fail to reach agreement in tactical situations in which the absence of a contract zone is not the major bar to agreement. In some of these cases, the fact that a contract zone is manifest is perhaps somewhat paradoxically the major source of difficulty. In other cases, there may be a contract zone which is not manifest, and agreement is impeded by communications problems. We may distinguish a number of agreement problems, and associated mediation tactics, falling within this general category.

Aspects of the "Pure"-Bargaining Game

It will be recalled that the pure-bargaining game features a manifest contract zone and the nonavailability to the parties of such tactical maneuvers as the bluff, commitment, and so forth. It was suggested in Chapter VI that instances of collective bargaining, particularly in the later predeadline stages, might approximate the pure-bargaining situation. The analytical problem is: What in an "indeterminate" situation such as this causes the expectations of the parties to converge upon some particular position as the solution? In the context of this chapter the analytical problem is: What, in an indeterminate situation such as this, can the mediator do to help the convergence of expectations upon some particular position? Mediation in the face of a manifest contract zone has been recognized as a difficult problem. Kerr remarks: "A particularly difficult controversy to mediate, strangely enough, is one in which the costs of aggressive conflict to each party are enormous. Then any one of many solutions is better than a strike, and the process of narrowing these possible solutions to a single one is an arduous task." [25]

In an indeterminate situation such as this the mediator can, generally speaking, attempt by argumentation to convince the parties that one particular position should be agreed upon. This sort of persuasion might succeed. However, it must be remembered that in the manifest contract zone situation, any position that the mediator argues for will be a position from which at least one party would be willing to retreat for the sake of agreement, and the other party knows this. In these circumstances, persuasion in the direct sense of this term will be difficult. The analysis of how the parties themselves may be led to coordination of expectations about the outcome in the pure-bargaining situation suggests that a more subtle mechanism than persuasion in the direct sense may be involved in the mediation of these disputes. (Whatever "actual" mechanism the mediator employs, his effort viewed *ex post* will have, superficially at least, the appearance of an instance of persuasion.)

Schelling has suggested that the "intrinsic magnetism" (connoting such properties as prominence, simplicity, uniqueness, precedent, and so forth) of a particular outcome may serve the coordination function. This suggestion stems from the notion that subjective phenomena present in instances of tacit bargaining may generalize to instances of negotiation with communication. Earlier, we considered the role of various factors, especially the basic criteria used in wage negotiation, in attributing focal point value to particular positions. That discussion in general, and the arbitration award example in particular, is directly relevant to the task of mediation. For example, a mediator might use a negotiation record built up on the basis of the basic criteria to attribute prominence to a particular position. More simply, the fact that the mediator favors a particular position (and none other) in the efficient range may be enough (because of the "uniqueness" the position thereby acquires) to recommend that position as a focal point for the convergence of expectations.

We now suggest that the mediation tactic of converting collective bargaining negotiations into instances of (quasi) tacit bargaining may be important in resolution of indeterminate situations of the pure-bargaining game kind. Tacit bargaining refers, generally, to games in which there is no explicit communication between the players.[26] In some such games there is no communication at all. This will be the case if there is no succession of moves and if the game is not iterated. A case in point is the game in which the players are told to divide a given sum—say 100—between themselves. Each writes his claim on a slip of paper, no communication permitted. If the two claims total 100 or less, each player receives the amount of his claim. If the claims total more than 100, each player receives nothing. If a play of a game is comprised of a succession of moves, or if a game is iterated, then some communication is possible because of the information content of the moves themselves, but explicit communication is not permitted.

An aspect of tacit games relevant to mediation tactics is the possibility that resort, in mixed games, to tacit rather than explicit bargaining may force elements of cooperation to the fore. The game of "divide a sum" is, as is collective bargaining negotiation, a mixed game. There are elements of competition and important elements of cooperation. Experiments conducted by Schelling indicate that players can usually "win" this game, the characteristic configuration of claims being 50–50.[27] The nature of the common tacit solution suggests that resort to tacit play has led to domination of the conflict of interest by the need to coordinate, by the cooperative element. One suspects that the players would find it harder to resolve an explicit bargaining variant of this game. Freedom of communication would facilitate dominance by the competitive elements. Each party would now have the opportunity to support various division criteria favoring himself—division according to the ratio of their incomes, assets, debts, number of children, and so forth. If the sum were large and if there were no deadline, a play of this game might continue for a very long time. Suppose that for this reason, or because of an impending deadline, the parties in disagreement call in a third party. On the definition of a "good" arbitration award as one that does not "surprise" either party very much, this would be an easy game to arbitrate. What about mediation? A mediator attempting persuasion by the device of simply sitting in with the parties, moderating and contributing to their discussion, might not get very far. A mediator who separated the parties, who forced them to play a tacit bargaining variant of this game, might rather quickly resolve the dispute, particularly if he had suggested in a prior joint conference that in his opinion a particular division (say 50–50) was reasonable.

In pursuing the above line of thought there is no suggestion that any particular instance of collective bargaining negotiation is a close analogue to so simple a game situation as that of divide 100. Nevertheless, the point illustrated in the above—that tacit bargaining may facilitate domination of a conflict of interest by the necessity for coordination—may have some relevance to the workings of the mediation process. One of the prominent features of mediation, and one of the most interesting analytically, is the mediator's control over the communications structure of the negotiations. We saw in the previous section, that control over the flow of information between the parties may enable the mediator to bring certain "pressures" to bear on the parties, as in the technique termed "unselling" and "selling," for example. Beyond this, however, is the point emphasized in this section. The fact that the mediator can separate the parties, suppress the flow of information between them, that is, oblige them to play a tacit variant of their negotiation game, may itself be of some importance in those instances of failure of the parties to reach agreement in the tactical context of the pure-bargaining situation. (There is always the possibility, of course, that even though the mediator attempts to separate the parties they will go around him, that is, establish lines of communication outside his cognizance.)

Characteristically, the parties will have negotiated for some time before the mediator comes on the scene. The fact that they have failed to converge upon a solution does not necessarily mean that no position in the contract zone has the power to compel agreement in a tacit variant of this same game. Nevertheless, this may be a part of the difficulty. This suggests that a mediator wishing to use the tacit bargaining approach may first have to "set the situation up" by playing an active role, that is, by deliberately contriving to attribute "prominence" to a particular position. In so doing, he may attempt to rationalize a particular position, perhaps in terms of various criteria which have already been adduced by the parties. In order for a position to compel a convergence of expectations in tacit bargaining, it is necessary that it be clearly differentiated from all the others. The actual function of "rationalization" in an operation of this kind is that of differentiation of a position, distinguishing it *per se*— rather than that of persuasion. Following this operation, he may separate the parties. If he elects to suppress completely the flow of information between the parties, he in effect tells them to write their claim on a slip of paper.

The fact that tacit bargaining precludes the parties from pursuing their conflict of interest in the usual way is a permissive feature of the situation which may facilitate bringing cooperative elements to the fore. There must also be an active feature—namely, that failure to concert involves a significant penalty. In consequence, the mediator using this approach may have to build a "threat" of his own devising into the situation. He might set a deadline and tell the parties that if their proposals are not approximately convergent by that time he is "through." Such a failure of mediation may spell economic warfare for the parties (or it may spell appointment of a fact-finding board with the power to subpoena witnesses and records), and in consequence may be effective.[28] If the mediator has clearly differentiated a position (or if there was a "natural" resting place in the situation as he inherited it), the parties may converge upon it by tacit negotiation.[29]

It is clear from the above discussion that a manifest contract zone, while perhaps necessary, is not a sufficient condition for convergence upon a solution by tacit bargaining. In addition, some candidate for the role "solution" must be clearly differentiable. If the dispute involves a complex multi-item package, such differentiation may be difficult. It may be difficult for other reasons.

Problems of Definition and Measurement

We saw in Chapter VI that agreement in collective bargaining negotiation may be impeded by the inability of each party to define his equilibrium position in institutional terms. This bar to agreement was suggested by considering application of the avoidance–avoidance conflict model to non-wage issues. Reverting to the previous example, suppose that the parties are negotiating a union security clause. The employer's announced position is the open shop; the union's announced position is the closed shop. Let us further suppose that the employer occupies an equilibrium position such as D_1, Figure 1, Chapter II. The question that arises is: How, in this context, are we to interpret the concept "distance" (from goals)—the horizontal axis in Figure 1? Scrutiny of Figure 1 reveals that position D_1 is about one-third of the way from an open shop to a closed shop. This is the position which the employer is willing to accept. But what particular institutional arrangement (the "X" shop) represents a position one-third of the way from an open shop to a closed shop?

In the mediation context, the important distinguishing feature of this situation is that the actor, although ready to compromise, is unable to do so because of inability to define his equilibrium position in institutional terms. Let us suppose that in our example the parties occupy approximately the same equilibrium position. Then the mediator has to define the equilibrium position in institutional terms. This definition function is the key to dispute resolution in this particular kind of tactical situation, a function calling upon the mediator's "inventiveness."

Evolution of the maintenance-of-membership provision in collective agreements seems to be an excellent case of resolution of conflict by definition of an equilibrium position. On the eve of World War II, a bitter labor dispute was certified to the National Defense Mediation Board (predecessor to the National War Labor Board).[30] The crucial issue in the case was union security. The union representatives were demanding a union shop—the management representatives an open shop. The positions of both sides were rationalized in terms of "principles." Finally each side confided in the public member of the board the minimum provision it would accept in a settlement. Frank Graham's description of the result is worth quoting:

The union representatives told the public member that they wanted to be sure that their union, for which they had worked so hard, would not be destroyed in the defense period or in the possible war period which loomed ahead; that they would be guaranteed their voluntarily acquired union membership for the duration of the contract, which would recognize their union as their bargaining agent in their particular plant. The representatives of the company told the public member that they wanted to be assured the right to hire, fire and direct the working force and that workers would not be compelled to join the union by any closed or union shop provision.

When these provisions, separately asked for, were put in a joint package, they added up neither to an open shop nor to a closed shop, but to the maintenance of voluntarily acquired membership for the duration of the contract.

The maintenance-of-membership provision was accepted (with only *pro forma* dissent by both sides) and generally adhered to by both labor and management throughout World War II.

The maintenance-of-membership provision is a compromise between an open shop and a union shop. George W. Taylor has stressed the "art of proposing the alternate solution" as the crucial aspect of mediation.[31] It should be clear that proposing an "alternate solution" will by itself resolve conflict, achieve agreement, only in particular circumstances. If such a proposal is, by itself, to work, the parties must already be in a kind of covert "agreement" in the sense that they both occupy the equilibrium position which receives its institutional definition in the proposal. Although willing to accept the proposal in this sense, the parties cannot reach overt agreement because they cannot define the equilibrium position, and the crucial contribution of the mediator is the ingenuity and inventiveness he brings to the definition problem. Proposing an alternate solution will not, by itself, resolve a conflict in which the equilibrium positions of the parties are not consonant with each other and with the proposed alternate solution. In this latter case, if mediation is to be effective it must bring "pressure" to bear which will move the equilibrium positions of the parties. Nor will proposing an alternate solution by itself resolve conflict in the pure-bargaining-game situation discussed in the previous subsection.

We saw in Chapter VI that, in addition to the definition problem just discussed, problems of dimensionality and measurement may constitute bars to agreement in collective bargaining negotiation. A typical instance of collective bargaining negotiation is concerned with a multi-item package, and it is the total cost of the package that matters when it comes to settlement. Even if all the items in the package are dimensionally commensurable in some terms, such as dollars and cents, it may be difficult as a practicable matter to calculate the total cost, or to calculate the trading value of one item in terms of some other. For example, what is the trading value in terms of the wage rate of a concession on work rules? What is the total cost of a multi-item package comprised of wage, quasi-wage, and nonwage items? It is difficult to see what peculiar contribution the mediator, *qua* mediator, can make in cases where agreement is impeded by measurement problems *per se*. In cases of this kind where three heads are better than two, he might be of assistance in a general way. More particularly, those aids to the mediator's vision which stem from his occupying a disinterested position *vis-à-vis* the dispute may prove helpful in resolution of this aspect of the measurement problem.

There is, however, another aspect of the measurement problem in which, it seems possible, the mediator might make a unique sort of contribution to the resolution. This involves the possibility that agreement is impeded because of nonunidimensionality of the items in a package—because of the lack of a common denominator in terms of which the items may be made commensurable. In brief, the point is that certain issues (union security, work rules, supplemental unemployment benefits, and so forth) while clearly involving dollars and cents, also involve much more. For example, in addition to a monetary flow "pie," a power "pie" is being divided in collective bargaining negotiation, and the significance of one's share may inhere more in the direct ego satisfaction from recognition of status, and so on, than from the indirect monetary implications of the division.

Whatever the substantive case for nonunidimensionality of options in collective bargaining negotiation, the implication relevant to mediation functions is that if an actor confronts noncommensurable options, he may be conflicted—unable to choose (literally unable to rank in terms of preference) for want of a common denominator. One way to resolve such a choice is simply to let someone else, who is for some reason perceived as an "authority" adequate to the task, make it.[32] The suggestion is that the mediator may serve this function where nonunidimensionality of choice options is a bar to agreement. In the mediator's value system, detached as he is from the role positions of the actors, there may be no conflict, that is, he *can* have a relative preference and can choose. Following the lead of a third party may provide at least a short-run answer. It would seem that effectiveness with respect to this particular mediation function would be enhanced if the mediator had considerable prestige.[33]

MEDIATION AS A WAY TO "COME CLEAN" WITHOUT PREJUDICE

Analysis of the later predeadline stages of collective bargaining negotiation reveals that there are a number of tactical bars to full freedom of communication between the parties. The tactical bars in question give rise to the problem identified in Chapter VI as that of how to "come clean" without prejudice. How may a party announce his equilibrium position without prejudice, that is, without, by the very act of the announcement, making the ultimately to be agreed-upon position less favorable to himself than might otherwise have been the case? We may briefly recapitulate the reasons why such an announcement may be prejudicial.

(1) Such an announcement involves retreat from the ostensible posi-

tion, a retreat which may be interpreted by the opposite number as a sign of weakness, or even as a sign of impending collapse and capitulation.

(2) Operating under the deadline rule, the solution of the negotiation game is the equilibrium position occupied by the party who "gives" at 11:59. At 11:59 (the last "moment" before a strike) the time has come for "last" proposals. In the nature of the case, one of these proposals is an offer, the other, if there is a contract zone, is agreement. There is a tactical asymmetry in this situation in the sense that the advantage may well have gone to the one who waited.

(3) Even though a party does not wish to strike or to take a strike, it may be forced upon him, and this consideration may cause him to be concerned about the *status quo* which strike negotiations will inherit from the prestrike negotiations, therefore, he may for these reasons be reluctant to announce his true equilibrium position.

An implication of these tactical bars to full freedom of communication is that the parties may be in (covert) "agreement" in the sense that their equilibrium positions are consonant but may fail to reach overt agreement. Thus, because of these bars, a party's final prestrike proposal may not state the least favorable terms (to himself) upon which he is willing to settle but terms more favorable to himself. In such cases, if the parties would have settled had each stated the least favorable terms upon which he was (or would have been) willing to settle, the intervention of a mediator may be of real assistance.

Another aspect of these tactical problems is also relevant to mediation functions. They all have in common the fact that each is an influence making for the photo-finish, making for delay in an announcement of equilibrium position—the least favorable terms upon which one is willing to settle. The approach of the deadline brings with it an 11:59, the last moment at which a change in ostensible position may be made, and a 12:01, the moment beyond which a strike is inevitable. However, as we saw, the deadline is not a knife edge in time. Rather, it is a sort of zone in time, if only in consequence of the fact that if a strike is impending various preparations must be made. This means that under the influence of these forces for delay by the time one party has decided that 11:59 has arrived, it may already be 12:01. Thus, an inadvertent strike may take place, which might have been precluded by the intervention of a mediator.

It should be noted that the tactical problems adverted to here may constitute bars to agreement in cases in which there are also other bars to agreement. Hence, discussion of mediator's function in this context is also relevant to mediation in those other contexts. However, in what follows, we may proceed as if we were considering the "pure" cases of bars to agreement on the grounds suggested in this section. That is, in these cases, the parties are supposed to be in (covert) "agreement" in that their equilibrium positions are consonant. They have not achieved overt agreement because their ostensible positions have not, for the reasons adduced, incorporated the least favorable terms upon which each is willing to settle.

In these instances, the critical function of the mediator stems in large part from the role he plays as part of the communications structure of the negotiations. For example, he can receive information from each party without passing that information on to the opposite number. If, on the basis of such information, it turned out that the equilibrium positions of the parties were indeed consonant, he could simply announce to the parties that they were in agreement, and thereby resolve the dispute. That is, in such a case, even though the ostensible positions of the parties were divergent, they would not have to alter these positions at all—prior to the moment of actual agreement.

Even if the mediator enters the picture prior to a strike, resolution of the situation is not apt to be so simple as above suggested. The parties may hesitate, at least early in the game, to reveal their true positions to the mediator. There is no reason, for example, for A to suppose that because he has revealed his true position to the mediator that B has done likewise. If the mediator simply passes this information on to B, the difficulties discussed remain. However, the mediator may do much more than simply pass information along. Peculiarly appropriate to agreement difficulties of the sort here considered, he may appear to be the author of proposals which are in point of fact originated by (and even represent the true equilibrium positions of) the parties. Or each side may give the mediator something to use as he sees fit. The major advantage here is that a party need not (appear to have) become committed to a position (his own) since it appears to be the mediator's position. Indeed, if the tactical situation should demand it, he might denounce the "mediator's" position as stoutly as he does that of his opposite number. Thus the parties can make ostensible concessions via the mediator with much less hazard than would be the case in making such concessions directly, and we might expect such concession to be made. As the mediation progresses, the confidence of the parties in the mediator will become established. Especially if he has implied a deadline of his own (having been appropriately patient with what has gone before), the parties will be encouraged to reveal their true positions to him. This, in the nonmanifest contract zone cases here under consideration, will be sufficient to resolve the dispute.

The function of the mediator in suppressing information may also be important in these cases. An existing contract zone may be wiped out if, for example, A, learning of B's true equilibrium position (considerably less favorable to B than was his ostensible position), interprets this as a sign of B's collapse and promptly revises the terms upon which he is willing to settle. Thus the mediator may have to slow down the pace of B's retreat.[34]

Particularly in cases of this kind, the timing of the mediator entering the dispute may be critical. In light of the possibility of negotiation failures of the nonmanifest contract zone type, it may be argued that mediation (of a sort) should be a part of many negotiation proceedings from their inception.[35] Thus it might be required that the parties continuously submit information regarding their true equilibrium positions to a neutral third party. It would be understood and agreed that the sole function of this third party would be to receive the information in question and announce the fact of conditions necessary for bilateral compromise—if and when such conditions should eventuate. The value of employing mediation of this sort from the outset is that it might prevent the parties from destroying a condition necessary for bilateral compromise in their unaided attempts to discover the fact of its existence.

In any event, whether or not mediation of this sort is employed from the outset, the mediator should enter the picture prior to the deadline and occurrence of a strike. Once the strike has begun, the picture changes. What may have begun as an "unnecessary" strike may not be as easy to terminate as this genesis would imply. Misunderstandings are easy, and tensions created by the uncertainty of the situation may lead to violent reactions. Once the strike has begun, the nonmanifest contract zone may evaporate, and the mediator's task will be complicated.

Leiserson has suggested that there should be a period between the end of collective bargaining and the beginning of a strike in which the mediator can work.[36] Such an arrangement might be very helpful in some cases. It would not seem, however, that it should be generalized as a rule to apply to all cases. In some situations, mediation might be helpful during the predeadline negotiation. In other cases, where there is no contract zone and the parties appear quite intractable, perhaps only the actual experience of a strike will lead the parties to a correct estimate of the cost involved and the probable gains to be had thereby. In such instances, mediation may be more effective after the strike has run its course for awhile. In general, however, and particularly in the nonmanifest contract zone case, there is a case for the mediator's entering the picture prior to the beginning of a strike.

Intraorganizational Problems

The negotiators are the representatives of organizations. Ultimately, whatever package they come up with must be sold by each to his own constituents. We have noted that these considerations might pose a bar to agreement. Thus it may be the case that, insofar as the negotiators as delegates are concerned, a manifest contract zone has emerged in the course of negotiation. However, difficulties may arise in the effort to tailor a package which is as "salable" as possible (salable at all, in the extreme case) to the respective constituencies. In such a case, the negotiators in a sense share a common problem. A mediator may be helpful in this situation. For one thing, he brings with him the fresh view of a disinterested third party and (if the parties are fortunate) a facility for the invention of alternative proposals. He may come up with an ingenious solution which, although it was inherent in the situation, neither party had seen. In this kind of situation, the mediator operates as a kind of maximizer of "total welfare." He must attempt to get more for A without getting less for B, and vice versa. Equally important in this kind of situation is the "face-saving" function discussed previously. The negotiator may find it difficult to endorse a given package, which he is willing to accept, to his constituents because the package may appear to discriminate in an awkward way as among the various interest groups represented in his organization. In such a case, if the mediator can appear to shoulder some of the responsibility for the outcome, the negotiator's problems in relation to his constituents may be eased.

A Note on the Avoidance–Avoidance Model and Pen's Theory of the Wage Rate under Collective Bargaining

The traditional and still largely prevailing view of the wage rate under collective bargaining (and of the price under bilateral monopoly generally) is that it is indeterminate—within limits prescribed by a contract zone. A notable recent exception to this is Pen's theory.[1] Pen, critical of the "prevailing agnosticism about wage determination," develops a theory which exhibits an equilibrium for the wage rate. His is a utility-theory-type analysis in which choice (in the bargaining situation) depends upon maximization of the expected value of the outcome.

The avoidance–avoidance conflict-choice-theory model of collective bargaining negotiation (presented in Chapter II) also represents an exception to the prevailing view. With this theory, the outcome of negotiation is determinate in the sense that an equilibrium condition is exhibited.

These theories have in common one principal formal characteristic, namely, that the bargaining equilibrium depends upon consonance of equilibria separately arrived at for each of the parties. The purpose of this appendix is to compare certain aspects of these theories.[2] In order that the discussion be reasonably self-contained, we first sketch the central notions of Pen's formal analysis. Since a general critique is not intended, the presentation will be simplified, with the supporting argument and discussion accompanying Pen's own presentation omitted. Further, Pen's notation will be somewhat rephrased and certain of the points somewhat recast in an effort to get as clear a picture as possible of the central ideas.

PEN'S THEORY

Exposition will be facilitated by developing the analysis (as does Pen) with respect to one of the bargainers, the union leader. An analogous argument then applies to the company representative.

The union's rate preferences are fully described by a cardinal ophelimity (that is, utility) function (L) which is generally increasing and has a maximum value at $L(W_1)$. The ophelimity function is not invariant during bargaining—rather, it may be shifted by that process, particularly if "ludic" elements (for example, emotional involvement, necessity to "save face," and so forth) enter the picture.

At choice points in the bargaining, the union must decide whether to accept a given rate W and its associated ophelimity $L(W)$ or to continue bargaining for the most favorable rate W_1. The rate W is supposed to be one which has (somehow) "come under discussion," that is, we might suppose it to be a tentative proposal by the bargaining opponent. Continuing to bargain means a possible gain of $L(W_1) - L(W)$.

Continuing to bargain also involves some expected risk (r) of a conflict (bargaining strike or lockout) with which a conflict ophelimity of Lc is associated. The conflict ophelimity is importantly influenced by the *post bellum* wage rate expected to rule. Ludic elements may also influence conflict ophelimity. Continuing to bargain, therefore, involves a possible loss of $L(W) - Lc$, since, in the event of conflict, $L(W)$ is lost and Lc takes its place.

The basic equilibrium postulate (for the individual bargainer) is now this: The union will continue to bargain at the rate W, that is, continue to strive for W_1, only so long as the *expected* value of the gain hoped for is at least equal to that of the loss feared. That is, so long as:

1a. $$(1 - r) [L(W_1) - L(W)] \gtrless r [L(W) - Lc]$$

In utility-analysis terms, and assuming an actuarial mentality, we may say that the choice confronted is between the "certain option" $L(W)$ and the "lottery option" involving $(1 - r)L(W_1)$ and $(r)Lc$. In these terms, we may rewrite (1a) as:

1. $$L(W) \gtrless (1 - r)L(W_1) + (r)Lc$$

For the union, the expected risk of conflict (r) depends upon the employer's net contract ophelimity (at the rate W which has come under discussion). Where E denotes the employer's ophelimity function, $E(W)$ the ophelimity he associates with the given rate, and Ec his conflict ophelimity, the employer's net contract ophelimity is given by $E(W) - Ec$. If this value is below 0, the employer prefers conflict to contract at W, and if above 0, vice versa. Were this value known to the union, r would always have a value of 1 or 0. However, an important basic assumption is uncertainty about the ophelimities of the opponent. In consequence, r has values between 0 and 1, increasingly as the union's perception or estimate of $E(W) - Ec$ lies closer to 0. The "correspection" function (F_1), describing the union's estimate of $E(W) - Ec$, relates this net contract ophelimity to the union's estimate of r:

2. $$r = F_1 [E(W) - Ec]$$

By argument analogous to that pertaining to the union, an equilibrium equation can be developed for the employer:

3. $E(W) \lessgtr (1 - r)E(We) + (r)Ec.$

Analogously, the employer's perception of r depends upon his estimate of the union's net contract ophelimity at the rate W under discussion:

4. $r = F_e [L(W) - Lc]$

The above equilibrium conditions apply one to each of the bargainers. It takes two to conclude a contract. The point of equilibrium of bargaining will be reached when equations (1) and (3) are consonant, realized (as equalities) at a common W. At the outset, (1) and (3) will be in conflict. According to Pen "the function of the bargaining process is to transform the relevant magnitudes and relations in such a way that the equilibrium conditions are no longer in conflict. At the moment when both equations, which originally gave different values for W, are transformed to such an extent that the solutions of W display the same value, equilibrium has been reached *and the contract is concluded at this value of W.*" [italics supplied] [3]

It may be noted that Pen's discussion implies that the point of equilibrium in bargaining (the equilibrium solution of the bargaining process) is reached when equations (1) and (3) are equalities at the same value for W. Indeed, this interpretation is necessary if the theory is to exhibit an equilibrium condition for the outcome of bargaining. However, it is not clear to this writer why the outcome must be so characterized. As Pen indicates, if the W under discussion is such that the left-hand side of equation (1) is greater than the right-hand side, the union will be quick to conclude the contract at that W. The same may be said analogously for equation (3) in the case of the employer, and if the wage rate W "under discussion" was a proposal made by the employer, we would expect this to hold. In other words, it is sufficient for an outcome by agreement that equations (1) and (3) be consonant as inequalities. Pen's assumption seems to be that with (1) and (3) in conflict at the outset (that is, with only one of these equalities favoring the left hand side) the parties will gradually converge upon that W for which these are consonant as equalities.

COMPARISON OF THEORY FORMATS

It will be instructive to attempt to interpret Pen's theory in terms of the format of the avoidance–avoidance model. Refer to Figure 1, Chapter II, and assume that it now represents the choice problem as confronted by the union (goal A now becomes "settle on employer's terms"). The model is cast in terms of "avoidance" tendencies whereas Pen's model is cast in terms of "ophelimities." From a formal point of view, however, we may neglect the implied signs.[4]

Pen's actor is supposed to focus upon a conflict ophelimity and upon the ophelimity associated with his optimum rate. The analysis is then concerned with achievement of the equilibrium conditions with respect to some particular W, conceptualized as the wage rate under discussion. Pen indicates that the way in which W comes under discussion does not matter. However, we are permitted to assume that it represents a proposal made by one of the parties. If we assume W to be a proposal by the bargaining opponent (the employer), we might identify W with Figure I's goal A, and L(W) with the intercept on the goal A axis. It will be recalled that the tendency to avoid Figure I's goal B was based on the consideration that to "maintain own position" (at the deadline) involved risk of conflict (strike). In consequence, if we assume W_1 to be "own position," we might identify $(1 - r)L(W_1) + (r)Lc$ with the intercept on the goal B axis. These identifications of Pen's constructs with Figure I's goals A and B select the closest analogues available for purposes of this comparison, but do not imply precise analogues. Thus, for example, in Figure I, goals A and B both represent rates "under discussion," that is, these are the announced bargaining positions of the parties, and goal B ("own position") is not supposed to be an optimum rate in Pen's sense. There appears to be no very direct analogue in Pen's formulation to Figure I's avoidance-gradients, and no very direct analogue to Figure I's equilibrium positions, that is, positions such as D1, which are rates somewhere in between the rates under discussion.

If this translation of Pen's constructs into their closest analogues in the avoidance–avoidance model does not misrepresent Pen's formulation, we must conclude that his formulation neglects the whole conflict-choice problem suggested in Figure I. In Figure I terms, Pen's actor is either at goal A or goal B. If the former, the bargaining is over, that is, he simply accepts his opponent's proposal. If the latter, he "goes on bargaining," but (as Pen puts the argument) no equilibrium position analogous to D1 seems to be suggested. The closest Figure I analogue would perhaps be found in situations such as represented by avoidance-gradient A'A'—situations in which one gradient is everywhere above the other and, hence, in which, in spite of the avoidance nature of the choice, there is no conflict.

Perhaps another way to put the matter is this. Pen's actor confronts this (simple) nonconflict choice: (a) accept bargaining opponent's proposal, or (b) go on bargaining. The avoidance–avoidance model deals with the choice problem involved in the situation "go on bargaining." That is, the avoidance–avoidance model actor in any event goes on negotiating until the necessary and sufficient conditions for agreement are met. While negotiating, he confronts this choice: (a) accept bargaining opponent's proposal, or (b) insist upon own position. He does not simply elect either of these goals; he is conflicted—which yields an equilibrium position such as D1, the rate he would be willing to accept if there were some way to do so. The negotiation process involves a resolution of this intrapersonal conflict in the context of an interpersonal conflict.

NECESSARY AND SUFFICIENT CONDITIONS
FOR AGREEMENT

These two analyses have one major feature in common. In each, consonance of equilibrium positions (one occupied by each party) is depicted as at least a necessary condition for reaching an agreed price in bargaining. In Pen's theory, this consonance is also a sufficient condition, ". . . and the contract is concluded at this value of W." Here is a major difference in the two approaches. With the avoidance–avoidance analysis, consonance of equilibrium positions was deemed to be only a necessary, not a sufficient condition for agreement. Beyond this, it is necessary for the parties somehow to inform each other of the fact of this consonance in order that it constitute a route to actual, overt agreement. As we saw, establishing mutual awareness that the necessary conditions for agreement have been met may involve a delicate problem in communication. In other words, in the terminology used in Chapter II, Pen's analysis deals only with the first task to be accomplished in negotiation (bringing the equilibrium positions into consonance) but neglects the second major function of the negotiation process.

Pen's neglect of this second aspect of the analysis is not inherent in an approach to equilibrium through maximization of expected utility. Instead, it stems from the particular way in which the choice problem is posed in this context. Pen indicates that the way in which W (conceptualized as the wage rate under discussion) comes under discussion does not matter. Actually, as we have seen, if W is to constitute the outcome of the negotiations, it very much matters how it comes under discussion. In any event, it is clear that as long as the equilibrium rate is identified as a rate under discussion, there is no communication problem with respect to it.

An alternative would be to treat equations (1) and (3) as equalities which determine equilibrium rates (those the parties would be willing to accept), rather than as inequalities which determine whether the parties go on bargaining given some rate W. On this interpretation, the equations would state that there is for each party and at each choice point in the negotiation some equilibrium rate W (determined by the ophelimities and r). This rate could be treated as unannounced and unknown to the opposite number, and in general different from the announced (ostensible) rate of each. This view would recognize the fact that usually in negotiation there will be two rates under discussion—the announced positions of the parties at that time.

AD HOC RELATION OF TACTICAL ENTITIES
TO FORMAL THEORY

In comparative statics analysis generally, equilibrium models are of interest because they permit (at least formal) prediction of the direction of shift in the variable of interest consequent, *ceteris paribus,* upon shifts in certain environmental parameters of interest. From this point of view, the analysis may be useful to the extent that it directs the investigator's attention to factors which are significant determinants of the variable of interest.

Looking, for example, at equation (1), we observe that a Pen-type employer can attempt to move the union's equilibrium position in his own favor by operating upon the various ophelimities therein included and/or upon the risk of conflict factor, r. Equation (2) then tells us that the employer's operations upon r will involve his operations upon the union's perception of the employer's net contract ophelimity at the rate under discussion. Pen feels that although attempts to influence the opponent's ophelimities may be a common part of negotiation, these attempts are not apt to be very effective. Much more effective will be operations upon r (that is, by attempting to exaggerate the risk of conflict).[5]

The kinds of tactical entity to which Pen's theory would direct the investigator's attention would seem, in general, to be the same as the tactics discussed in this inquiry. That is, the classification of tactics we have developed would seem to be consistent with any such classification suggested by Pen's theory, and the particular tactics discussed in the various chapters would seem to be consistent with the implications of his formal theory.

From the point of view of relation of tactics to the formal theory, these theories share a common weakness. In both theories, particular tactics are related to the formal theoretical structure in a rather *ad hoc* fashion. This is a greater deficiency with the avoidance–avoidance analysis. In this analysis, the various tactics adduced have simply been treated, without formal theoretical structure, as shift parameters in the avoidance functions. In Pen's theory, the equations (2) and (4) incorporate the tactic of exaggerating the risk of conflict more directly into the formal theoretical structure.

APPENDIX II

Collective Bargaining Negotiation
and Game Theory: Summary
and Special Topics

Comments about the applicability of game theory to analysis of collective bargaining negotiation have been made at various points throughout the text. One function of this appendix is to collect and summarize certain of these observations for a more general comment. Secondly, certain special topics are developed briefly. This discussion is generally intended for investigators interested in negotiation problems, and particularly for the student of collective bargaining who may wish to review his thinking about the applicability of game theory to his own analytical problems.[1]

GENERAL ORIENTATION

Initially we should be clear that whatever use one might make of game theory in analysis of collective bargaining negotiation, this (probably) will not include the attempt literally (formally) to represent (an instance of) collective bargaining negotiation as a game in the technical sense. There are a number of reasons why this is so—some of which may be briefly suggested.

Formal definition of a game must specify the range of response options (choices, acts) available to each player at each choice point (move) of the game. Hence, in thinking about representation of any interaction as a game, the first problem confronted is one of response definition, that is, specification of the "domain of choices" supposed to constitute the options available at each move. In relation to the negotiation game, this is a problem of what might be termed the "instrumental" significance of a "negotiation response," that is, what the players "do" while negotiating. In many simple games, this may be no special problem. For example, in certain parlor games the instrumental significance of a response is defined in terms of a certain physical apparatus. However, in complicated social games, and in negotiation games in particular, this may be a perplexing problem.[2]

Even if the problem of ambiguity with respect to the choices available at each move could be overcome, there are other general problems involved in attempted formal representation of collective bargaining negotiation as a game. The structure of a game (in normal form) is represented by the familiar payoff matrix—the set of outcomes (payoffs) associated with the various strategies represented by the rows and columns of the matrix. Generally speaking, in the reduction of a game to normal form, each strategy must be supposed to consist of a sequence of the choices provided for in the definition of the game. Each strategy represents a complete sequence of choices appropriate for a peculiar sequence of contingencies (opponent's order of choices). That is, each strategy (row or column) is a complete prescription for a play of the game (in extensive form) under a given situation. Even if unambiguous strategies could be defined in terms of the choices, if the number of choices available at each move is more than just a few—a most likely case with any adequate representation of collective bargaining negotiation—the number of strategies implied (rows and columns of the payoff martix) is enormous. This, in turn, makes actual solution of the game impracticable.

The fact that we cannot reduce particular instances of collective bargaining negotiation to games in normal form does not by itself mean that game-theory analysis can be of no use in this context.[3] We might still hope, for example, that by examination of simple, abstract games in normal form, we shall achieve some analytical insights by the analogy of features of these games with particular aspects of collective bargaining negotiation. Perhaps the appropriate general orientation for the student of collective bargaining with an interest in potential uses of game-theory analysis is that suggested by Luce and Raiffa: "Given the present state of game theory, we are indeed skeptical that many such problems [such as collective bargaining] can be given a realistic formal analysis; rather, we would contend that a case can be made for studying simplified models which are suggested by and related to the problem of interest. The hope is that, by analogy, their analysis will shed light—however dim and unreliable—on the strategic and communication aspects of the real problem."[4]

NEGOTIATION TACTICS AND GAME THEORY

Within the spirit of the proscriptions of the preceding section, we may now consider in more detail the relation of negotiation theory to game theory.

Games may be assigned to either of two (among other) classes depending upon whether they are: (1) cooperative games—the players are assumed to have complete freedom of preplay communication; (2) noncooperative games—the players are not permitted to communicate.[5] The aspect of game theory with which the theory of negotiation is most closely related is preplay communication in cooperative games. Although in principle the theory of negotiation is closely related to that of preplay communication, in practice this relationship has not been substantial because the format of conventional game-theory analysis is such as to exclude most important negotiatory phenomena from the analysis, notably, tactics of bluff, persuasion, and rationalization.

The exclusion of these tactical entities reflects difficulties which inhere in the rationality postulate of game theory, particularly the assumption concerning perfect knowledge. That is, game theory assumes that each player has full knowledge not only of his own utility function but of the payoff functions of the other players as well. Related to this is the assumption that the payoff matrix remains invariant under play and preplay of the game. For example, Luce and Raiffa, in their treatment of the two-person cooperative game, explicitly assume that: "iii. A player's evaluations of the outcomes of the game are not disturbed by these preplay negotiations." [6] Although we might readily agree that the parties to collective bargaining negotiation are not adequately characterized by the perfect-knowledge postulate, this does not mean, *per se,* that analysis based upon the perfect-knowledge assumption will be of no use. That is, we might proceed on the basis of a postulate that the parties behave "as if" they were so characterized, with the hope that the analysis would turn up some interesting results. In more particular terms, however, the difficulty with the perfect-knowledge postulate is that it rules out classes of tactics which are virtually ubiquitous to, and of critical importance in, negotiation. If, for example, in terms of the payoff matrix, a party's strategy 1 is preferred to his strategy 2, that party cannot, since the theory assumes that he and his opponent are fully informed maximizers, "pretend to prefer" strategy 2. Thus the tactic of bluff based upon misrepresentation of preferences is ruled out. Tactics of persuasion (defined in Chapter IV as A's attempts to influence the outcome by altering B's preferences) would also appear to be ruled out. Tactics of persuasion are eminently designed to operate on the payoff matrix and are not admissible to an analysis which assumes that the payoff matrix remains invariant under play and preplay of the game.[7]

Another negotiatory phenomenon which the game-theory format has difficulty accommodating is the fact that a player's evaluation of the outcomes may not be independent of the strategies employed by his bargaining opponent, that is, he may attach positive or negative value to elements in the process of play *per se.*[8] For example, he might react negatively to certain techniques his bargaining opponent used to coerce him, and this would imply a change in his preferences over the outcomes. In analysis of collective bargaining negotiation, this consideration may be rather important. We saw, for example, that in such negotiation "ultimatum" tends to be a "dirty" word. Tactics interpreted as instances of "bad faith" will not be neutral with respect to the utilities the parties associate with outcomes. Such considerations cannot be taken into account in game-theory analysis if the payoff matrix is to be assumed invariant during play of the game.

Game theorists are, of course, well aware that the format of the analysis excludes the various tactical entities alluded to in this section—an awareness well illustrated by this summary comment by Nash regarding his analysis of the bargaining problem in a game-theory context: "With people who are sufficiently intelligent and rational, there should not be any question of 'bargaining ability,' a term which suggests something like skill in duping the other fellow. The usual haggling process is based on imperfect information, the hagglers trying to propagandize each other into misconceptions of the utilities involved. Our assumption of complete information makes any such an attempt meaningless." [9]

We saw in Chapter V that the game-theory format does accommodate certain tactical entities of interest to negotiation theory, namely, coercive notbluffs, such as the threat. However, in the conventional treatment, the threat is treated as essentially external to the formal structure of the game. A player may threaten a given strategy of his own against a choice of strategy by his opponent, thereby limiting the options available to his opponent in the payoff matrix, but the matrix, defining the formal structure of the game, remains invariant. Further, the threat is treated in such a way as to abstract from many of the interesting problems associated with this tactic (and other coercive notbluffs). This is so because the threat is treated as binding by definition. Thus, for example, Luce and Raiffa, in their treatment of the two-person cooperative game, explicitly assume that: "ii. All agreements are binding, and they are enforceable by the rules of the game." [10] This treatment sweeps under the rug the interesting problems of how (by what devices) a threat may be in point of fact committed.

Schelling has suggested that coercive notbluffs (threat, promise, commitment) might (in principle at least) be brought within the formal structure of the analysis.[11] In a game-theory context, committing a threat essentially involves contriving by tactical maneuver to "rig" the payoff matrix to make the threatened strategy dominant over those the player wishes to abjure. Hence, a threat could be incorporated in a game matrix by appropriate alterations in the original matrix. Schelling shows how a "super-game" (in normal form) might be built up, constructing pure strategies out of the original strategies available and the sequence of "moves" (including tactical possibilities of threat, promise, and so forth, available). As he emphasizes, however, we cannot learn anything about these tactics by studying games in normal form. The interesting tactical problems are essentially buried in the concept of a strategy.

We may sum up the discussion in this section. Generally speaking, the format of game-theory analysis is such as to exclude from the analysis many negotiatory phenomena of prime importance and interest. Tactical entities which may be accommodated by the analysis, for example, coercive notbluffs, are treated outside the formal structure of the game and in such a way as to abstract from the most interesting problems associated with them. Although in principle some such tactics ("moves") might be incorporated in the game matrix, the analytical gain to be had thereby is not immediately obvious.

SOLUTION CONCEPTS

As the preceding discussion may imply, in the study of abstract games in general, the interest frequently is less in the process of play and more in the outcome, particularly in definition of the "solution" in terms of the outcome. We might grant that the format of game-theory analysis does not accommodate, and in consequence the analysis does not throw much light upon, many of the negotiatory phenomena in which the investigator of collective bargaining is apt to be interested. However, might the student of collective bargaining not gain some insights by scrutiny of solution concepts in the game-theory context, that is, notions which will help him to predict, or perhaps (normatively) to characterize outcomes—regardless of the tactical routes to these?

On this score, game theory at present does not seem to offer much help. The von Neumann-Morgenstern solution in the two-person cooperative game case yields a "negotiation set" (very roughly speaking, analogous to a "contract zone") within which multiplicity of payoffs the actual outcome selected is held to be indeterminate insofar as game theory is concerned.[12] The actual outcome, not specified, is then held to depend upon negotiation and bargaining behavior, and in a sense, the theory of negotiation begins where this sort of "solution" leaves off. To be very helpful, the solution concept must specify some unique point as the solution.

A well-known suggestion of this sort is that of John Nash.[13] Nash offers as a solution to the bargaining problem that point (pair of payoffs) for which the product of the utilities accruing to the two players is a maximum. This "solution" is not to be treated as a prediction of what the actual outcome of bargaining will be. Nor does it seem to carry normative connotations in any general social sense. Luce and Raiffa suggest that the Nash solution be treated as an arbitration scheme—a "rule" which yields a payoff consistent with certain principles of "fairness" or "reasonableness" in an arbitrated outcome of a bargaining conflict of interest.

Although an evaluation of the Nash solution from this point of view is not warranted here, this comment should be made. Students of collective bargaining primarily interested in "descriptive" science (theories which predict the occurrence of events) will tend naturally to turn away from any "solution" concept of cooperative games which conceptualizes the solution in terms of an arbitration scheme. However, even with the solution concept so envisioned, there are problems of considerable interest even to the descriptively oriented investigator. This is so because if arbitration occurs, the arbitrated interaction will be one variant in a game-variant sequence. We saw that an important aspect of the analysis of such sequences was concerned with the interaction between the variants in the sequence—the mutual influence of each variant in the sequence upon the play and solution of the others. Thus, for example, a game-variant 2 will not be "efficient" as a sequel to a variant 1 if the possibility of electing 2 leads to the virtual abandonment of 1. A case in point is the potential effect upon the prearbitration negotiation of a provision for binding arbitration in the event of a strike. Clearly, the rules which characterize any arbitration scheme are potentially important from this point of view. Also, we saw that for a game-variant 2 to be "relevant" as a sequel to 1, the former perhaps should reflect the sanctions upon which the play of 1 was based in the first place. This suggests the problem of the degree to which any given arbitration scheme reflects (in the outcome it yields) the basic power relationship underlying the prearbitration bargaining, and in consequence yields a result consonant with what would have been the outcome of the initial game-variant.

What is here suggested is that the concept of game-variant sequences, where the analytical concern is with the mutual influence of each variant in the sequence, provides a way in which to relate arbitration schemes to analysis of the whole of collective bargaining negotiation. Further, this relation is of interest to descriptively oriented inquiry, that is, of interest whether or not the investigator has particular interest in the normative implications of an arbitration scheme.

"UNNATURAL" GAMES AND THE MINIMAX THEOREM

It will be recalled from Chapter II that an unnatural game is one in which pressures generated in the choice situation impel the parties to seek strategies in addition to those made available by the existing rules for play. This concept is important because players of purposive social games have some control over the rules for play. Confronted with rules for play which create an unnatural choice problem, they may be expected to respond not only by attempting optimal play of the extant game, but also by operations on the rules for play themselves.

It may be argued that, since unnatural games evoke responses designed to eliminate them, such games will tend to be transitory phenomena in a historical sense. In consequence, game analysis intended to bear on social games should perhaps concentrate on natural games. At least, the game analyst should query, with respect to game formats which appear to be unnatural in the above sense, whether the response of operating upon the rules structure of the game is not apt to be prepotent as contrasted with optimal play of the extant game.

Notions analogous to that of the unnatural game appear in game-theory discussions. A case in point concerns "The Prisoner's Dilemma." This is a frustrating game in that what appear to be the optimal strategies yield results which are perverse from an intuitive point of view. Luce and Raiffa, in commenting on this game, observe: "The hopelessness that one feels in such a game as this cannot be overcome by a play on the words 'rational' and 'irrational'; it is inherent in the situation. 'There should be a law against such games.' Indeed, some hold the view that one essential role of government is to declare that the rules of certain social 'games' must be changed whenever it is inherent in the game situation that the players, in pursuing their own ends, will be forced into a socially undesirable position." [14]

Another unnatural-game concept, of particular interest in the light of the Chapter II discussion, is Ellsberg's characterization of the players envisaged by game theory as "reluctant duelists." [15] He points out that if we consider any game in which each matrix row contains at least one negative element, and add to it a strategy (row of zeros) which represents "standing pat" (not playing)—the minimax player would elect the latter, regardless of how small the possible losses or how great the possible gains with the other strategies. This leads to the query: Why should a player bother to play the game at all if he prefers the certainty of zero to the chance of winning or losing? In Ellsberg's view, the rationale of the minimax strategy is much more convincing if we assume situations in which the individual is forced to make decisions. That is, the minimax theorem directs the player to the least ominous choice in a game he would rather not play. Reporting the results of putting the above query to a prominent game theorist, he notes: "his unconsidered reply, presumably intended as no more than a partial answer, was that in many situations one *must* play a game, even against one's wishes." [16]

The same query might be presented with respect to the avoidance-avoidance conflict-choice model. Why should an actor "bother to" participate in an avoidance–avoidance choice at all? The answer is that an actor should be expected to escape from such a choice situation unless somehow constrained to participate in it. In social situations, important instances of such constraint are those in which the avoidance–avoidance choice is tied to a positive goal. [17] A case in point is collective bargaining negotiation. The parties are constrained to "play the game" by the fact that they are mutually dependent. However, given that they are thus constrained to make the choice, the analytically significant aspects of that choice may be comprehended under the rubric of the avoidance–avoidance model. Thus the quotation in the preceding paragraph contains an important element of truth.

In the preceding sense, the "reluctant duelist" may be a much more general social phenomenon than one might at first suppose. However, and reluctant though he may be, such a duelist will prefer not to resolve his conflict by playing an unnatural game. He will want a choice of weapons. Thus, it was argued earlier, an actor confronting an avoidance–avoidance choice set up by an interpersonal conflict will prefer to resolve the interaction by playing "negotiation" rather than, "take-it-or-leave-it." The difficulty with the game-theory formulation *vis-à-vis* this kind of choice may not be so much that its prescriptions for prudential play imply a reluctant duelist as it is that the duelist is not afforded an appropriate choice of weapons. From this point of view, the prisoner's-dilemma format represents a conflict-choice situation which generates pressures impelling the players to resolve their conflict through negotiation, with rules for play appropriate to the defection problems inherent in this matrix, and so forth. [18] The whole issue of what constitutes "rational" noncooperative play of a game format such as this may be rather less significant from the point of view of social science analysis than the game-design issue—that is, what rules for play are "natural" for a choice situation described by such a format.

From one point of view, the avoidance-avoidance conflict-choice model may be thought of as representing a (subjective) behavioral process which "resolves" a conflict-choice situation by the definition ("introduction") of intermediate points in what would otherwise be a "discrete" opportunity function. [19] A negotiation game related to such a choice may be considered a technique for making intermediate points so defined actually available to the actors (that is, facilitating the actual introduction of such points into an opportunity function which would be, under take-it-or-leave-it rules for play, discrete). These considerations have a bearing upon interpretation of those (zero-sum) games in which there are no pure-strategy equilibrium pairs. In these games, the minimax prescription in terms of pure strategies does not provide the players with a resting place.[20] That is, the expectations of each about his opposite number's choice of strategy do not lead them to converge upon a particular pair of strategies as an equilibrium pair. From each player's point of view, the reasons for electing a particular strategy turn out to be all the more reason for electing some other, and the chain of expectations goes in circles. Luce and Raiffa note that the argument in terms of players' expectations in such cases seems to lead to the position that the players should be indifferent as to their available choices. Such games do have an equilibrium solution in terms of mixed (randomized) strategies, a solution which raises the security level of each. A mixed strategy is supposed to select some one pure strategy from among those available for actual play of the game.

A question exists as to whether a player would ever (or would ever be well advised to) play a mixed strategy in this sense. Without general discussion of this question, the following aspect of it, suggested by the preceding considerations, may be briefly noted. In games where there are no pure-strategy equilibrium pairs, the argument in terms of players' expectations may lead to the conclusion that the players should be indifferent as to their available strategies. The argument in terms of players' expectations might better lead, however, to the conclusion that such players will be conflicted. In such games, the role of mixed (randomized) strategies may be viewed as precisely that of "resolving" (actually, that of representing) an intrapersonal conflict in somewhat the same way that the avoidance–avoidance conflict-choice model "resolves" (represents) such a conflict. That is, from one point of view, strategy randomization in game theory is a technique for "introducing" intermediate positions into what would otherwise be a discrete opportunity function.[21] The positions thus "introduced" are not available, however, since the randomization serves simply to select some one pure strategy for actual play. These considerations suggest the following line of argument:

(a) Conflict choice situations in which mixed strategies are appropriate impel the actors to "play" such strategies in the sense of "occupying" an equilibrium position analogous to a mixed strategy.

(b) But, the conflict-choice situation which impels "play" of a mixed strategy in the sense of (a) also makes play of such a strategy in the sense of using it to elect some pure strategy inappropriate.

(c) Rather than simply agree to play a mixed strategy in the conventional sense, the actor may respond by attempting to operate on the rules for play. He may devise techniques for incorporating mixed strategies into his opportunity function in the form of "physical" mixtures of the pure strategies—he may resort to negotiation.

Bibliography

Allen, James L., and C. Wilson Randle: "Challenge of the Guaranteed Annual Wage," *Harvard Business Review*, 32:37–48 (May-June 1954).

Backman, Jules: *Wage Determination, An Analysis of Wage Criteria* (New York: Van Nostrand, 1959).

Bakke, E. Wight: "Mutual Survival after Twelve Years," Presidential Address, Eleventh Annual Meeting of the Industrial Relations Research Association, IRRA *Proceedings*, December, 1958.

"The Basic Steel Companies and Steelworkers Agreement," *Monthly Labor Review*, 83:161–163 (February 1960).

Bloom, Gordon F., and Herbert R. Northrup: *Economics of Labor Relations,* 3rd ed. (Homewood, Ill.: Richard D. Irwin, Inc., 1958).

Bowles, George E.: "The G. A. W. Negotiations," *Labor Law Journal*, 6:566–571 (August 1955).

Chamberlain, Neil W.: *Collective Bargaining* (New York: McGraw-Hill, 1951).

———: *A General Theory of Economic Process* (New York: Harper & Brothers, 1955).

———: *Social Responsibility and Strikes* (New York: Harper & Brothers, 1953).

———: *Sourcebook on Labor* (New York: McGraw-Hill, 1958).

———: *The Union Challenge to Management Control* (New York: Harper & Brothers, 1948).

———, Frank E. Pierson, and Theresa Wolfson, eds.: *A Decade of Industrial Relations Research—1946–1956* (New York: Harper & Brothers, 1958).

Cole, David L.: "Observations on the Nature and Function of Mediation," University of Pennsylvania Conference, April 10, 1953.

Commons, John R.: *The Economics of Collective Action* (New York: The Macmillan Co., 1950).

Cox, Archibald, and John T. Dunlop: "The Duty to Bargain Collectively During the Term of an Existing Agreement," *Harvard Law Review,* 63:1097–1133 (May 1950).

Dollard, John, and Neal E. Miller: *Personality and Psychotherapy* (New York: McGraw-Hill, 1950).

Douglas, Ann: "What Can Research Tell Us About Mediation," *Labor Law Journal,* 6:545–552 (August 1955).

Downing, Thomas G.: "Strategy and Tactics at the Bargaining Table," *Personnel*, January-February 1960, pp. 58–63.

Dunlop, John T.: *Industrial Relations Systems* (New York: Henry Holt & Co., Inc., 1959).

———, ed.: *The Theory of Wage Determination*, Proceedings of a Conference held by the International Economic Association (London: MacMillan & Co., Ltd., 1957).

———, and James J. Healy: *Collective Bargaining: Principles and Cases*, revised edition (Homewood, Ill.: Richard D. Irwin, Inc., 1955).

Ellsberg, Daniel: "Rejoinder," *The Review of Economics and Statistics*, 41:42–44 (February 1959).

———: "Theory of the Reluctant Duelist," *The American Economic Review*, 46:909–923 (December 1956).

Flanders, Allan, and H. A. Clegg, eds.: *The System of Industrial Relations in Great Britain* (Oxford: Basil Blackwell & Mott, Ltd., 1954).

Golden, Clinton S., and Virginia D. Parker, eds.: *Causes of Industrial Peace under Collective Bargaining* (Washington, D.C.: National Planning Association, 1955).

Graham, Frank P.: "Maintenance of Membership: A Historical Note," *Labor Law Journal*, 6:560–1 (August 1955).

Gregory, C. O.: *Labor and the Law*, 2nd rev. ed. (New York: W. W. Norton & Co., 1958).

Harbison, Frederick H., and John R. Coleman: *Goals and Strategy in Collective Bargaining* (New York: Harper & Brothers, 1951).

Hicks, J. R.: *The Theory of Wages* (New York: Peter Smith, 1948).

Holzman, Mathilda: "Theories of Choice and Conflict in Psychology and Economics," *The Journal of Conflict Resolution*, 2:310–320 (December 1958).

Hull, Clark Leonard: *Essentials of Behavior* (New Haven: Yale Univ. Press, 1951).

Jackson, Elmore: *Meeting of Minds—A Way to Peace Through Mediation* (New York: McGraw-Hill, 1952).

Kerr, Clark: "Industrial Conflict and its Mediation," *The American Journal of Sociology*, 60:230–245 (November 1954).

Koo, Anthony Y. C.: "Recurrent Objections to the Minimax Strategy," *The Review of Economics and Statistics*, 41:36–41 (February 1959).

Kornhauser, A. W., R. Dubin, A. Ross, eds.: *Industrial Conflict* (New York: McGraw-Hill, 1954).

Kuhn, James W.: "Democracy in Grievance Settlement, the Workers' Challenge to the Union," (MS.) Columbia Univ., New York, 1959.

Landsberger, Henry A.: "Final Report on a Research Project in Mediation," *Labor Law Journal*, 7:501–510 (August 1956).

———: "Interim Report of a Research Project in Mediation," *Labor Law Journal*, 6:552–560 (August 1955).

Leiserson, William M.: "The Functions of Mediation in Labor Relations"

Industrial Relations Research Association, Proceedings of Fourth Annual Meeting, December 1951, p. 5.

Lewis, Ben W.: "Economics by Admonition," *The American Economic Review*, 49:384–398 (May 1959).

Lindblom, Charles E.: *Unions and Capitalism* (New Haven: Yale Univ. Press, 1949).

Logan, F. A., D. Olmsted, B. S. Rosner, R. D. Schwartz, C. M. Stevens: *Behavior Theory and Social Science* (New Haven: Yale Univ. Press, 1955).

Lovell, Hugh G.: "The Pressure Lever in Mediation," *Industrial and Labor Relations Review*, October 1952.

Luce, R. Duncan, and Howard Raiffa: *Games and Decisions* (New York: John Wiley & Sons, Inc., 1957).

Mason, Edward S., ed.: *The Corporation in Modern Society* (Cambridge, Mass.: Harvard Univ. Press, 1959).

McMurry, Robert W.: "War and Peace in Labor Relations," *Harvard Business Review*, 33:48–60 (November–December 1955).

Meyer, Arthur S.: "Function of the Mediator in Collective Bargaining," *Industrial and Labor Relations Review*, January, 1960.

Meyers, Frederic: "Right to Work in Practice," The Fund for the Republic, 1959.

Miller, Neal E., and John Dollard: *Social Learning and Imitation* (New Haven: Yale Univ. Press, 1941).

Monthly Labor Review, Volumes 79, 80, 81 and 82, December 1956 through April 1959.

Nash, John: "Two-Person Co-operative Games," *Econometrica*, 21:128–140 (January 1953).

The New York Times, April 1959.

The Oregonian-The Oregon Journal (Portland, Oregon) "Strike Facts," February 1960.

Papandreou, Andreas G., and John T. Wheeler: *Competition and Its Regulation* (New York: Prentice-Hall, Inc., 1954).

Pen, J., *The Wage Rate under Collective Bargaining*, translated by T. S. Preston (Cambridge: Harvard Univ. Press, 1959).

———: "A General Theory of Bargaining," *The American Economic Review*, 42:24–42 (March 1952).

Peters, Edward: *Conciliation in Action* (New London: National Foremen's Institute, Inc., 1952).

———: *Strategy and Tactics in Labor Negotiations* (New London: National Foremen's Institute, Inc., 1955).

Pigou, A. C.: *The Economics of Welfare*, 4th ed. (New York: The Macmillan Co., 1950).

Reder, M. W.: "The Theory of Union Wage Policy," *The Review of Economics and Statistics*, 34:34–45 (February 1952).

Report to the President by the Emergency Board (appointed pursuant to the Railway Labor Act), Emergency Board No. 130, June 8, 1960.

Reynolds, Lloyd G.: *Labor Economics and Labor Relations,* 2d ed. (New York: Prentice-Hall, Inc., 1954).

Ryder, M. S.: "Strategy in Collective Bargaining Negotiations," *Labor Law Journal,* 7:353–358 (June 1956).

Schelling, T. C.: *The Strategy of Conflict* (Cambridge, Mass.: Harvard Univ. Press, 1960).

———: "Bargaining, Communication and Limited War," *The Journal of Conflict Resolution,* 1:19–36 (March 1957).

———: "An Essay on Bargaining," *The American Economic Review,* 46:281–306 (June 1956).

———: "For the Abandonment of Symmetry in Game Theory," *The Review of Economics and Statistics,* 41:213–224 (August 1959).

———: "The Strategy of Conflict: Prospectus for a Reorientation of Game Theory," *The Journal of Conflict Resolution,* 2:203–264 (September 1958).

Selekman, Benjamin M.: *Labor Relations and Human Relations* (New York: McGraw-Hill, 1947).

———, Selekman, Sylvia Kopland, and Fuller, Stephen H., *Problems in Labor Relations,* 2nd ed. (New York: McGraw-Hill, 1958).

Shackle, G. L. S.: *Expectation in Economics* (London: Cambridge Univ. Press, 1949).

Siegel, Sidney, and Lawrence E. Fouraker: *Bargaining and Group Decision Making* (New York: McGraw-Hill, 1960).

Soffer, Benson: "The Effects of Recent Long-Term Wage Agreements on General Wage Level Movements: 1950–1956," *The Quarterly Journal of Economics,* 73:36–60 (February 1959).

Stagner, Ross: *Psychology of Industrial Conflict* (New York: John Wiley & Sons, Inc., 1956).

Stark, Arthur: Introduction to "New Vistas in Mediation," Proceedings of the Fourth Annual Conference Association of State Mediation Agencies, Ithaca, New York, June 1955, *Labor Law Journal,* 6:523–524 (August 1955).

Stevens, Carl M.: "A Note on Conflict Choice in Economics and Psychology," *The Journal of Conflict Resolution,* 4:220–224 (June 1960).

———: "On the Theory of Negotiation," *The Quarterly Journal of Economics,* 72:77–97 (February 1958).

———: "Regarding the Determinants of Union Wage Policy," *The Review of Economics and Statistics,* 35:221–228 (August 1953).

Taylor, George W.: *Government Regulation of Industrial Relations* (New York: Prentice-Hall, Inc., 1948).

———, and F. C. Pierson, ed.: *New Concepts in Wage Determination* (New York: McGraw-Hill, 1957).

Ulman, Lloyd: *The Rise of the National Trade Union* (Cambridge, Mass.: Harvard Univ. Press, 1956).

U.S. Bureau of Labor Statistics, Dept. of Labor, Bull. No. 908–9: *Collective Bargaining Provisions—Wage Adjustment Plans* (Washington, D.C.: Government Printing Office, 1948).

U.S. Dept. of Labor: *Termination Report of the National War Labor Board*, 3 vols. (Washington, D.C.: Government Printing Office, 1948).

Weisenfeld, Allan, and Monroe Berkowitz: "A New Look in Collective Bargaining," *Labor Law Journal*, 6:561–566 (August 1955).

Weschler, Irving R.: "The Personal Factor in Labor Mediation," *Personnel Psychology*, vol. 3, no. 2.

Willis, Richard H., and Myron L. Joseph: "Bargaining Behavior I: 'Prominence' as a Predictor of the Outcome of Games of Agreement," *The Journal of Conflict Resolution*, 3:102–113 (June 1959).

Wilson, Bernard: "Conciliation Officers' Techniques in Settling Disputes," paper prepared for discussion at the Eighteenth Annual Conference of the Canadian Association of Administrators of Labour Legislation, Quebec, September, 1959.

Notes

CHAPTER I. SUBJECT MATTER CONTEXT AND THE NEGOTIATION MODEL

1. *See* Neil W. Chamberlain, *A General Theory of Economic Process* (New York, 1955), esp. Chaps. 6, 7, and 8. As Chamberlain illustrates, the concept "bargaining power" may be elaborated with respect to numerous transactions in which no negotiation takes place.

2. The exchange of information need not be of the *vis-à-vis* variety, nor need it involve verbalization.

3. John T. Dunlop, *Industrial Relations Systems* (New York, 1958).

4. John R. Commons, *The Economics of Collective Action* (New York, 1950).

5. Clark Kerr, "Industrial Conflict and its Mediation," *The American Journal of Sociology*, 60:231 (November 1954). Kerr notes that although the expansibility of the income pie may be quite significant, the power pie is always fixed in dimensions. In this connection, Ross Stagner, *Psychology of Industrial Conflict* (New York, 1956), p. 291, has observed:

> The evidence has indicated two basic aspects of industrial conflict: first, conflicts over the distribution of economic returns from industry; second, conflicts over ego satisfaction, power, and recognition. If we concede, as seems almost necessary, that the significance of economic gain in American society is very largely related to the ego status of the individual and to his sense of power, and if we recognize also that economic power gives the individual an opportunity to increase his monetary return from industry, then we might even succeed in boiling down this formulation by saying that there is only one single type of industrial conflict, namely, conflict over power.

Conflict of interest inheres not only in the industrial relations system but also in the economy more generally. Ben W. Lewis, "Economics by Admonition," *The American Economic Review*, 49:385 (May 1959), has observed:

> Economizing by its very nature involves the disposition of conflicting claims, all of which may be reasonable and "good." All economic decisions are related and interdependent, and if our decisions are well taken, we purchase our satisfactions at the cost of other satisfactions foregone.

6. Collective bargaining is a symbiotic relationship, involving both elements of cooperation and elements of conflict. The functions of collective bargaining negotiation reflect this "mixed"-game nature of the underlying relationship. For

a discussion of this point *see* Benjamin M. Selekman, *Labor Relations and Human Relations* (New York, 1947), Chap. IX, "Conflict and Cooperation." For an excellent recent discussion of the antagonistic and cooperative elements in the bargaining relationship, *see* E. Wight Bakke, "Mutual Survival After Twelve Years," Presidential Address, *Eleventh Annual Meeting of the Industrial Relations Research Association, IRRA Proceedings,* December 1958, pp. 2–18. Harbison has expressed the view that although collective bargaining has its roots in a conflict of interest between capital and labor, it is really an instrument for furthering industrial peace. *See* Frederick H. Harbison, "Collective Bargaining and American Capitalism," *Industrial Conflict,* A. W. Kornhauser, R. Dubin, A. Ross, eds. (New York, 1954), p. 271.

7. In this connection it has been noted that union awareness of its responsibility to the membership ("bringing in" the membership by one technique or another) is one of the important factors making for peace in collective bargaining negotiation. F. H. Harbison and John R. Coleman, "Procedures and Methods," *Causes of Industrial Peace under Collective Bargaining,* Clinton S. Golden and Virginia D. Parker, eds. (Washington, D.C., 1955), p. 45.

8. Frederick H. Harbison and John R. Coleman, *Goals and Strategy in Collective Bargaining* (New York, 1951). *See also* the typology of bargaining relationships (in terms of "patterns of power bargaining") developed by Selekman. Benjamin M. Selekman, Sylvia Kopland Selekman, and Stephen H. Fuller, *Problems in Labor Relations* (2d ed.; New York, 1958).

9. The distinction between contract negotiation and contract administration raises important problems for interpretation of the statutory (L.M.R.A.) requirement of the parties "to bargain collectively" (Sections 8 [a] [5], 8 [b] [3], and 8 [d]). For an excellent discussion of this matter, *see* Archibald Cox and John T. Dunlop, "The Duty to Bargain Collectively During the Term of an Existing Agreement," *Harvard Law Review,* 63:1097–1133 (May 1950). The authors feel that clear recognition of this distinction by the NLRB is important to the proper functioning of collective bargaining.

10. It must be recognized that the line between contract negotiation and contract administration is not as finely drawn as the text may suggest; at some point the two tend to shade one into the other. Further, in some cases the parties, while not openly disavowing the grievance procedure, may subvert that machinery to the ends of substantive negotiation and may resort to such pressures as the wildcat strike, slowdown, overtime ban, and so forth, between periodic agreement conferences. An interesting discussion of this matter is James W. Kuhn, "Democracy in Grievance Settlement, the Workers' Challenge to the Union," (MS) Columbia University, New York, 1959.

11. Stagner, *Psychology of Industrial Conflict,* Chap. XIII.

12. Although collective bargaining is game-like, it is neither feasible nor (at this stage of development of the analysis) analytically helpful to represent the process as a game in the technical sense of this term. This does not mean, however, that consideration of simple, abstract games may not be of some use in analysis of aspects of collective bargaining. (*See* Appendix II for discussion of application of game theory in analysis of negotiation.)

13. T. C. Schelling, "The Strategy of Conflict: Prospectus for a Reorientation of Game Theory," *The Journal of Conflict Resolution,* 2:206 ff. (September 1958), has remarked upon the difficulty in finding a sufficiently "rich" name for the mixed game, observing that we have no very good word for the relationship between the parties in such cases. Perhaps the words symbiotic and symbionts

fill this need. They are suggested for use in this context by Chamberlain, *A General Theory*, pp. 74 ff.

14. *See* John T. Dunlop and James J. Healy, *Collective Bargaining: Principles and Cases*, revised edition (Homewood, Ill., 1955), pp. 61 ff., for a discussion of the "stages" of typical contract negotiations.

CHAPTER II. CONFLICT-CHOICE MODEL OF NEGOTIATION

1. This chapter is in part adapted from the author's previous article, "On the Theory of Negotiation, "*The Quarterly Journal of Economics,* 72:77–97 (February 1958).

2. *See,* for example, a list of "Questions to be Answered by a Theory of Bargaining," suggested by G. L. S. Shackle, "The Nature of the Bargaining Process," *The Theory of Wage Determination,* Proceedings of a Conference held by the International Economic Association, John T. Dunlop, ed. (London, 1957), Chapter XIX. Shackle comments upon the weakness from a theory-construction point of view of any such list of questions intended to define the task of a theory.

3. In modern-utility theory, "preference" is operationally defined in terms of overt choice behavior. The empirical input to the theory is generalization on a sample of choice behavior. Interest in the analysis inheres in the matter of consistency of (patterns of) choice behavior—"explanation" of choice behavior entering only in this sense. In this chapter, technical aspects of utility theory—distinctions between utility analysis and preference analysis, between cardinal and ordinal utility, and so forth—may be neglected.

4. Although of considerable interest in this context, a general discussion of conflict *vs.* nonconflict choice theory in economic and psychological analysis is beyond the scope of this inquiry. The reader is referred to Mathilda Holzman, "Theories of Choice and Conflict in Psychology and Economics," *The Journal of Conflict Resolution,* 2:310–320 (December 1958); also to the author's comment upon Holzman's article, "A Note on Conflict Choice in Economics and Psychology," *The Journal of Conflict Resolution,* 4:220–224 (June 1960).

5. The model described is that developed by Neal E. Miller. *See* John Dollard and Neal E. Miller, *Personality and Psychotherapy* (New York, 1950). Dollard and Miller do not apply this model to the negotiation problem.

6. *See* Dollard and Miller, *Personality and Psychotherapy,* for a discussion of the inductive and deductive bases for these hypotheses.

7. Figure 1 is adapted from Dollard and Miller, *Personality and Psychotherapy,* p. 364. The linear assumptions incorporated in this figure are not intended to be significant; that is, any functions with continuous negative slopes yield the results adduced.

8. With respect to Figure 1, if A and B were positive goals, and AA and BB approach (rather than avoidance) gradients, then the model would be of the unstable-equilibrium type. Given a displacement from equilibrium, the actor would continue to the goal.

9. Such considerations as the existence of a statutory requirement to bargain are not at this point relevant.

10. This was indeed very much the way in which collective bargaining was carried on in this country in the early nineteenth century. As far as the point made in this section is concerned, we might alternatively suppose the company to quote the terms unilaterally. The analysis herein applies to both cases.

11. This way of looking at the matter is in line with Hicks' depiction of the em-

NOTES   169

ployer's position in the bargaining situation: "Either he must pay higher wages than he would have paid on his own initiative [and this generally means a prolonged reduction in profits] or on the other hand must endure the direct loss which will probably follow from a stoppage of work." *See* J. R. Hicks, *The Theory of Wages* (New York, 1948), pp. 141 ff. *See also* Neil W. Chamberlain, *Collective Bargaining* (New York, 1951), Chap. X. Chamberlain adopts a modification of Hicks' view.

12. Such a rationality-principle argument can be made. Suppose that a solution "no deal" has an extremely low value. Suppose further that, as contrasted with negotiation, take-it-or-leave-it greatly increases the chance of such an outcome. Then one might choose to resolve the transaction by negotiation precisely because this increases the expected payoff.

13. Adaptation of the avoidance–avoidance model to analysis of collective bargaining results in visualizing that process as similar in many ways to approaches suggested in the literature. *See* Hicks, *The Theory of Wages*, pp. 141 ff. Compare also Chamberlain's definition of "bargaining power." Chamberlain, *Collective Bargaining*, Chap. X. Using Hicks' analysis as a point of departure, Chamberlain defines A's bargaining power *vis-à-vis* B as the ratio of the cost to B of disagreeing with A on A's terms to the cost to B of agreeing with A on A's terms. The significant thing about Chamberlain's concept of bargaining power is not that it results in a coefficient of that power in any particular situation. Rather, it is the theory of the negotiation process implied by it. His scheme, unlike much discussion of bargaining, recognizes both what we have termed Class I and Class II tactics. Beyond such similarities to the avoidance–avoidance model, there are also important differences. For example, Chamberlain does not develop any explicit equilibrium theory of conflict-choice situations. Thus his scheme does not explain why it is that if, in his terms, A's coefficient of bargaining power *vis-à-vis* B is greater than one, B doesn't simply settle on A's terms—rather than go on bargaining (as, he indicates, may indeed be the case).

14. It might be objected that these classes of tactics are not really independent. That is, that a tactic which will increase the company's tendency to avoid its own position (Class I) will, at the same time, decrease the company's tendency to avoid the union's position (Class II). The implications of this way of putting the matter are misleading. It is true, of course, that a union tactic which will move the company's equilibrium position farther from the company's goal B (maintaining its own position) will, at the same time, move that equilibrium position closer to the company's goal A (settling on the union's terms). However, tactics of Classes I and II are not distinguished in terms of movements of equilibrium position, but in terms of movements of the avoidance gradients. In these latter terms, the independence of the two classes seems plausible. In the instant example, the company's avoidance tendencies are based upon calculation of expected cost associated with paying a higher rate, on the one hand, and a strike, on the other. Let us suppose, for example, that the information exchanged during negotiation will revise downward the company's estimate of the cost associated with paying a higher rate (a successful union Class II tactic). There is no *prima facie* reason to suppose that this tactic must necessarily have a Class I effect.

15. J. Pen's theory of bargaining bases theoretical determinacy of the wage rate under collective bargaining upon an equality of equilibrium conditions (these developed in terms of utility theory). His analysis appears, however, to neglect the second major function of negotiation as above distinguished. *See* J. Pen,

The Wage Rate under Collective Bargaining, translated by T. S. Preston (Cambridge, 1959). Pen's theory is discussed in Appendix I.

16. There has been considerable discussion of the determinacy of the outcome under collective bargaining. For recent comments on this issue, *see* Shackle, "The Nature of the Bargaining Process," Chap. XIX, Dunlop, ed., *The Theory of Wage Determination. See also* Pen, *The Wage Rate under Collective Bargaining.*

17. Although this factor is important in some negotiations, Edward Peters, *Conciliation in Action* (New London, 1952), pp. 28–29, after warning against an overemphasis upon the emotional factor and pointing out that disputes are based first and foremost upon the relative strengths of the parties, goes on to point out: "This does not mean that deadlocks are not marked by a tense emotional atmosphere. It does mean taking into account that the contestants usually exhibit strong emotions because of the issues between them, and not, as is often supposed, that there are issues between them because of angry passions and deep emotions. The emotions are not the cause of the deadlock. They are one of its effects." Quoted by permission from National Foremen's Institute, division of Prentice-Hall, Inc. Waterford, Connecticut.

18. This matter is discussed in Appendix II.

19. On this point, *see* T. C. Schelling, "For the Abandonment of Symmetry in Game Theory," *The Review of Economics and Statistics,* 41:213–224 (August 1959).

20. George W. Taylor, *Government Regulation of Industrial Relations* (New York, 1948), p. 362.

21. "Unnatural" games will be further discussed, in connection with game theory, in Appendix II.

CHAPTER III. RULES FOR PLAY OF THE NEGOTIATION GAME

1. There is a problem here in distinguishing periodic negotiation of the contract and administration of the contract under the grievance machinery. Whether in fact an existing agreement serves as a bar to further substantive negotiation depends, in part, upon NLRB interpretation of the statutory obligation (National Labor Relations Act) to bargain collectively. Section 8 (d) of the act requires each party to serve written notice of proposed modification of an existing contract sixty days prior to its expiration date (or sixty days prior to the time it is proposed to make the modifications in question). This section further provides that the parties must continue in full force and effect the terms of the existing contract, with no resort to strike or lock-out, for a period of sixty days after such notice, or until the expiration date of the contract, whichever occurs later.

2. For a discussion of wage adjustment plans, see U.S. Bureau of Labor Statistics, Dept. of Labor, Bull. No. 908–909, *Collective Bargaining Provisions—Wage Adjustment Plans* (1948).

3. *See Monthly Labor Review,* 79:1452 (December 1956); 80:80–81 (January 1957).

4. *See* Allan Flanders and H. A. Cleggs (eds.), *The System of Industrial Relations in Great Britain* (Oxford, 1954), pp. 291–292. Flanders notes that this aspect of collective bargaining in Great Britain is one "which we are inclined to take for granted," but he does not then go on to elucidate. He does imply that widespread willingness in England to resort to arbitration of labor disputes may be a factor involved. Dunlop has suggested that collective agreements of indefinite duration can be accommodated in an industrial relations system where

the process of setting new terms and conditions of employment is of uncertain and lengthy duration. John T. Dunlop, *Industrial Relations Systems* (New York, 1958), pp. 70–71

5. With many nonpurposive games, the relative "power" position of the players is not significantly a function of the extra-game environment. In consequence, game theory elaborated with respect to such games may well afford to neglect the rule for beginning each play in the sense developed in the text. This should not, however, lead investigators of social games to similar neglect.

6. One issue of interest in this context is that of the relative effect, if any, of the longer-term General Motors-type agreements (as contrasted with conventional agreements) on the general level of wages. For a discussion of this matter, *see* Benson Soffer, "The Effects of Recent Long-Term Wage Agreements on General Wage Level Movements: 1950–1956," *The Quarterly Journal of Economics,* 73:36–60 (February 1959).

7. *See Report to the President by the Emergency Board* (appointed pursuant to the Railway Labor Act), Emergency Board No. 130, June 8, 1960, p. 7.

8. *See* Lloyd Ulman, *The Rise of the National Trade Union* (Cambridge, 1956), Chap. XIV, "National Strike Policies"—from which this account of national union policies was derived; 144.

9. Prior to the recent steel strike, *The New York Times,* April 6, 1959, p. 39, said few steel users were betting that there would not be a strike and that soon most steel users would have accumulated substantial steel inventories.

10. *See* Dept. of Labor Bull. No. 908–9, *Collective Bargaining Provisions,* pp. 22 ff.

11. John T. Dunlop and James J. Healy, *Collective Bargaining: Principles and Cases,* revised edition (Homewood, Ill., 1955), p. 54.

12. Although the major alternative to the large demand is the minimum demand, the "small" demand is possible as a rule for beginning. The small demand is a party's initial bargaining demand less favorable to himself than the least favorable terms upon which he expects to settle. Specification of a minimal acceptable bid in opening an auction is an example of the small demand. The small demand may be useful in setting up subsequent negotiations. This would be the case in negotiations in which there existed no *status quo* upon which to begin the bargaining, or in which, although there existed an inherent *status quo,* it had been made irrelevant. Collective bargaining is a continuing relationship, contract negotiations are frequent, and usually there does exist a relevant *status quo* upon which to base the negotiations. Further, the small demand is inappropriate to negotiations in bilateral monopoly generally. A seller's (or a buyer's) small demand is an efficacious way to start the ball rolling in a context in which he may feel quite sure that subsequent competition among buyers (or sellers) will set the agreed price satisfactorily above (or below) the initial level, a circumstance which bilateral monopoly precludes. The European institution of successive or pyramided wage bargains would seem to be related to the small-demand approach. In this case, there is an initial national wage policy agreement on some increase in rates. The national wage policy bargain then serves as a *status quo* upon which subsequent industry and company bargains are built.

13. For a discussion of Boulwareism, *see* Allan Weisenfeld and Monroe Berkowitz, "A New Look in Collective Bargaining," *Labor Law Journal,* 6:561–566 (August 1955); *see also* Robert W. McMurry, "War and Peace in Labor Relations," *Harvard Business Review,* 33:48–60 (November-December 1955).

14. On the union side, a close analogue to the minimum demand may arise when a local union negotiates under constraints imposed by international union "law."

A dramatic case in point is provided by the 1959 newspaper negotiations between the International Stereotypers' Union (and other unions) and *The Oregon Journal* and *The Oregonian*. These negotiations culminated in a strike, November 10, 1959, a strike which was still in progress more than a year later. Although several issues were involved, the principal one seems to have been the problem of manning requirements on a new M.A.N. (automatic) plate caster *The Oregonian* intended to install. W. R. Morrish, *The Oregonian* negotiator, has contended that: "From the very first the Stereotypers' committee said they couldn't bargain on manning or other subjects covered by their union laws." *See* "Strike Facts," a special section printed by *The Oregonian–The Oregon Journal,* undated, about February 15, 1960.

15. Clark Kerr, "Industrial Conflict and Its Mediation," *The American Journal of Sociology,* 60:237 (November 1954).
16. Edward Peters, *Strategy and Tactics in Labor Negotiations* (New London, 1955), pp. 101, 110.
17. McMurry, "War and Peace in Labor Relations," pp. 53, 59.
18. T. C. Schelling, "An Essay on Bargaining," *The American Economic Review,* 46:281–282 (June 1956).
19. T. C. Schelling, "The Strategy of Conflict: Prospectus," *The Journal of Conflict Resolution,* 2:224 (September 1958).
20. Weisenfeld, and Berkowitz, "A New Look," p. 564.
21. Schelling, "An Essay on Bargaining," p. 281.
22. R. Duncan Luce and Howard Raiffa, *Games and Decisions* (New York, 1957), pp. 110–111.
23. Schelling, "The Strategy of Conflict: Prospectus," pp. 237 ff. discusses this and other tactical aspects of communication and its destruction in game situations.
24. For discussion of these points, *see* Schelling, "An Essay on Bargaining," p. 290.
25. Although it is useful to comprehend some aspects of collective bargaining negotiation in terms of separable, successive "moves," in general such negotiation does not feature successive moves. *See,* for example, the discussion of the "commitment" in Chapter V.
26. For an interesting discussion of the GAW demand, *see* James L. Allen and C. Wilson Randle, "Challenge of the Guaranteed Annual Wage," *Harvard Business Review,* 32:37–48 (May-June 1954).
27. Unfortunately, sometimes demands also appear in the public press before they make a formal appearance at the bargaining table. *See* Chapter V for a discussion of this matter.
28. For discussion of this, *see* Archibald Cox and John T. Dunlop, "The Duty to Bargain During the Term of an Existing Agreement," *Harvard Law Review,* 63:1097–1133 (May 1950).
29. Contract between General Motors and the UAW-CIO, May 29, 1950. Cited in Dunlop and Healy, *Collective Bargaining: Principles and Cases,* p. 483.
30. One solution in a case of this sort is to submit the nonnegotiable item to arbitration, or to set up a committee to undertake study of the item. A prominent recent instance of the latter procedure was the joint committee to study the "local working conditions" provisions of collective agreements in the steel industry provided for under the terms of the 1960 settlement. *See* "The Basic Steel Companies and Steelworkers Agreement," *Monthly Labor Review,* 83:163 (February 1960).
31. *See* George W. Taylor, *Government Regulation of Industrial Relations* (New York, 1948), pp. 358 ff.

32. Peters, *Strategy and Tactics,* pp. 219–220.
33. Thomas G. Downing, "Strategy and Tactics at the Bargaining Table," *Personnel,* January-February 1960, pp. 58–63, observes with respect to this division of items that it makes "good common sense—when it comes to the question of wages and fringe benefits, you do not want to have seniority problems hanging fire." Whether it similarly makes good tactical sense, however, would seem to vary from situation to situation.
34. Peters, *Strategy and Tactics,* p. 164.
35. Dunlop and Healy, *Collective Bargaining: Principles and Cases,* p. 65.
36. There is also a legal obligation here. Section 8 (d) (4) of the National Labor Relations Act obligates the parties to continue "in full force and effect, without resorting to strike or lockout, all the terms and conditions of the existing contract for a period of sixty days" after notification of his opposite number by a party proposing to modify an existing agreement.
37. *See Monthly Labor Review,* 81:779 (July 1958); 81:1023 (September 1958); 81:1284 ff. (November 1958).
38. *See* Schelling, "The Strategy of Conflict: Prospectus," pp. 248–249. Here he suggests that if there is a determinate variant on an indeterminate game (pure-bargaining game), the solution to the former may serve to focus convergence of expectation in the latter. *See also* T. C. Schelling, "For the Abandonment of Symmetry," *The Review of Economics and Statistics,* 41:213–224 (August 1959). Here he says that if we scrutinize the rule for termination of a cooperative game upon which perfect move symmetry has been imposed by definition, we may find that the game degenerates into a tacit game. This point suggests the extreme importance of careful consideration of the rules for termination of social games under analysis. These rules may be, as in the case of the deadline rule, essentially rules for setting up a game-variant on the original game.
39. An exception to the prevailing view is Pen's theory which does exhibit an equilibrium condition for the outcome under collective bargaining. J. Pen, *The Wage Rate Under Collective Bargaining,* translated by T. S. Preston (Cambridge, 1959), p. 144. Pen's theory is discussed in Appendix I.
40. Although the policy was resisted by employers, the National War Labor Board considered retroactivity to be a "well established principle" in collective bargaining negotiation and applied it to its own determinations. *See* U.S. Dept. of Labor, *Termination Report of the National War Labor Board* (Washington, D.C., 1948), vol. I, Chap. XIV.
41. In the event of a breakdown of the negotiation process, there may be a situation subsequent to negotiations when the parties maintain their relationship but where there has been no agreement, and in consequence the only outcome of the negotiation process is abandonment of it. For example, suppose that a strike is broken. In such a situation, the union may ultimately sign a contract on company terms if only to salvage its status as bargaining agent. Such an eventuality is not an outcome of negotiation (there is no "agreed" position properly speaking) but rather represents a destruction of the organizational integrity of one side. That is, the "outcome" is achieved in consequence of the abandonment of the negotiation process.
42. For an excellent general discussion of the emergency strike problem, *see* Neil W. Chamberlain, *Social Responsibility and Strikes* (New York, 1953).
43. C. O. Gregory, *Labor and the Law,* 2nd revised edition (New York, 1958), pp. 508 ff.
44. Richard A. Lester, in testimony before the Senate Committee on Labor and

Public Welfare (83rd Cong., 1st Sess., 1953) pointed out that "By such means as . . . levy of financial penalties on both sides, some of the pressures of the strike may be created in cases where work stoppage cannot be permitted to run its course." Cited in Neil W. Chamberlain, *Sourcebook on Labor* (New York, 1958), p. 757.

45. Peters, *Strategy and Tactics*, pp. 209, 222.

CHAPTER IV. CLASSIFICATION OF TACTICS, EARLY STAGES OF NEGOTIATION, AND PERSUASION VERSUS RATIONALIZATION

1. Ann Douglas, "What Can Research Tell Us About Mediation," *Labor Law Journal*, 6:546–548 (August 1955), reporting tentative conclusions of extensive field observation. With respect to these early stages, she remarks:

Those psychologists who have tried to analyze behavior of this phase as though they were clinicians confronted with anxious, aggressive personalities have, I think, gone considerably off base and done actual disservice to research in this field. The invective and seeming antagonism of this stage do not, I think, represent psychological hostility as we normally conceive of it in individuals under clinical surveillance. Our data indicate quite the reverse, in fact. As far as negotiators to negotiators are concerned, there may be warm undercurrents of good will and good feeling between and among *individuals* at the conference table at the same time the institutional *parties* at that same table are engaged in a sharp conflict of interests.

2. Ross Stagner, *Psychology of Industrial Conflict* (New York, 1956), pp. 241–242.

3. *See* John T. Dunlop and James J. Healy, *Collective Bargaining: Principles and Cases*, revised edition (Homewood, Ill., 1955), p. 54.

4. Edward Peters, *Strategy and Tactics in Labor Negotiations* (New London, 1955), pp. 112–114. In discussing this example, he notes that in such a situation (area of hard bargaining from five to ten cents) the employer has very little mobility (of ostensible position). He comments: "At a time when the employer is only two or three cents away from the area of hard bargaining, the union is miles away, enjoying, it supposes, a genuine tactical advantage. The union is profoundly in error, however: the advantage is only illusory. What is in reality merely a failure to join the issue has been mistaken for a bargaining advantage."

5. *See* G. L. S. Shackle, *Expectation in Economics* (London, 1949), Chap. VI. Also, his statement in *The Theory of Wage Determination;* Proceedings of a conference held by the International Economic Association, John T. Dunlop, ed. (London, 1957), pp.311–312.

6. I have elsewhere postulated that such a relationship between the effective minimum price and the absolute minimum price is characteristic of the "mature" collective bargaining relationship. Carl M. Stevens, "Regarding the Determinants of Union Wage Policy," *The Review of Economics and Statistics*, 35:221–228 (August 1953).

7. Dunlop and Healy, *Collective Bargaining: Principles and Cases*, p. 55.

8. For discussion of this point, *see* Peters, *Strategy and Tactics*, Chap. VIII.

9. *See* J. Pen, *The Wage Rate under Collective Bargaining*, translated by T. S. Preston (Cambridge, 1959), pp. 139–140.

10. *See* George W. Taylor, "Wage Determination Processes," *New Concepts in Wage Determination*, G. W. Taylor and F. C. Pierson, eds. (New York, 1957), p. 107.

11. F. H. Harbison and John R. Coleman, "Procedures and Methods," *Causes of Industrial Peace under Collective Bargaining,* Clinton S. Golden and Virginia D. Parker, eds. (Washington, D.C., 1955), p. 45.

12. Opinion expressed in conversation with the writer.

13. *See* Jules Backman, *Wage Determination, An Analysis of Wage Criteria* (New York, 1959), p. 15. Backman cites this as further evidence of the importance which must be attached to the wage criteria.

14. In Chapter V we consider the possibility that appeal to these standards may serve as a device whereby a party may imply commitment to a particular position. In Chapter VI the possibility that a negotiation record built up on the basis of these criteria may, by attributing "prominence" to a particular position, facilitate mutual convergence of expectation upon that position as a solution, is given consideration. Thus we wish to establish that in this section we are concerned with only one of several tactical functions of the basic criteria.

15. This consideration, plus the tendency of the parties to shift from criterion to criterion depending upon the circumstances, are adduced by Reynolds as evidence of the "lack of substance" and "frailty" of arguments involving these criteria. *See* Lloyd G. Reynolds, *Labor Economics and Labor Relations* (2nd erd.; New York, 1954), pp. 575 ff.

16. *See* Charles E. Lindblom, *Unions and Capitalism* (New Haven, 1949), Chap. III.

17. Reynolds, *Labor Economics and Labor Relations,* p. 575.

18. M. S. Ryder, "Strategy in Collective Bargaining Negotiations," *Labor Law Journal,* 7:353-358 (June 1956), p. 355.

19. Bloom and Northrup say:

> This is not to say that criteria do not have their place in wage negotiations. Man prides himself on his rationality. Explanations are needed to fortify needs, wants, or demands, and to gain support for them. Every battle must have its slogans. The slogans should not, however, be confused with the practical realities of union-management wage determination however important they might be in crystallizing these realities in the form of policies.

Gordon F. Bloom and Herbert R. Northrup, *Economics of Labor Relations,* (3rd. ed: Homewood, Illinois, 1958, pp. 322-323. Is one to conclude from this that the basic criteria used in wage negotiations are or are not important (determinants of the outcome) in wage negotiations?

20. Jules Backman, *Wage Determination, An Analysis of Wage Criteria* (New York, 1959), p. 17.

21. Dunlop and Healy, *Collective Bargaining: Principles and Cases,* p. 99. These authors do feel, however, that economic analysis can make some contribution to wage determination, largely by pointing to the impact of wage decisions upon other variables—prices, output, and employment. In this way, economic analysis can serve "as the conscience of the parties as to many of the less immediate effects of a wage-rate decision."

22. Considerable care would be required in the formulation of an inquiry designed to get at this matter. I have discussed some of the difficulties in my article, "Regarding the Determinants of Union Wage Policy," *The Review of Economics and Statistics,* 35:221-228 (August 1953).

23. Professor George W. Taylor, suggesting that "rationalization" is not a "dirty word," has stressed to the writer the importance of rationalization as a negotiation technique. More particularly, he pointed out that the functions of ration-

alization may be found in considerations relating to the relationship between the negotiators and their constituents.

24. This was the case in the 1959 steel negotiations when two months before the contracts were due to expire, few steel users were betting that there would not be a strike. See *The New York Times*, April 6, 1959, p. 39.

25. This longer-run implication of the rationalization tactic was pointed out to the writer by Professor William G. Bowen.

26. See *Monthly Labor Review*, 82:428-429 (April 1959); 83:161-163 (February 1960).

27. This aspect was pointed out to the writer by Professor George W. Taylor.

Chapter V. Tactics of Coercion: Bluff and Notbluff

1. John T. Dunlop and James J. Healy, *Collective Bargaining: Principles and Cases*, revised edition (Homewood, Ill., 1955), p. 53, observe: "The collective bargaining process has been caricatured in a variety of ways. It is said to be like a poker game. The largest pots go to those who combine deception, bluff, and luck or ability to come up with a strong hand on the occasions they are challenged or 'seen' by the other side."

2. T. C. Schelling has provided extended discussion of this aspect of the tactical problem in "An Essay on Bargaining," *The American Economic Review*, 46:281-306 (June 1956), and "The Strategy of Conflict: Prospectus," *The Journal of Conflict Resolution*, 2:203-264 (September 1958).

3. I have elsewhere suggested that the "legitimate" strike is probably best viewed as an effective way of communicating information. See Carl M. Stevens, "On the Theory of Negotiation," *The Quarterly Journal of Economics*, 72:91 ff. (February 1958).

4. One might argue that such a strike called at 12:00 will be over at 12:01—as soon as the information point has been put across—and that in consequence the possibility of the information strike is not of great importance. This is not a compelling argument, however. For one thing, technical considerations in some industries make it impossible to turn a strike on and off with zero costs. Of more importance, once a strike has actually begun, the "atmosphere" in which negotiation takes place is significantly altered. Once it has begun, what was initially an information strike (from this point of view of legitimate function) is very apt to degenerate into economic warfare of another sort. See Ross Stagner, *Psychology of Industrial Conflict* (New York, 1956), Chap. XIII.

5. For a brief discussion distinguishing these functions, see Abram Chayes, "The Modern Corporation and the Rule of Law," *The Corporation in Modern Society*, Edward S. Mason, ed. (Cambridge, 1959), pp. 28 ff.

6. Schelling, "The Strategy of Conflict: Prospectus," pp. 223, 225.

7. It may be noted that the distinctive character of the game-theory-type threat arises in consequence of the basic assumption of the analysis. In game theory, a notbluff without this distinctive character, that is, a party's assertion that he will do (in a contingency) what he would prefer to do in event of that contingency, has no status as a tactical move since it is already a (tautological) part of the postulational structure of the analysis. That is, by postulation, A assumes that B will do what he would prefer to do.

8. I speak now of the use of such a threat in a general negotiation context. It should be noted that in the usual game-theory context, the threat is subsumed

in the concept of the "binding agreement," that is, it is by definition a binding agreement, and in consequence the problem of means to commitment does not arise. For example, R. Duncan Luce and Howard Raiffa, *Games and Decisions* (New York, 1957), p. 114, in their discussion of two-person cooperative games, explicitly assume: "ii. All agreements are binding, and they are enforceable by the rules of the game." Schelling's treatment of the threat in a game-theory context, striving for some reorientation of the traditional game theory format, does not sweep the commitment problem under the rug by making agreements binding by definition. *See* Schelling, "The Strategy of Conflict: Prospectus," pp. 203–264.

9. Schelling has paid particular attention to the commitment problem. *See* his "An Essay on Bargaining," pp. 281–306. Among other devices he mentions the practices of nailing a demand to a principle.

10. In this discussion of commitment tactics, I have adduced certain events in the recent steel negotiations as examples. These events might be differently interpreted. For example, the publicized stands upon principle in this case might be viewed as "rationalizations" intended to secure public support for positions. Even if these were the intentions of the negotiators, the (possibly inadvertent) commitment potential of such tactics should not be overlooked. Generally speaking, the theory of negotiation suggests that negotiation tactics may each serve a number of tactical functions simultaneously. The theory puts the investigator in a position systematically to distinguish and elucidate these functions.

11. In game theory, the payoff matrix is generally assumed to be invariant under play (and preplay) of the game. Hence, such an adverse reaction to a commitment tactic, which in effect alters the payoffs, cannot systematically be taken into account. *See* Luce and Raiffa, *Games and Decisions,* p. 91.

12. Edward Peters, *Strategy and Tactics in Labor Negotiations* (New London, 1955), p. 44.

13. Elmore Jackson, *Meeting of Minds—A Way to Peace Through Mediation* (New York, 1952), p. 133.

14. *See* George W. Taylor, *Government Regulation of Industrial Relations* (New York, 1948), pp. 355, 359. Of course, with tactics of deliberately contrived coercive commitment, the precise objective of the tactics is to force a party "out on a limb."

15. *See* Peters, *Strategy and Tactics,* Chap. VII.

16. Thomas G. Downing remarks, "One must always be conscious of whose turn it is to act. It may not be fatal to act out of turn—but it may result in some undesirable complications," in "Strategy and Tactics at the Bargaining Table," *Personnel* (January-February 1960), p. 61.

17. Schelling has considered the possibility of progressive commitment; *see* "An Essay on Bargaining," *The American Economic Review,* 46:296 (June 1956).

18. Threats may fail for any number of reasons, and the risk of failure provides an incentive to use moderate rather than extreme threats. Schelling has suggested that game theory can take account of this consideration by randomization of threats. That is, an actor can reduce the "size" of any given threat by attaching to it some specified probability less than 1.0 that it will be carried out. *See* T. C. Schelling, *The Strategy of Conflict* (Cambridge, 1960), Chap. VII.

19. Schelling has suggested this explanation for the strike over a few cents. *See* "An Essay on Bargaining," p. 293.

20. Luce and Raiffa, *Games and Decisions,* pp. 110 and 120.

21. Schelling, "The Strategy of Conflict: Prospectus," p. 228.
22. For this definition, *see* Neil W. Chamberlain, *A General Theory of Economic Process* (New York, 1955), Chap. VI.
23. For example, John Nash, "Two-Person Co-operative Games," *Econometrica*, 21:138 (January, 1953), observes:

> With people who are sufficiently intelligent and rational, there should not be any question of "bargaining ability" a term which suggests something like skill in duping the other fellow. The usual haggling process is based on imperfect information, the hagglers trying to propagandize each other into misconceptions of the utilities involved. Our assumption of complete information makes such an attempt meaningless.

24. *See,* however, Note 18. Even randomized threats may be viewed as binding commitments in the sense that the player may be bound to the course of action which attaches to the threat the specified probability that it will be carried out. Of course, in this case, the threat may never be carried out, but the player is committed in the sense that no freedom of choice has been reserved, the eventualities being up to chance.
25. This was pointed out to the writer by an official of a large west coast union whose opinion it was that bluff played only a minor role in the negotiations with which he was familiar.
26. In Pen's theory of bargaining, this tactic is emphasized. More particularly, the risk of conflict assigned by a party to a particular rate is made a function of his estimate of the satisfaction his bargaining opponent associates with that rate. *See* J. Pen, *The Wage Rate under Collective Bargaining,* translated by T.S. Preston (Cambridge, 1959).
27. Stevens, "On the Theory of Negotiation," pp. 89 ff.
28. *See* Schelling, "An Essay on Bargaining," p. 283.
29. Pen, *The Wage Rate under Collective Bargaining,* pp. 140 ff., alludes to this as an important problem.
30. *See* Schelling, *The Strategy of Conflict,* Chap. VIII. He employs the example of limited war as a generator of the risk of total war.
31. This has been recognized in the literature. Pen, in *The Wage Rate under Collective Bargaining,* for example, in discussing the importance of "atmosphere" in the collective bargaining process has noted on p. 141: "In particular, each of the two bargainers must try to give his opponent ample opportunity to withdraw sham demands and pave the 'way back' for him as much as possible." Schelling has observed that the use of casuistry to release an opponent from a commitment is an interesting problem in bargaining generally. *See* Schelling, "An Essay on Bargaining," p. 291.
32. Schelling has observed that the distinction between the threat and the promise is not clear, and that although the promise might seem to be a commitment that the second party welcomes, it is probably best to consider these names for different aspects of the same tactic, "which in certain simple instances can be identified in terms of the second party's interests." Schelling, "The Strategy of Conflict: Prospectus," pp. 229–230.
33. *See* Chamberlain, *A General Theory,* p. 160.

CHAPTER VI. THE LATER (PREDEADLINE) STAGES OF NEGOTIATION

1. John T. Dunlop and James J. Healy, *Collective Bargaining: Principles and Cases,* revised edition (Homewood, Ill., 1955), p. 58, have taken a similar posi-

tion, observing that: "A work stoppage is much less effective pressure for settlement when it is weeks off than when it is scheduled for midnight. Looking down the barrel of a strike or lockout causes negotiators on both sides not only to make the best they planned in advance but also to reappraise their positions and even to make more acceptable offers to the other side than they had intended. It is this genuine change in position, induced by the immediacy of the shutdown, that frequently produces settlement."

2. A precise equality of equilibrium positions is probably too stringent a necessary condition in the sense that the condition might provide just that the equilibrium positions be "nearly" the same. This implies that there is a threshold problem, that as the equilibrium positions approach each other, at some point short of precise equality, the difference between them becomes small enough to be neglected by the parties. Just what this threshold is need not detain us in this context.

3. We should point out that this analysis supposes that the negotiator announces his equilibrium position at 11:59—not just some bargaining position other than his then announced position. Also, the analysis here abstracts from the previously discussed tactics of coercive commitment by means of which a party might "win" by seizing first move.

4. See Dunlop and Healy, *Collective Bargaining: Principles and Cases*, p. 59.

5. T. C. Schelling has pointed out that breaking a threatened act down into a sequence of small steps provides a demonstration of intention and may increase credibility of each step. "An Essay on Bargaining," *The American Economic Review*, 46:298 (June 1956).

6. In Chapter III, I discussed the "tentative proposals" rule: All proposals made during the course of negotiations are understood to be provisional and may be withdrawn without prejudice if final agreement upon all items in dispute is not reached prior to a strike or lockout. We saw that the status of this rule was ambiguous, that is, in many cases it tends to be more a ritual than a fact in the sense that proposals once made are seldom effectively withdrawn.

7. Dunlop and Healy, *Collective Bargaining: Principles and Cases*, p. 57, in discussing the last-minute settlement have observed, "The frequency of these photo-finishes suggests that something may be involved fundamental to the process of collective bargaining."

8. See Edward Peters, *Strategy and Tactics in Labor Negotiations* (New London, 1955), pp. 153–154, Chap. IX.

9. These examples are from Peters, to whom the reader is referred for an illuminating discussion of the use of sign language in negotiation. *Strategy and Tactics*, Chap. IX, "Sign Language," and pp. 153–154.

10. This kind of reciprocity, although a move-like phenomenon, should not be taken to imply that collective bargaining negotiation features "moves" in the formal sense of clearly delineated alternating choices. Some negotiations do not feature this kind of reciprocity.

11. See Peters, *Strategy and Tactics*, Chap. IX, pp. 153–154.

12. See Dunlop and Healy, *Collective Bargaining: Principles and Cases*, p. 63.

13. See Ann Douglas, "What Can Research Tell Us About Mediation," *Labor Law Journal*, 6:545–552 (August 1955). Her observations suggest this interpretation of the early stages.

14. For emphasis, I have described the transition as if there were a sharp break, as if the "divide" were knife-edged. Actually, however, the transition is better viewed as a gradual one, marked by shifting emphasis in the tactic mix that is from competitive to more coordinative tactics.

15. *See* T. C. Schelling, "The Strategy of Conflict: Prospectus," *The Journal of Conflict Resolution*, 2:246 ff. (September 1958).
16. T. C. Schelling, "For the Abandonment of Symmetry," *The Review of Economics and Statistics*, 41:219 (August 1959).
17. *See* T. C. Schelling, "Bargaining, Communication, and Limited War," *The Journal of Conflict Resolution*, 1:19–36 (March 1957). He has observed that generally speaking this concept receives some elucidation and support from Gestalt-type theorizing about perception phenomena. *See* "The Strategy of Conflict: Prospectus," pp. 248–249. For discussion of an experiment designed to test Schelling's suggestion with respect to convergence of expectations in tacit bargaining, *see* R. H. Willis and Myron L. Joseph, "Bargaining Behavior I: 'Prominence' as a Predictor of the Outcome of Games of Agreement," *The Journal of Conflict Resolution*, 3:102–113 (June 1959).
18. *See* M. W. Reder, "The Theory of Union Wage Policy," *The Review of Economics and Statistics*, 34:34–45 (February 1952). In general, to "explain" A's behavior simply on the grounds that he imitates B does not get very far. Beyond this, it is necessary to explain why A resorts to imitation, and why A selects B as the model to imitate rather than some other model, and so forth. *See* Neal E. Miller and John Dollard, *Social Learning and Imitation* (New Haven, 1941). Schelling's suggestion that a "mutually perceived analogue" may, through the "power of suggestion," focus expectations might be made more definite if we ·substituted for "power of suggestion" an analysis in terms of factors involved in social learning through imitation.
19. *Amalgamated Association of Street, Electric Railway and Motor Coach Employees of America, AFL* v. *Indianapolis Railways, Inc.* This case is presented in Dunlop and Healy, *Collective Bargaining: Principles and Cases*, pp. 361 ff.
20. Table 2 summarizes, as the arbitrators saw it, the negotiation record built up by the parties. The arbitrators themselves might have applied these standards very differently. The interest here is in the record available to the parties in consequence of their own negotiation, a record which might (or might not) serve to focus expectations.
21. This is not a criticism of the board. In a case such as this the arbitrator may deliberately not supply a single rationalization of his own in order to reserve the major role for the parties' own judgments.
22. *See* Mathilda Holzman, "Theories of Choice and Conflict," *The Journal of Conflict Resolution*, 2:310–320 (December 1958), for a very illuminating discussion of the implications of nonavailability of intermediate positions in the opportunity function for conflict choice. She makes the important distinction between economic and psychological theory turn on the properties of the opportunity function. She characterizes the psychological view as one of uniqueness of goals and (hence) conflict, and the economic view as one of compromise (a variety of positions in the opportunity function) and (hence) resolution of conflict. I agree that this is an important distinction. I think, however, that emphasis upon it alone is rather misleading as regards a general comparison of psychological and economic theories on this score. *See* my "Note on Conflict Choice in Economics and Psychology," *The Journal of Conflict Resolution*, 4:220–224 (June 1960).
23. Operational definition of the concept "distance" (the horizontal axis in the avoidance–avoidance model) in nonspecial contexts poses some problems. In a previous discussion I suggested that the concept of distance from goal A be interpreted as "nearness to having made up one's mind" to elect goal A. In

the absence of a natural metric in terms of which to scale the horizontal axis, this concept of distance is perhaps susceptible to operational definition only in terms of an individual's responses upon interrogation, and it seems probable that in many instances a subject would only be able to testify on this matter in an ordinal sense. That is, he might be able to rank his equilibrium position among a list of institutionally defined alternatives, even though he could not himself supply an institutional definition of that position.

24. Holzman, "Theories of Choice and Conflict," pp. 310–320, has contended that conventional economic-choice theory and Miller's conflict-choice models share this assumption, and, further, that the empirical generality of this assumption is questionable. Technical discussion of this contention would be out of place here. However, the nature of some of the problems involved in this interpretation may be suggested. Whether economic-choice theory may be said to assume a "unidimensional continuum" depends in part upon the operational definition of "preference" (utility) employed in the theory. As developed in earlier years, economic-choice theory did assume that utility was a subjective psychological phenomenon, amounts of which were "assigned" to choice objects. In modern "utility" analysis, however, preference is operationally defined in terms of overt choice behavior. If on a series of A versus B trials (costs zero or equal), an actor consistently chooses A, he is said to prefer A. As a convention in formalizing the choice problem, we may assign a higher number to A than to B, and talk of A's having a higher utility (index). But the existence (or nonexistence) of utility as a subjective phenomenon is not at issue in the analysis. Whether such an operational definition of preference is properly characterized by saying that it assumes an unidimensional continuum is questionable.

Similar problems exist in interpreting Miller's models from this point of view. To get at this we really should go back to the basic theory (of C. L. Hull) from which the models are derived. The underlying learning theory is an intervening variable model. An index of strength of tendency to perform is made a function of such variables as drive, habit strength, incentive motivation, and so forth. The theory indeed assumes that a subject's response to all goal objects will involve these variables—but in what sense this can be said to assume a unidimensional continuum is not at all clear to this writer. For a concise presentation of the central ideas in C. L. Hull's learning theory, *see* his *Essentials of Behavior* (New Haven, 1951). For a brief self-contained exposition of Hull's theory, the reader might also consult F. A. Logan, D. Olmsted, B. S. Rosner, R. D. Schwartz, C. M. Stevens, *Behavior Theory and Social Science* (New Haven, 1955), Chap. II.

Neil W. Chamberlain, in his *A General Theory of Economic Progress* (New York, 1955), pp. 84–85, makes choices between bargains depend upon "greatest inducement to agree" rather than upon a conventional maximizing concept. He notes the absence of a meaningful common denominator for all satisfactions, and feels that "in the absence of a common denominator of satisfactions the conception of a person's balancing a variety of aspirations is less misleading than a conception of maximizing."

25. As implied in Note 24, one problem with the concept of nonunidimensionality of choice is that of operational definition of nonunidimensionality. More particularly, this concept needs an operational definition independent of the choice behavior in question (ability or inability to resolve a choice problem) if demoniac explanation is to be avoided. Also, not all conflict in choice is due to dimension problems.

26. For an excellent discussion of these issues, *see* Neil W. Chamberlain, *The Union Challenge to Management Control* (New York, 1948).
27. A recent study of "right to work" legislation in Texas advanced the conclusion that the legislation has had minimal direct effect, that the important meaning of the statute seems to be symbolic. *See* Frederic Meyers, "Right to Work in Practice," The Fund for the Republic, 1959.
28. *See* George E. Bowles, "The G. A. W. Negotiations," *Labor Law Journal*, 6:566–571 (August 1955).

CHAPTER VII. MEDIATION: FUNCTIONS AND TACTICS

1. Joseph Shister, "Collective Bargaining," *A Decade of Industrial Relations Research—1946–1956*, Neil W. Chamberlain, Frank E. Pierson, and Theresa Wolfson, eds. (New York, 1958), p. 35.
2. Arthur Stark in his Introduction to "New Vistas in Mediation." Proceedings of the Fourth Annual Conference Association of State Mediation Agencies, Ithaca, New York, June 1955. *Labor Law Journal*, 6:523 (August 1955).
3. David L. Cole, "Observations on the Nature and Function of Mediation," University of Pennsylvania Conference, April 10, 1953.
4. William M. Leiserson, "The Functions of Mediation in Labor Relations," Industrial Relations Research Association, Proceedings of Fourth Annual Meeting, December, 1951, p. 5.
5. Ann Douglas, in commenting on the invention of "fictions" with respect to the mediation process, has observed:

> There are, for example, oft-heard claims about the uniqueness of every dispute that comes to mediation. As a result, cases supposedly defy categorizing and mediators must be such free-lancing artists that the secret of their successes is non-communicable. All human and social situations, of course, are in some respects always unique, but the first article of faith of all the behavioral sciences declares that human phenomena also share enough in common to warrant the search among them for general organizing principles. Ann Douglas, "What Can Research Tell Us About Mediation," *Labor Law Journal*, 6:550 (August 1955).

6. My impression from the literature is that most investigators interested in the theory and function of mediation think it most appropriate to focus their studies upon the mediation process itself and/or the mediator himself. Such studies may be valuable, but this orientation of the research tends to obscure the fact that mediation is an integral part of collective bargaining negotiation. A good theory of collective bargaining negotiation is an essential prerequisite to elucidation of the functions of the mediator.
7. Elmore Jackson, *Meeting of Minds—A Way to Peace Through Mediation* (New York, 1952), p. 27.
8. Thomas G. Downing, "Strategy and Tactics at the Bargaining Table," *Personnel* (January-February 1960), p. 62.
9. William A. Leiserson, "The Functions of Mediation in Labor Relations." Industrial Relations Research Association, Proceedings of Fourth Annual Meeting.
10. *The American Journal of Sociology*, 60:230–245 (November 1954).
11. *See* David L. Cole, "Observations on the Nature and Function of Mediation," University of Pennsylvania Conference, April 10, 1953.

12. *See* Kerr, "Industrial Conflict and its Mediation," pp. 230–245.
13. Bernard Wilson, "Conciliation Officers' Techniques in Settling Disputes," paper prepared for discussion at the Eighteenth Annual Conference of the Canadian Association of Administrators of Labour Legislation, Quebec, September, 1959.
14. Henry A. Landsberger, "Interim Report of a Research Project in Mediation," *Labor Law Journal,* 6:552–560 (August 1955), and "Final Report on a Research Project in Mediation," *Labor Law Journal,* 7:501–510 (August 1956). Another interesting study is that by Irving R. Weschler, "The Personal Factor in Labor Mediation," 3.2 *Personnel Psychology.* Weschler explores the personality variables which distinguish a "good" mediator from a "poor" mediator.
15. Landsberger, "Interim Report of a Research Project," p. 554. The basic technique was then to rank a group of subjects (mediators) in accordance with these criteria as judged by the parties. The same mediators were ranked in accordance with a battery of psychological tests—and the correlation between the two rankings secured. The correlation was quite high.
16. Bernard T. Wilson, "Conciliation Officers' Techniques in Settling Disputes," "With respect to the prestige factor in mediation, there was a time when any highly placed amiable fathead could mediate with some assurance of effectiveness, but that time is now long past." He goes on to point out that prestige is now important only if combined with other qualifications.
17. This is a part of what Kerr terms "removal of nonrationality." "Industrial Conflict and its Mediation," pp. 230–245. This is an unfortunate choice of terms. The concept "rationality" usually refers to the appropriateness (in some sense) of decision criteria, or the appropriateness of problem solving behavior in the light of such criteria as given—not to problems associated with perception of the environment. Kerr points out that while the task of assisting the negotiators to a more realistic appraisal of the situation is ordinarily not too difficult, the task of reaching and influencing the constituencies on both sides may be very difficult. The latter may be brought to a realistic appraisal only through actual experience of strike or lockout (p. 237).
18. T. C. Schelling has suggested that a mediator is probably best viewed as an element in the communications arrangements. *See* "The Strategy of Conflict: Prospectus," *The Journal of Conflict Resolution,* 2:236 (September 1958).
19. *See* Bernard Wilson, "Conciliation Officers' Techniques in Settling Disputes," for discussion of this tactic.
20. *See* Hugh G. Lovell, "The Pressure Lever in Mediation," *Industrial and Labor Relations Review* (October 1952). In Lovell's view, the mediator's primary role is that of forcing the parties to change positions (as contrasted with the "human-relation-type" role of resolving personality clashes, and so forth, so often emphasized in discussion of mediation). He feels that the mediator's ability to control the level of pressure stems from his control over the flow of information between the parties.
21. Douglas, "What Can Research Tell Us About Mediation," p. 550.
22. Kerr has observed that "much of the fascination of collective bargaining is in the tactics of retreat." *See* "Industrial Conflict and its Mediation," p. 237. Schelling has discussed the use of casuistry to release an opponent from a commitment in "An Essay on Bargaining," *The American Economic Review,* 46:281–306 (June 1956).
23. Kerr discusses the face-saving function of mediation, including the aspect of sharing responsibility of the outcome. *See* "Industrial Conflict and its Mediation," p. 238.

24. Schelling, "An Essay on Bargaining," pp. 281–306.
25. Kerr, "Industrial Conflict and its Mediation," p. 239. He attributes this point to A. C. Pigou, *The Economics of Welfare* (4th ed.; New York, 1950).
26. Schelling has provided discussion of what he terms tacit bargaining. *See* "Bargaining, Communication and Limited War," *The Journal of Conflict Resolution,* 1:19–36 (March 1957), and "The Strategy of Conflict: Prospectus," pp. 203–264. In game-theory terminology, the term "noncooperative" is used to refer to games in which there is no preplay communication.
27. *See* Schelling, "Bargaining, Communication and Limited War," pp. 19–36.
28. Arthur S. Meyer, "Function of the Mediator in Collective Bargaining," *Industrial and Labor Relations Review* (January 1960), p. 164 mentions this kind of mediator threat as a rarely used tactical aid to dispute settlement.
29. Resolution of a dispute by tacit bargaining convergence upon a *somehow* distinguished position may lend a quality of "arbitrariness" to the outcome. In this context, the following comment is of interest: "Labor disputes are exhausting processes and the mediator, like the participants, will think of nothing so much as of a settlement, any settlement, for according to the conventions of the game, each settlement is a victory and there is little to choose between one and another." Meyer, "Function of the Mediator," *Industrial and Labor Relations Review* (January 1960), p. 165.
30. This account is taken from Frank P. Graham, "Maintenance of Membership: A Historical Note," *Labor Law Journal,* 6:560–561 (August 1955). The dispute in question was in the lumber industry in the Pacific Northwest.
31. *See* "The Role of Mediation in Labor-Management Relations" (Address at a Conference of Regional Directors of the Federal Mediation and Conciliation Service, Washington, D.C., 1952), cited in Kerr, "Industrial Conflict and its Mediation," pp. 230–245.
32. *See* Mathilda Holzman, "Theories of Choice and Conflict," *The Journal of Conflict Resolution,* 2:317 ff. (December 1958), for a discussion of resolution of conflict stemming from nonunidimensionality of choice options.
33. "The mediator as a respected authority" was one of the ten areas of mediator behavior cited in the Landsberger study as the areas to which the parties had most frequent reference when attempting to evaluate a mediator as "good," "not so good," and so forth. *Labor Law Journal,* 6:552–560 (August 1955); 7:501–510 (August 1956). The mediation function of resolving conflict stemming from nonunidimensionality of choice options has a quasi-therapeutic flavor to it. That is, there is an analogue here to the case of the conflicted individual who seeks out his teacher, or his minister, or his physician, and so on, to resolve a conflictful choice.
34. Kerr, "Industrial Conflict and its Mediation," p. 238, makes this point.
35. *See* Stevens, "On the Theory of Negotiation," *The Quarterly Journal of Economics,* 72:77–97 (February, 1958).
36. Leiserson, "The Functions of Mediation in Labor Relations."

Appendix I

1. *See* J. Pen, *The Wage Rate Under Collective Bargaining,* translated by T. S. Preston (Cambridge, 1959); also Pen's article summarizing the theory: "A General Theory of Bargaining," *The American Economic Review,* 42:24–42 (March 1952).

2. There are other equilibrium formulations of the bargaining problem. For example, *see* Hicks' theory of labor negotiation J. R. Hicks, *The Theory of Wages* (New York, 1948), pp. 140 ff.; also, for example, G. L. S. Shackle's bargaining theory in *Expectation in Economics* (London, 1949). Pen discusses these theories as well as that of Zeuthen, which he acknowledges as the starting point for his own reasoning (*The Wage Rate Under Collective Bargaining,* Chap. VI and Appendix).

For a brief review of bilateral monopoly theories generally, and a report on some experiments conducted by the authors designed to test certain bilateral monopoly equilibrium theories, *see* Sidney Siegel and Lawrence E. Fouraker, *Bargaining and Group Decision Making* (New York, 1960). These experiments were essentially tacit bargaining experiments with most negotiatory phenomena suppressed (that is, direct communication between the players was not allowed, tactical "moves," except perhaps as implied in the exchange of offers, were not involved, and so forth).

Our purposes in this appendix will be served by confining the discussion to Pen's theory and the avoidance–avoidance-model analysis. Portions of the following account of Pen's theory are adapted from the author's review of his book, in *Review of Economics and Statistics,* February 1961.

3. Pen, *The Wage Rate Under Collective Bargaining,* p. 137. An attempt has been made to present the essential central notions of Pen's formal analysis while at the same time keeping the discussion and notation as simple as possible. This has demanded some simplification and rephrasing of notation. To avoid confusion and possible misrepresentation, we may here sketch Pen's actual presentation a bit more closely.

Equations such as (1a) imply a maximum risk of conflict which the parties can accept if they are to go on bargaining, that is, a maximum value for r. This maximum risk of conflict is related to the ophelimities by a "risk valuation" function (Φ). This function takes account of the fact that the parties, rather than having actuarial mentalities, may attach some positive or negative value to the gambling situation *per se*.

To be distinguished from this maximum acceptable risk of conflict is the expected risk (r) which is given by the equations (2) and (4). Now the equilibrium condition may be put: Each party will be in equilibrium *vis-à-vis* any W when the maximum acceptable risk of conflict is equal to the expected risk, that is, when in Pen's notation and for the union and employer respectively:

5. $$\Phi 1 \left[\frac{L(W_1) - L(W)}{L(W_1) - Lc} \right] - F_1 [E(W) - Ec] = 0$$

6. $$\Phi e \left[\frac{E(W_e) - E(W)}{E(W_e) - Ec} \right] - F_e [L(W) - Lc] = 0$$

The quotation in the text applies in Pen's presentation to these equations (5) and (6).

4. From a substantive point of view, however, it is essential not to suppress this distinction. This will be so if, as argued in Chapter II, choices involving avoidance give rise to conflict in the choice situation whereas choices involving approach tendencies do not.

5. A more complete statement of the theory reveals a possibility of operations upon

the opposite number's "risk valuation" function. Pen does not consider this a very important tactical possibility.

APPENDIX II

1. An excellent treatment of game theory (and related decision theory) is to be found in R. Duncan Luce and Howard Raiffa, *Games and Decisions* (New York, 1957). This is a most valuable reference for the student interested in potential applications of game theory to labor negotiations.

   T. C. Schelling's treatment of bargaining and negotiation problems within the context of game theory (striving for a reorientation of traditional approaches to game theory) is of particular interest to students of collective bargaining. His work has been treated extensively in the text and comments upon it will not, for the most part, be summarized in this appendix.

2. Of course, the problem of response definition is one that confronts any analysis of collective bargaining negotiation. However, what is germane here is that this problem creates special difficulties for attempted formal representation of negotiation as a game, for, in order to be defined adequately as a game, the choices available at each move must be specified.

3. Luce and Raiffa, *Games and Decisions,* p. 53, comment:
   The reduction of any specific game, except the simplest, to normal form is a task defying the patience of man; but since the normal form of *all possible games* is comparatively simple, one may hope to carry out successfully a mathematical examination of all possible games in normal form. The study of specific games may be close to impossible, but it may now be quite feasible to classify, analyze, and determine the features of all games. For some empirical purposes that may be sufficient.

4. Luce and Raiffa, *Games and Decisions,* p. 115.

5. Games may also be classified as: (1) strictly competitive (zero-sum) games— the players' interests are strictly opposed, what one gains is precisely matched by what the other loses (that is, the players' utility functions sum to zero); (2) non-strictly competitive (non-zero-sum) games—the players' interests are not strictly opposed; what one gains is not precisely offset by his opponent's loss, and there is a possibility of mutual gain by cooperation. Generally speaking, if collective bargaining is to be considered a game, it will be of the non-zero-sum class. Schelling has commented upon the inadequacy of the conventional game classification scheme. *See* "The Strategy of Conflict: Prospectus," *The Journal of Conflict Resolution,* 2:206 ff. (September 1958).

6. Luce and Raiffa, *Games and Decisions,* p. 114.

7. In a previous comment upon the relation of game theory to analysis of negotiation, the writer observed:

   the game-theory format is essentially inappropriate to the analysis of negotiation . . . Game theory emphasizes a rationality-type solution with the calculation of optimal strategy elaborated with respect to a supposedly known or somewhat arbitrarily assumed payoff matrix. But in most negotiated, purposive games, precisely the major task of the exchange of information during negotiation is to change the negotiators' perception of the values comprising the payoff matrix. Herein lies the essence of the analysis. Elaboration of techniques for the calculation of optimal strategies on the basis of known payoffs would not seem to add much to the analysis of this type of situation. *See* Carl M. Stevens, "On the Theory of Negotiation," *The Quarterly Journal of Economics,* 72:96–97 (February 1958).

8. *See* Luce and Raiffa, *Games and Decisions,* p. 91.
9. *See* John Nash, "Two-Person Co-operative Games," *Econometrica,* 21:138 (January 1953).
10. *See* Luce and Raiffa, *Games and Decisions,* p. 114. Also Nash in "Two-Person Cooperative Games," observes:

> Supposing A and B to be rational beings, it is essential for the success of the threat that A be *compelled* to carry out his threat T if B fails to comply. Otherwise it will have little meaning, for, in general, to execute the threat will not be something A would want to do, just by itself.

11. *See* T. C. Schelling, "The Strategy of Conflict: Prospectus," *The Journal of Conflict Resolution,* 2:240 ff. (September 1958). Schelling's treatment of such tactics as the threat, promise, etc., in a game-theory context is discussed at some length in the foregoing chapters. It should be clear from that discussion that he does not sweep the commitment problem under the rug by making coercive notbluffs binding by definition. Rather, he advocates, as a desirable reorientation of game theory, recognition of the tactical problems involved in commitment, conveying the truth, and so forth.
12. *See* Luce and Raiffa, *Games and Decisions,* pp. 115 ff.
13. *See* Nash, "Two-Person Co-operative Games," pp. 128–140; also Luce and Raiffa, *Games and Decisions,* pp. 121, 124ff.
14. Luce and Raiffa, *Games and Decisions,* pp. 96–97. It may be noted that the unnatural-game concept developed in Chapter II does not turn upon the undesirability of the actor's position from a social point of view but rather upon the undesirability (unnaturalness) of the game format from the actor's point of view.

    Andreas G. Papandreou and John T. Wheeler, *Competition and Its Regulation* (New York, 1954), introduce unnatural-game-type concepts in their development of criteria for antitrust policy. Rejecting "perfectly" free competition as policy objective, they comment: "The participants, in other words, will refuse to play the game. In what follows, it will be argued that we must give up some freedom of competition in order to induce the participants to engage in the game—in other words, in order that we have competition," p. 191.
15. *See* Daniel Ellsberg, "Theory of the Reluctant Duelist," *The American Economic Review,* 46:909–923 (December 1956). For a comment on Ellsberg's position, *see* Anthony Y. C. Koo, "Recurrent Objections to the Minimax Strategy," *The Review of Economics and Statistics,* 41:36–41 (February 1959); Ellsberg's "Rejoinder," pp. 42–44.
16. Ellsberg, "Theory of the Reluctant Duelist," p. 922.
17. Carl M. Stevens. *See* "Note on Conflict Choice in Economics and Psychology," *The Journal of Conflict Resolution,* 4:220–224 (June 1960), for a more extended discussion of this point.
18. In terms of conflict-choice theory, the prisoner's-dilemma format represents a double-approach-avoidance, or what I have termed a two approach-avoidance conflict. For brief discussion of these concepts, *see* Stevens "A Note on Conflict Choice in Economics and Psychology," pp. 220–224.
19. For a discussion of the bearing of such properties of the opportunity function

on conflict choice, see Mathilda Holzman, "Theories of Choice and Conflict in Psychology and Economics," *The Journal of Conflict Resolution,* 2:310–320 (December 1958).

20. *See* Luce and Raiffa, *Games and Decisions,* p. 69, for discussion of this point; also pp. 74 ff. on actual play of mixed strategies.

21. Strategy randomization in a game-theory context is frequently rationalized in terms of the security function; that is, selecting a strategy for play by some chance device may preclude the opponent from gaining valuable intelligence. *See* Schelling, *The Strategy of Conflict,* Chap. VII, for a discussion of the role of randomization in zero-sum and non-zero-sum games.

It is perhaps worth noting in connection with this discussion that there is considerable formal analogue between the geometrical representation of the avoidance–avoidance conflict choice and the geometircal solution of a two-person zero-sum game. (On geometrical solutions for such games, *see* Luce and Raiffa, *Games and Decisions,* Appendix 3.)

Index